ELEMENTARY TEACHER'S LANGUAGE ARTS HANDBOOK

Techniques and Ideas for Teaching Reading, Writing, Speaking, and Listening

Robert L. Hillerich

PRENTICE HALL
Englewood Cliffs, New Jersey 07632

Prentice-Hall International (UK) Limited, *London*
Prentice-Hall of Australia Pty. Limited, *Sydney*
Prentice-Hall Canada, Inc., *Toronto*
Prentice-Hall Hispanoamericana, S.A., *Mexico*
Prentice-Hall of India Private Limited, *New Delhi*
Prentice-Hall of Japan, Inc., *Tokyo*
Simon & Schuster Asia Pte. Ltd., *Singapore*
Editora Prentice-Hall do Brasil, Ltda., *Rio de Janeiro*

© 1988 *by*

PRENTICE-HALL, Inc.

10   9   8   7   6   5   4   3   2   1

Library of Congress Cataloging-in-Publication Data

Hillerich, Robert L.
  Elementary teacher's language arts handbook: techniques and ideas for teaching reading, writing, speaking, and listening / Robert L. Hillerich.
    p. cm.
  Bibliography: p.
  Includes index.
  ISBN 0-13-259391-2
  1. Language arts (Elementary)—United States. 2. Reading
(Elementary)—United States. I. Title.
LB1576.H42 1988
372.6'044—dc19   87-37579
                                                     CIP

ISBN 0-13-259391-2

PRENTICE HALL
BUSINESS & PROFESSIONAL DIVISION
A division of Simon & Schuster
Englewood Cliffs, New Jersey 07632

Printed in the United States of America

to Dottie

Acknowledgment

I am truly grateful to the teachers with whom I have taught, and especially to the many former graduate students of the National College of Education, at Bowling Green State University, and of the University of Florida, as well as to hundreds of teachers around the country. These professionals have shared their views and concerns about helping children learn to read and write. Their contributions have significantly added to the emphasis and interpretations presented here.

About the Author

Robert L. Hillerich has been an elementary teacher, an elementary principal, and an assistant superintendent for instruction. After earning an undergraduate degree in English and humanities, he went on to earn his doctorate in elementary education from Colorado State College. Until recently, he was a professor of education at Bowling Green State University, where he taught graduate courses in reading and language arts. He currently is a visiting professor at the University of Florida and serves as a consultant to the Pinellas County (Florida) Schools. Prior to his tenure at Bowling Green, he was chair of the Department of Reading and Language Arts at the National College of Education, where he established and directed the reading clinic.

Dr. Hillerich writes a monthly article for *Teaching K–8* (formerly *Early Years*), and is the author of more than one hundred journal articles, six professional books, a picture dictionary, an elementary spelling/writing series, a readiness program, a beginning reading program, and a variety of other instructional materials for teachers and children, including *Teaching Children to Write, K–8: A Complete Guide to Developing Writing Skills* (Prentice-Hall, 1985). In addition to teaching graduate courses in the teaching of reading and written composition, he has been director of the Northwest Ohio Writing Project and is a regular speaker at national, regional, and state conferences of many professional organizations, including the National Council of Teachers of English, the International Reading Association, and the National Association of Elementary Principals. Consultant to several publishers and state offices of education, he is also prominent as a director of in-service workshops for principals as well as for teachers throughout the United States and Canada.

About This Book

The *Elementary Teacher's Language Arts Handbook* is not just another book about how to teach reading. It is a book about teaching reading as a language art that is unique in several ways. First, it presents reading instruction in the framework of the total language picture—speaking, listening, and writing, as well as reading. Second, it does not offer a smorgasbord of various techniques; rather, it presents a research-supported direction with many ideas on how to implement that approach. Third, it offers extensive treatment of two often-neglected topics: oral language diagnosis/development and critical reading.

The *Elementary Teacher's Language Arts Handbook* is directed primarily to in-service teachers. It presents a sequence of essential skills and methods—from oral language development to decoding and comprehension skills, from prereading to critical reading.

Although benchmarks referring to the "typical" are included here, such age or grade designations are merely reference points since any given skill may have been mastered by an astute, well-prepared four-year-old or may still be needed by a teenager or adult who has not had the necessary experience or instruction.

The fact that individuals differ prescribes that this book deal with the *what, how,* and *why* of instruction, rather than with the *when*. Much has been debated about *when* instruction should begin, but the fact remains that *when* is most often a function of *how*, and the *how* is determined by the previous background of the individual. For example, it has been demonstrated that most four-year-olds in a typical, nonselect group learned skills traditionally reserved for seven-year-olds, but the former were taught these skills as four-year-olds.

What Should Be Taught

The content of reading instruction (the *what*) is seen as a sequence of skills and understandings needed by anyone learning to read. In some instances, the sequence is rigid. For example, no one can be taught to read or write if that person does not yet comprehend the oral language. In other instances, the sequence is loose. Work on word identification and comprehension skills can be simultaneous or interchangeable, and who is to say whether students should be taught to infer cause/effect relationships before or after they're taught to predict an outcome.

How to Instruct

Methods (the *how*) are based on research dealing with both the relative effectiveness of techniques and with how children learn. Those methods dealing with the specific skills to be mastered are precisely outlined in terms of research. There are other aspects of reading, however, that are suggested as open, unstructured experiences. It is here that writing comes into strong focus. The most important aspects of method cannot be determined or controlled through any book. To ensure that children learn to use language effectively— whether in reading or in writing—the teacher must enjoy working with children and with language, must ensure the success of each child at each step of the process, and must help children to discover that reading, writing, and the manipulation of language can be fun! Only a teacher—not a book—can truly integrate the language arts as that teacher leads students to examine and manipulate ideas through the variety of language modes: listening, speaking, reading, and writing.

The *Why* of Instruction

The *why's* expounded in *Elementary Teacher's Language Arts Handbook* are of two types: sometimes they are the research foundation on which a given method is based; at other times, they are the logical or philosophical foundation underlying a given skill or understanding. While trying to keep citations to a minimum, I have attempted to identify those methods and techniques supported by research and to distinguish them from my own biases based on past experience.

Specifically:

- Chapter 1 identifies a research-based direction for instruction.
- Chapters 2 and 3 present the kinds of skills and methods that are appropriate for typical kindergarten children or for any younger or older individuals working at the very beginning level of language development. These skills are the foundation upon which any future success in language must be built. Chapter 2 presents the background evidence on debates about formal versus informal instruction in kindergarten, while Chapter 3 deals with methods and skills involved in oral language development.
- Chapter 4 deals with specific prereading or beginning reading skills for

decoding, as they can be developed in the typical kindergarten. Methods in all these skills incorporate work in oral language and in writing.

- Chapter 5 completes the presentation of the basic decoding skills, those skills needed in order to interpret print. Beginning with the concerns usually classified as "first grade," it continues with additional phonic understandings related to vowels and with a discussion of syllabication and affixes, thereby rounding out the decoding skills that most basal reading programs assume will be accomplished by the "average" child by the end of grade two.

- Chapter 6 includes evidence and techniques for developing vocabulary of all kinds and at all levels, from the recognition vocabulary of beginning readers through the increased meaning vocabularies (both expressive and receptive, oral and written) of literate adults. The dictionary skills also presented in this chapter serve as a bridge from basic decoding to maturity in reading, as students move into material that includes words outside their listening/speaking vocabularies.

The remaining chapters deal with the application of reading. They are the *raison d'être* for teaching those preceding decoding skills. Nor is their placement after the decoding skills intended to imply that they not be attended to until after decoding has been developed. In fact, as should be abundantly clear, these comprehension skills (1) are the means of communication and begin before youngsters enter school; (2) are continued simultaneously with the decoding skills; and (3) their development never ceases. It is here that the language arts can truly be interrelated, and it is here that writing becomes effectively integrated with reading.

- Chapters 7 and 8 deal with this application of reading as it involves the comprehension skills: literal, inferential, and creative in Chapter 7, and the sadly neglected critical reading and study skills in Chapter 8. These chapters present the crucial skills, techniques to improve their development with children, and current thinking in some new directions. It is in these areas that the record is not good, and it is here that the language arts can be and should be integrated.

- The heart of reading—the use of skills in trade-book reading—is presented in Chapter 9. This chapter discusses background needs and suggests over two hundred ideas for stimulating library reading in the classroom. It is in this use that the teacher has the greatest opportunity for interrelating the language arts and for youngsters to read, speak, listen, and write about information of interest to them. More important, this chapter offers the most effective application anyone can provide for a reader: the opportunity to use language skills in order to read and write for pleasure. It is in this portion of the reading program that youngsters not only get enjoyable practice of the skills taught but also develop the necessary interest that produces the essential and lifelong *desire* to read.

- While techniques throughout this book imply a diagnostic approach to instruction, Chapter 10 deals specifically with the individualization of that instruction. After clarifying differences (strangely enough, misunderstood even by experienced educators), this chapter discusses simple classroom means of determining the needs of a typical youngsters and of working effectively with them.

Although every effort has been made to provide direction consistent with research that will lead to successful as well as enjoyable experiences in language for youngsters, only you, the teacher, can assure that this will happen. The *Elementary Teacher's Language Arts Handbook* will assist you in this all-important goal of developing youngsters who can read, who do read, and who enjoy reading.

Robert L. Hillerich

Contents

Chapter 1

Approaches
to Beginning
Reading

If you were to walk into the typical elementary classroom today during a "reading" class, what would you see? Most likely you would find the teacher working directly with one group of youngsters, teaching a particular reading skill. Meanwhile, another group might be independently filling in blank spaces in a workbook while a third portion of the class is reading in their readers, library books, or possibly studying their spelling, completing a math assignment, or preparing to dramatize a story.

Basal reading programs have been seen as the salvation of reading instruction, and they have been blamed for its supposed demise. Certainly basals deserve much of the credit or blame for the status of reading achievement in this country, since ninety percent of school districts use them to some extent, and most use them exclusively. Regardless of their training, most beginning teachers will walk into their first elementary teaching positions to find they are expected to use a basal in their teaching of reading.

This chapter is neither a condemnation nor a blind acclamation of basals. No program is perfect. However, used properly—that is, with good judgment—a basal series can be an important tool and a valuable asset to even the most highly trained teacher. Properly selected—using a carefully orchestrated evaluation procedure (Hillerich, 1983)—the basal is a valuable tool in any classroom, school, or district. Most often the lists of "weaknesses" of basal reading programs are actually tabulations of thoughtless reliance on or misuse of a basal, a weakness that deserves to be criticized.

1

WHAT IS A
BASAL READING PROGRAM?

A "basal reading program" is more than a series of books. It is a carefully structured and integrated collection of materials designed to provide not only the reading matter for students but sequence and direction for the teaching of skills from kindergarten through grade six or, in most cases, grade eight. A modern basal program usually contains:

- teacher's guides
- accompanying pupil books ("readers") and practice books ("workbooks")
- word, letter, and picture cards for the beginning levels
- duplicating masters
- a management system
- filmstrips, records or tapes, games, and activities
- supplementary reading books

No basal program today is written by *one* author. Unfortunately, in a few instances, programs are written by the editors "in-house," and a "senior author" is hired after the fact merely to promote that program. In most cases, however, programs are cooperative works requiring large teams of authors and editors. Authors provide the research base, philosophical foundation, pedagogy, and practical knowledge of children; editors add knowledge of the market (what is acceptable), sequence and continuity, and often a great deal of educational soundness as well.

Basal programs today are well constructed, expensive, and highly competitive. They offer a wealth of good reading material for students and an overabundance of instructional suggestions and aids for teachers. It is the teacher's guides, along with the accompanying pupil books and workbooks, that are the heart of a basal reading program. In fact, the "program" itself—the content of skills and methods—is in the teacher's guide, with the pupil books serving as a vehicle for their instruction and practice, the workbooks providing specific follow-up skill practice, and a variety of ancillary materials offering additional instruction and/or practice.

As noted by many writers on the subject, the printed page has an abundance of redundancy. The mature reader processes print in a manner that takes advantage of only as many of the superfluous clues as are needed to reduce uncertainty and to approximate the meaning intended by the author. Conversely, the beginning reader—and especially the nonreader—doesn't have a repertoire of skills to use. That person certainly doesn't have any words in a recognition vocabulary; that is, there are no words that can be recognized instantaneously to be used as context in reading. Further, such an individual may have no knowledge of the sounds that any of the letters represent in print. And so the question is: Where does one start with an individual who is not yet reading at all?

There are many approaches to beginning reading. Aukerman (1971, 1984) listed about one hundred from the age of innovation in the 1960s, although one is hard pressed to find many of the programs in use today.

It certainly is not the purpose of this chapter to examine a hundred different approaches. However, it is important to examine in greater detail the major philosophies represented, since the names and details may change, but old programs continue to be resurrected under new labels. This chapter will clarify the basic differences in approaches to beginning reading and identify the strengths and weaknesses of the different philosophies.

Any of the approaches to beginning reading can be classified on a continuum from the extremes of decoding emphasis to meaning emphasis. In no program has phonics ever been completely eliminated, and in only a few has meaning been omitted. Let's examine some examples of these two emphases and then look at what research and common sense suggest as the most favorable direction in beginning reading.

PROGRAMS OF DECODING EMPHASIS

Programs at this extreme present reading as a matter of learning to convert print into speech, hence the term "decoding," changing from the printed code to the oral code. Most such approaches can be classified as teaching sounds for letters (phonics)—usually in a stimulus-response fashion—before learners are exposed to complete words. As a result, such programs are often referred to as *synthetic phonics* programs: Upon seeing a word such as *boat*, the beginner is expected to synthesize (blend) the sounds—to "sound it out"—"buh, oh, tuh." Such noises do not result in the word "boat." In their strong focus on decoding, such programs tend to ignore semantic context or meaning.

Programs at this extreme are also currently referred to as "explicit" phonics programs in that they overtly tell the learner—and drill that learner—on the fact that a given letter represents a given sound. This is in contrast to most of the meaning emphasis approaches that are also referred to as "implicit" phonics programs because they teach words first and through these words *imply* to the learner the sound a letter stands for.

There are a number of types of decoding programs, ranging from a few basal reading programs, through coded approaches that manipulate the orthography to those that manipulate structure. Let's look at a few examples of each of the major types.

Decoding Emphasis Basals

Whether basal or a beginning approach similar to basals, the method in decoding emphasis is essentially the same—a behaviorist, stimulus-response learning. At the extreme, the beginning reader is shown a letter, for example *h*, and told that it says "huh." Then a vowel is added and pronounced (e.g., *a*), another consonant sound "taught" (*m*), and one supposedly can read the word *ham*.

Consistent with this lack of use of context is this same approach in the few regular basals at this extreme. However, instead of the rote drill on letter and sound, some add a mnemonic device, teaching sounds through the use of a picture beside each letter where the picture represents the sound that letter stands for. For example, for the letter *s*, there might be a picture of a tire with a nail in it going "ssss."

Coded Approaches

Some educators see the problem of learning to read as one aggravated by the fact that English has only twenty-six letters to represent forty-five sounds. Further, not only must a letter be used to represent more than one sound, some sounds are represented by more than one letter. To overcome this "problem," such individuals have attempted to achieve and maintain regularity at the beginning stages of reading by inventing additional symbols for sounds and reserving only one symbol for each sound.

One such invention was the Initial Teaching Alphabet or i/t/a (Downing, 1964), which was initiated in Britain originally as a remedial program and which experienced some popularity in the United States in the 1960s. In i/t/a forty-four symbols were used initially for the sounds of English; however, there was not a one-to-one correspondence between spelling and sound because if there had been, the print would not have looked like English. Even some basal reading materials and the Stanford Achievement Test in Reading were published in i/t/a.

Since i/t/a is a type face, some users have objected to its being classified as an approach to beginning reading. However, while it may not require a specific approach, it certainly implies a decoding emphasis. Otherwise, why would anyone want to mutilate the orthography to attain the possibility of a one-to-one correspondence between symbol and sound?

While i/t/a's impact on reading achievement was certainly not impressive, it did result in one interesting finding: Children using i/t/a wrote more, wrote better, and enjoyed writing more than did children in traditional programs. Who could criticize spelling when children wrote in i/t/a! Yet, we need not adopt i/t/a in order to gain this value; we need merely to recognize that the first task in improving writing is to free children to write, rather than to be concerned with their initial efforts at spelling. Furthermore, we also learned that experience in writing reinforces the recognition vocabulary of beginning readers.

Very similar to i/t/a, but without ever having gained its popularity, is UNIFON. The major difference lies in the fact that UNIFON has no lower-case form: an advantage according to its proponents since it reduces the number of letter forms by half; a disadvantage if one considers that most letters in English print are met in lower-case form and that lower case provides the ascending and descending shapes that make for "configuration."

In the same vein as these two programs, but differing by avoiding the invention of new letters, is Words in Color (Gattegno, 1962). Here the author used forty-four colors so that each letter sound was represented by its usual letter but in a color consistent for that sound. Anyone entering a classroom where Words in Color was in use might think they were in a music room as the teacher pointed to a chart of the colored letters, and children, in unison, made the appropriate noises for each color.

These coding approaches rose and fell in the 1960s—or did they? Spache (1965) reported on Nellie Dale's use of color in 1899 and on the appearance of forerunners of i/t/a and UNIFON in the eighteenth and nineteenth centuries. And Writing to Read, a reincarnation of i/t/a dressed up in computer hardware (discussed later in this chapter), arose in the 1980s.

"Linguistic" Programs

As one linguist stated, "Once again it must be emphasized that there can be no such method as a linguistic method of teaching reading" (Wardhaugh, 1969, p.14). Perhaps it is even more appropriate to question how there might be a non-linguistic method—which is about like asking how there could be a non-language method of teaching language. While linguists do have methods, these are means of studying the language itself. Reading programs obviously include language and therefore ought to draw upon the findings of linguists for guidance in what is taught about language, not for direction in method.

The so-called "linguistic" programs do not classify clearly at either extreme of decoding or meaning. The fact that they do not isolate individual letter sounds distinguishes them from the synthetic phonics programs. Instead of teaching children to read by the synthetic approach of sounding out letter by letter, "linguistic" approaches use patterns. They do, however, classify as implicit phonics, since they teach words and then attempt to teach inductively the generalizations that are often taught deductively in the synthetic programs. For example, instead of teaching that "*a* says /a/" or teaching a rule that the letter *a* between two consonants stands for its "short sound," "linguistic" programs provide pattern experience with stories about "Nan can fan Dan" or "A fat cat sat on a mat" with the intent of having the children, through this experience, generalize that when they see the letter *a*, or especially the phonogram -*an*, they can use their understanding of that phonogram to decode a strange word.

As can be seen from the example sentences, "linguistic" programs certainly do not fit in the meaning emphasis extreme (which will be discussed later), since one will get little meaning from sentences such as those used in pattern stories. In fact, the vocabulary of "linguistic" programs consists of words chosen to fit the patterns taught rather than in terms of their frequency of use or the likelihood of children understanding their meaning. For example, if the phonogram -*ig* had been taught, *fig, jig*, and *rig* were seen as appropriate words for beginning readers, since children are supposed to use nothing more than their knowledge of this pattern to decode the new words.

I recall seeing a demonstration of how this was to work with the beginning reader. The exposed word was *clown*. The child was supposed to figure out the word by seeing that it began like *climb* and ended like *town*. Not only does such an approach rest on a very tenuous foundation in logic, it also has little support in research. In fact, the whole basis for a "linguistic" program seems unfounded if, from such experience, one expects children to apply this pattern approach to unlock a strange word. It does not appear to be an independent word attack skill, nor is its use supported by evidence from studies with children (Murray, 1974; Lyttek, 1974) which revealed that children tended to recognize more commonly used words than less commonly used words, regardless of whether or not they recognized the phonogram from which the words were generated.

Programmed Instruction and Computer Assisted Instruction (CAI)

Programmed instruction, with or without a computer, is an outgrowth of Skinnerian behaviorist philosophy. Its major strengths are considered to be that instructional elements are broken down to their smallest parts, all responses are immediately reinforced, and rate of progress is individualized. However, even though the rate of progress is individualized, content is not: Students are forced to go through each step, whether they need it or not; there is no room for insightful learning in programmed material.

Although Programmed Reading (Buchanan and Sullivan, 1963) is seldom found in general use these days, the insertion of programmed material into computers as computer assisted instruction (CAI) seems to be making a comeback. There apparently is nothing new under the sun, and CAI certainly is not new (Hillerich, 1973). We saw the rise and fall of many efforts at CAI in the 1960s and early 1970s.

A recent revival is represented by IBM's Writing to Read (WTR). This is a system that uses typewriters, computers, and additional adults as a means of teaching a combination approach that has elements of i/t/a (initial instruction in phonetic spelling, actually encouraging misspelling), DISTAR (consonant sounds are pronounced in isolation and need to be blended together), language experience (children are to learn to read from their writing), and neurological impress method (daily practice in listening to and following recorded stories).

WTR uses ten program disks to develop phonetic spelling of thirty words—ranging from *cat* to *uniform*—through repetitive drill on the spelling of each isolated sound. Most of the time is spent away from the computer as children make words, write sentences, copy them on a typewriter, and make other words on their own. Suggestions in the manual are limited but sound in directing teachers to encourage writing without concern for mechanics.

A two-year evaluation by Educational Testing Service (Murphy and Appel, 1984) suggested what one would expect from knowledge of research on i/t/a and other programs of this type: Because children were encouraged to write and were not criticized for their spelling, they wrote better than children in a control group. In fact, WTR might reinforce our knowledge that any computer or word processor can ease the writer's chore of transcribing. However, in evaluating reading achievement, no control group was used. Here the report indicated that WTR children read significantly better at the end of first grade than they did at the beginning! In fact, while no comparison of reading achievement was made, 85 percent of non-WTR teachers surveyed reported their students were reading as well as or better than previously; only 73.9% of WTR teachers felt the same.

PROGRAMS OF MEANING EMPHASIS

Meaning emphasis programs are often referred to by critics as "look-say" or "sight," but are more accurately designated as "analytic" approaches. Pupils first learn to read some words, then they are led to "analyze" these words in order to develop phonic generalizations. For example, after learning to recognize *but, be*, and *boy*, youngsters can be taken back to see that these words all begin with the same letter, and they can pronounce the words to recognize that they all begin with the same sound. As a result of this analysis, they "discover" that the given letter stands for the identified sound. In contrast to the earlier reference to "explicit phonics," this technique may also be called "implicit phonics," since letter-sounds are implied through experience with words rather than explicitly taught.

Most of the isolated, nonbasal approaches to beginning reading have a decoding emphasis, while most basals have been meaning-emphasis programs.

In addition to meaning-emphasis basal programs, there are at least two additional meaning-emphasis approaches that ought to be discussed here. Both can be classed as even more toward the meaning extreme than any of the basals; or, to put it another way, more away from the decoding extreme than any basal. They are the Language Experience Approach and Individualized Reading.

Language Experience Approach (LEA)

LEA has been best promoted by Van Allen (1968), who stated the basic understanding to be achieved through it with children:

> What I can think about, I can talk about.
> What I can say, I can write (or someone can write for me).
> What I can write, I can read.
> I can read what others write for me to read. (p.1)

Children are to dictate their story, the teacher will write it for them, and that story will then become the material used for learning to read. Who could argue with a philosophy that encourages use of the natural language patterns of children, along with their own words on topics of their choosing, as beginning reading materials?

Unfortunately there is also room for debate here in all but the most unusual circumstances. While I see LEA as an excellent supplement, especially with older—remedial—students, it has severe drawbacks as the only approach to initial reading instruction.

First of all, young children speak in much more involved sentences and use a much more varied vocabulary than any teacher is going to use for the first reading material. Hence, the teacher most often paraphrases what the children say. As a result, one of the basic strengths of LEA is lost: The story is no longer in the words or sentence patterns of the children. Take a look at some of the beginning LEA stories. They usually go something like this:

> We went to the zoo.
> We saw the tigers.
> We saw the lions.
> We saw the monkeys.
> We had a good time.

When have you heard a five- or six-year-old speak like that? Yet, to do otherwise—to write the involved sentences and to use the varied vocabulary of such children—would present an impossible piece of prose for them to use for beginning reading. Also, one of the most important reasons for reading anything is lacking in this setting: Since the children dictated the story, they already know what it is about and have no reason for reading it to find out. Furthermore, unless the teacher is very knowledgeable about reading instruction, that teacher is likely to "teach" reading as a matter of memorizing the words.

Yet a valuable part of LEA is the initial demonstration that print represents the same language that these youngsters have been hearing and speaking for several years. That advantage can be achieved by having young children dictate an experience, writing it as they dictate it, reading it back several times to check for revisions, and then pointing out, "We'll save this story. Later in the year, after you've learned to read, you might want to read about some of the things we did at the beginning of the year."

Also, for older students, LEA offers an opportunity to deal with topics of interest to them and enables the joint construction of reading materials. Since such youngsters are usually in the care of a reading specialist, there is also less concern that the skills will be neglected in the process of instruction without the assistance of a teacher's guide.

Individualized Reading (IR)

Another approach at the extreme meaning end of the scale is Individualized Reading. This is not a reference to the individualization of reading that arose in the 1970s. In fact, it is almost a direct opposite in basic philosophy in that the latter focused on the atomization of reading into its most minute skill elements whereas IR just about lost the skill portion of the program in many instances.

IR grew out of a rebellion against the lock step of basal reading programs. Educators such as Lazar (1957) and Veatch (1959) said, in effect: Children aren't all interested in the same stories; let's have self-selection. They don't all move at the same rate; let's have self-pacing. They don't all need the same skills; let's teach them individually. Let's throw out those old basal readers and teach reading using nothing but library books.

The teacher was then to go about the room, holding individual conferences with each child and teaching that child whatever skill was needed at the time. As any experienced teacher might guess, with twenty-five to thirty students in a class, very few skills got taught in such a one-to-one effort. On the other hand, children did a lot of reading and discussing—they had fun really reading! Furthermore, any examination of research on this approach (Sartain,

1960) will reveal at least two important points: Children using IR did about as well in reading achievement as did those locked in basal reading programs, and the individual conferences, however superficial, contributed to enthusiasm and interest in reading. Both of these advantages can be incorporated into the use of any basal series if the total program in reading is seen as a combination of basal and library reading, as described in Chapter 9.

Of course, because use of basal readers is so widespread, these programs periodically come under attack. Most often the "weaknesses" pointed to—the lock-step approach, for example—are in reality examples of *misuse* of basal.

For example, most valid criticisms come from the common *misuse* of basals by allowing the basal reading program to become the *total* reading program: With its emphasis on management systems and its fragmentation of skills, the basal could allow no time for children to *read* anything. Teachers think they must use every bit of material in the program. Here again, the teacher's judgment and creativity must come into play. Any basal has more suggestions for instruction and practice than almost any child needs, partly because there may be the one who needs that much extra help, but also partly because no publisher wants to be outdone by the others; there are undoubtedly more errors of inclusion than of omission in any published program.

Educators must recognize that any basal program is nothing more than a vehicle, designed for the convenience of a knowledgeable, sensitive teacher, for teaching necessary skills in an organized, consistent, and sequential manner. As such, any basal is only half of a total program. The other half lies in the enjoyable application and practice of the skills in library books. Again, however, making the basal the entire reading program is not a weakness inherent in any program; it lies in the hands of the teacher.

EVALUATION OF APPROACHES TO BEGINNING READING

As you examine most basals today, you will find some phonics taught initially and some meaning included. Few classify neatly into either extreme as pure examples. However distinctions, best exemplified by the explicit/implicit criteria, do exist. In any given program you may find:

- specific instruction on the sounds letters represent (explicit)
- patterns and words emphasized (implicit)

Context may be:

- stressed as a means of guessing words (implicit)

- stressed as a tool to be used along with phonics to assure attention to meaning
- ignored (extreme explicit)

Improved reading instruction must rest on both logic and research. That research cannot be the global comparison of programs to see which is better, such as was attempted in "The Cooperative Research Program in First-Grade Reading Instruction" (Bond and Dykstra, 1967). In this massive study, two or three different reading programs, from i/t/a to LEA and from Words in Color to basals, were compared in various combinations in twenty-seven centers around the country. Some of the studies were extended through second grade and a few through third grade. The results, collected and blessed by computer statistics, should have surprised no one: In terms of the reading achievement of children, there was more difference between teachers in the same program than there was between programs.

This finding is often interpreted to mean that "the teacher makes all the difference." While few would disagree that teachers make an important difference and that good teachers are essential, programs also make a difference if teachers will only follow them. The findings also indicate that such specific comparisons of reading programs are not feasible for research. Anyone who has been in the classrooms of other teachers knows that too many teachers do not follow the program they and their children are holding in their hands; teacher and students may be holding a meaning emphasis program in their hands, but the teacher is teaching that program as if it were a synthetic phonics program. It is this fact that keeps us from succeeding in such specific comparisons of reading programs.

Are Any Programs More Effective Than Others?

While we cannot point to research to prove that one specific approach is better than another, we can look to the broader collection of studies to get some direction, to find the compass point toward improving reading instruction.

Programs of the 1960s. The research on the many programs that arose in the 1960s indicated that, at best, those programs were no more effective than existing approaches and in many instances not as effective (Smith and Strickland, 1969). Probably more telling than all of the research is the fact that we are hard pressed to find many of these programs in use today.

Basal Reading Programs. In contrast, basal reading programs on both sides of the continuum (explicit/synthetic and implicit/analytic) continue to be used. Hence, common sense suggests that these must work or they could not have survived over time.

In examining the broad collection of research and summaries, we find a general tendency for the extreme decoding emphasis programs (explicit phonics) to result in higher reading achievement at the end of first grade (Bliesmer and Yarborough, 1965; Chall, 1967). Part of the reason for this finding, however, is the fact that reading achievement scores at the first-grade level rely heavily on word recognition; if the youngster can sound out the word, that is, say the word, that child can most likely respond successfully on the first grade reading achievement test. Although there is a section called "comprehension," how much understanding is measured by a three-sentence paragraph with five words to a sentence? Any youngster who can say all the words can score well on such a test. However, by third grade or so that is no longer true; by that level one must truly understand what is read in order to score well on such tests. Hence, not measured in the case of that young decoder is the long-range effect of the extreme phonics emphasis, where youngsters make noises or say words without using context or being concerned about reading for meaning.

An Unplanned Study. One of the few longer-range studies (Morgan and Lightfoot, 1963) was a natural study, not planned in advance. The authors compared third-grade reading achievement in four schools, two that used a rule-oriented phonics program and two that used a meaning-emphasis basal reading series. They found a significant difference in favor of the meaning-emphasis program in both reading vocabulary (significant at .05) and reading comprehension (.01).

Meaning Emphasis vs. Synthetic Phonics. Sparks and Fay (1957) compared two schools in the same community with similar students and staff; one used a meaning emphasis basal series while the other used that same series along with a synthetic phonics program. Pupils were followed and tested from first grade through fourth. The investigators found that at the end of the first grade, the children enrolled in the school with the extra program in phonics had higher scores in total reading achievement as well as in the various subtests. At the end of second grade, differences were not clear-cut: on some subtests the phonics-emphasis children were ahead; on others, the meaning-emphasis pupils scored higher. By the end of fourth grade, there was no significant difference in achievement of the two groups, despite the use of two reading programs by the phonics group.

Sparks and Fay also found that by the end of fourth grade, the "fast learners" in the single basal program were superior to those in the phonics program. The point is that once children reach higher levels, where comprehension becomes a more important factor in the testing of reading achievement, the extra phonics is of little value. An extreme phonics emphasis may become a handicap because the reader has developed the habit of processing all the letters in print and is too often satisfied with saying the words rather than getting the meaning.

Extreme Phonics Programs. The artificial isolation of the sounds in words, as advocated by the extreme phonics programs also leads to another problem. Teachers of such programs actually create the problem of "blending," a problem that could not otherwise exist. Obviously, the child who is taught to read by making noises letter-by-letter—"sounding out"—must then find a way to "blend" those isolated sounds back together into words. When has a two-year-old ever had a problem of blending sounds together to make words? Only when children are taught the artificial technique of pronouncing the sounds of words in isolation do they then have to get those sounds blended back together. Of course, while the problem is avoidable, it certainly is serious when present. I recall a fourth grader who had been drilled on this kind of phonics. Larry knew more phonics than I could ever learn, but he could not read. When presented with the word *nest* in a test situation and asked to sound it out, Larry was quite at home. He looked at the word and very clearly grunted "nuh" "eh" "suh" "tuh" five times before he recognized what the word was. With such an approach, how could anyone pay attention to the meaning of a word, much less of a selection?

Long- and Short-Term Memory. From another standpoint, investigators have pointed out the influence of long- and short-term memory on understanding. Long-term memory holds a nearly unlimited amount, but items are slower to call up as compared with short-term memory. Short-term memory can hold only about five chunks of information for about five seconds (Mandler, 1967) before they are lost or reinforced and sent into long-term memory. For us as mature readers, the five chunks of information in short-term memory are five ideas as we read along, for the child learning to read through a letter-by-letter approach, however, those five chunks of information are five letter sounds. The poor youngster who comes to a six-letter word will lose the beginning of that word before getting to the end. What is that child to make of reading?

Comprehension Monitoring. We know what such children described above make of reading. Studies of comprehension monitoring (discussed as part of metacognition in Chapter 7) indicate the difference in attitude between good readers and poor readers. The good readers are accustomed to silent reading and follow-up discussion; the poor readers are accustomed to oral reading. When asked how they know when they are doing a good job, good readers consistently respond with statements such as "When I understand what I am reading." Poor readers respond with statements such as "When I know all the words."

The Best of Both Worlds. In summary, both analytic and synthetic phonic programs seem to have a strength and a weakness when viewed in their extreme. On the one hand, the extreme phonics-emphasis programs—synthetic phonics—give youngsters a fast start in reading because they can say all the words; they also too often give young readers the impression that they are reading well if that is what they do—say all the words. On the other hand, extreme meaning-emphasis programs—analytic phonics—usually have the handicap of getting children off to a slower start; conversely, youngsters learn from the very beginning to pay attention to meaning—they know that reading is a matter of reconstructing ideas represented on the printed page.

Does the approach to beginning reading instruction have to be an either/or situation? I believe we can have the best of both worlds without the weakness of either. We can teach explicit phonics but also teach children to use their phonics along with context in order to attend to meaning. In fact, my criteria for a beginning reading program are two: I want a program that (1) gets youngsters started as quickly and as efficiently as possible, but (2) in a manner that doesn't become a handicap at more mature levels of reading. Let's use common sense and research to investigate such an approach.

FOUNDATION FOR AN APPROACH TO BEGINNING READING

Let's begin by examining logically what is necessary for success in reading. We know, for example, that no literate adult would have any difficulty in reading the following:

W– m–st t– –ch –ll ch–ldr–n t– r– –d w–ll.

In reading the foregoing sentence, you may not know exactly what you did. However, probably no one—after noting that the dashes stood for vowels— looked at the first word and decided that the letter *e* was the only letter that made sense, then, on coming to the word *must*, went through the process of "mist," "mast," "most," "must" and gave up in despair. In fact, many readers may not have consciously noticed that dashes were substituted for vowels.

Most likely you identified the word *children*, possibly associated *teach*, and from there went on to build context, which indicated that the last word had to be *well*, not *will* or *wall*. In other words, as adults we still use the consonant sound associations that we've established automatically through our experience with print, and we still use context to anticipate words that would make sense. We certainly do not process words letter by letter in our reading.

The importance of this use of consonants can be demonstrated further by repeating the above sentence using only the vowels instead of the consonants:

–e –u– – –ea– – a– – – –i– – –e– –o –ea– –e– –.

Obviously no one could read the sentence presented with only the vowels.

There are at least three good reasons why the consonants in the first example provided more reliable information than did the vowels:

1. Consonants tend to be more limited in their sound representations; that is, if readers see the letter *m* at the beginning of a word, they can be relatively certain that the word is going to begin with the same sound as that heard at the beginning of *must*. In dealing with vowels, if we see the letter *a* at the beginning of a word, all we can be certain of is that its name is "a." That letter might stand for the sound heard at the beginning of *at, ate, all, about, avocado*, or even *aye!*

2. English has roughly two consonant sounds for every vowel sound represented on a page of text. The trigrams *can, Nan, fan, Dan* represent the approximate proportion of consonants to vowels. Therefore, the reader has twice as many clues from the consonants.

3. The consonant letters provide the ascenders and descenders, while the vowels are all neatly the same size. Hence, it is the consonants that provide the quick recognition clues referred to as configuration. For example, notice the greater difficulty in reading when the type is all in caps:

W– B–L– –V– TH–T –LL CH–LDR–N C–N L– –RN T– R– –D.

To avoid any misunderstanding about configuration, I should point out that it is a helpful device that adds speed for the experienced reader; even mature adults do not make configuration a major clue in word recognition (Williams et al., 1970). Therefore, there is no intent here to suggest that youngsters be given experiences with interpreting those funny boxes that some teachers draw on the chalkboard. For example, what word is this?

There is no way that you could know what word that box represents any more than I could—and I drew it! In fact, the evidence indicates that experience with such boxes is of no help in either reading or spelling (Gorelick, 1965).

Going a step further, from logic to research with children, Williams and others (1970) and Marchbanks and Levin (1965) used three-letter and five-letter nonsense words to investigate what clues beginning readers did use in word identification. They found that youngsters used the initial letter as their first cue to word identifications, then the final letter, and ultimately other letters in the word.

Hence, context continues to be useful; consonant sound associations are dependable; and the first letter of a printed word is the one most used. Putting this together, we have an efficient start for beginning reading, and one that does not have to be unlearned at more mature levels. In fact, we can begin with a skill that any four-year-old, English-speaking child already has: the ability to use oral context. Such youngsters expect what is said to them in their native language to make sense, and they anticipate words from a speaker, much as an adult does. When being read to, many preschool children will supply a missing word if the reader stops before reading the final word in a sentence. We can help four- or five-year-olds to become consciously aware of what they are doing: They are using the sense of the other words that are spoken to them in order to anticipate or predict a word that would make sense; they can supply a word that might be missing in a sentence that is spoken to them.

If we make children consciously aware of their intuitive ability to use spoken context and if we also teach them the sounds that consonant letters usually stand for in the initial position in printed words, they can begin reading at this very point. For example, consider yourself a nonreader. Nevertheless, if you were provided orally with the words printed in regular English in the following sentence and if you had been taught that ——◯ stands for the sound you hear at the beginning of "wagon" and "wind," you should be able to read the strange word in the following sentence:

It was a hot day, so we decided to go for a swim in the ——◯ ⅄ ♯.

In the foregoing case you were able to read a strange word using only the context and the first consonant letter. You didn't really care what sounds the other letters represented because you knew that the word had to be *water*. This is also an important point to teach children from the very beginning: They need not—in fact, should not—use every possible phonic understanding they have in order to identify a strange word; they should use the meaning and only as many of the letter sounds as they need in order to read that printed word. As pointed out earlier, it is a handicap to overprocess words—to sound them out letter by letter.

Obviously this is a primitive stage of reading, but it is a beginning and one that doesn't have to be unlearned at later stages of development. However, to carry the point a bit further, if ——◯ represented the sound heard at the beginning of "path" and "pan," then the printed word in the same context might be *pond* or *pool*. Now the reader must use the final consonant as well, in order to determine which word was correct. In any event, that reader still doesn't need to be concerned about what sound the vowel letter stands for in that particular word.

In fact, if one uses context, there are very few examples where knowledge of the vowel sound is essential to successful reading. And it is also very seldom that anyone does any reading *in the real world*—the world outside of school—where that person doesn't have context. Even a grocery list provides context of a sort: The reader doesn't expect to find *cloud, airplane,* or *house* on that list. Perhaps about the only reading without any context would be street signs as one drives along, seeing *Washington, Monroe, Lincoln,* and then suddenly *Oak* and *Elm* or *First* and *Second.*

Of course, one might argue that vowels are essential in some contextual situations, such as "We wanted to go fishing but couldn't find the b–-t" (*boat, bait*). However, even here, if this was a realistic reading situation, there would undoubtedly be enough context to make that kind of overanalysis unnecessary. For example, a preceding or following sentence would likely be "We knew we tied it up here at the dock before we left" or "We knew we put the can under that old stump."

The effectiveness of this combination of context and initial consonant sound associations was demonstrated from another standpoint. Hillerich (1967) compared this approach with an extreme phonics program, using two neighboring school districts that were very similar in socioeconomic background, IQ's of children, teacher training and experience, and so on. With a total of 722 children in the two school districts, results indicated that children learning to use context and consonants scored significantly higher in reading achievement at the end of grade one, despite the fact that the other district had the presumed advantage of a synthetic method at grade one and also used two reading programs. The most interesting result was that the entire difference in reading achievement was reflected in one subtest—the subtest of comprehension—and that that difference was great enough to make a significant difference in the total test score. Such a finding suggests that too much attention to vowels can lead to an overprocessing of words and a resultant distraction from meaning.

This argument for combining the strengths of both extremes is further reinforced by trends in basal reading programs of the 1980s, as compared with their 1960s and 1970s versions. The extreme synthetic approaches have attempted to incorporate some comprehension at the early stages; meanwhile, the extreme analytic approaches—represented best by "Dick and Jane"—introduce some phonics earlier.

THE WORLD OF PHONICS

The preceding explanation lays the foundation for what I see as the best of both worlds: capitalizing on the strengths of both the phonics and the meaning-emphasis programs; that is, teaching phonics *explicitly* by developing consonant letter-sound associations, but using these only to the extent ncessary, along with context, to figure out a strange word.

Such an approach provides skill for early independence in decoding words, and it develops the habit of reading for understanding from the very beginning. Children learn that reading is a meaning-getting act; it is neither a matter of making noises for letters nor one of memorizing words. Furthermore, the reader is not taught to be a context guesser nor a letter-by-letter "sounder-outer" of words. That beginning reader *is* taught to use context and phonics together in order to get meaning from the printed page.

To carry this one step further, however, we must recognize the limited role of phonics in the process of reading: Phonics is helpful only if the word is already in the reader's listening-speaking vocabulary, since phonics enables beginning readers to approximate the sound of a word that they know the meaning of when they hear that word. Further than this, phonics is of no help. For example, the child who has been taught both sounds represented by *th* (*th* as in *the* and *th* as in *thumb*) may, upon seeing the word *the*, recall only the sound heard at the beginning of *thumb*. That youngster would attempt to say *the* with that beginning sound, recognize that there is no such word, and be close enough to realize what the word was.

Conversely, if a word is outside the reader's listening-speaking vocabulary, then phonics is of no value at all. For example, the italicized word in the following sentence may be strange to you:

She decided to *parget* the brick wall in the kitchen.

If you've never heard the word *parget*, no amount of phonics is going to help you decide what that word means—and meaning should be your primary concern as a reader. The only alternatives are to use the context, which in this case is very weak, or to use context and a dictionary.

Of course, as a mature reader you know enough to check one more step. You know that often there is more helpful context after a strange word than there was before it, so you might read on before getting the dictionary. Then you might find:

... because she didn't like the rough surface.

Using this additional context, you may be satisfied with the very general meaning you get for *parget*; that is, you know it has to do with eliminating the rough surface of the brick wall, whether by smoothing it over, covering it up, or blowing it up. Then you may continue reading, unless it is important to you to know exactly what the meaning is, in which case you are still faced with the necessity of using a dictionary. Sometimes, of course, you may have very strong context that satisfies this need, as in the remainder of the sentence:

... and decided that plaster would be better.

In this case, you have a synonym for *parget* and you are completely satisfied in terms of meaning. However, if you are asked to read that portion to the group, your concern would be expanded to include the pronunciation of that word. Does phonics help the reader to pronounce the word? As stated previously, phonics will only enable approximation of the word. If the reader has never heard that word before, there is no way of knowing whether the attempted pronunciation is correct or not.

Of course, we could go through the usual kinds of rules a second or third grade teacher might subject pupils to if they came upon the word *parget*. First of all, it's a long word, so we might use our structural analysis to decide if it is one syllable or two. Certainly, any second grader should know the rule: "If there are two consonants between two vowels, we divide between the two consonants unless they are a digraph or cluster, in which case we never divide them but use the next rule." Well, the business of "digraph or cluster" is already a tough decision for a second or third grader, but let's proceed to use the rule and identify the word as having two syllables.

Now the children can use their phonics. They certainly should have no difficulty in knowing what sound *p* stands for at the beginning of the word. Then they find a vowel between two consonants; in fact, they have the same situation in both syllables. The rule: "When there is a single vowel between two consonants, it has its short sound, unless it is followed by *r*, in which case it has a sound that is neither long nor short." This rule suggests that children should know what the vowel sound is in the second syllable, and they should know exactly what it is NOT in the first. Incidentally, that rule is true only 57 percent of the time! How would you like to gamble in public TWICE with odds like that?

Of course, a few other questions still remain before the word can be pronounced: Does the *g* represent its hard or soft sound? (One of my graduate students helped to answer that question by indicating that when *g* is followed by *e*, it has its soft sound, as in *gem*. All I could do was point to the second syllable and ask, "As in *GET*?" No, that's an exception!) One might also ask, should *-et* have the regular English pronunciation or the French /ā/ ending? And finally, how does one accent the word, as in *TARget* or as in *forGET*? It is truly doubtful that anyone, relying only on a knowledge of the rules we foist on children, would want to pronounce *parget* in public.

COMPREHENSION

Of course, if a teacher looks upon learning to read as a matter of learning words or learning to make noises in response to printed letters, then a discussion of comprehension is irrelevant. However, if one sees reading as a process whereby the reader is gaining information and reacting to information on a printed page, then the topic of comprehension is at the heart of reading instruction.

Comprehension skill actually begins long before the beginning of reading instruction since reading comprehension skill is nothing more than thinking skill applied in the reading act. Therefore, preliminary to any actual reading, the prospective reader can begin to develop—and should be developing—thinking skills in the oral language: the ability to draw conclusions, to make judgments, to predict outcomes, and so on. This means that long before any formal skill related to reading is introduced, young children can be responding orally in terms of these thinking skills. They should be responding to stories read to them and to ideas told to them; they should be responding in terms of their own telling of experiences and thoughts. Practically all the skills called "reading comprehension skills" can be taught at the listening-speaking level before children ever begin to read. In fact, if they cannot perform these thinking skills at the oral level, they can hardly be expected to perform them in reading. Furthermore, the more experience children have with these skills at the oral level, the more proficient they will be when applying them in a reading situation.

Even more basic to beginning reading is the assumption that individuals already speak and understand the language in which they are expected to learn to read. At best, those who don't speak the language can do no more than learn to parrot noises for printed words; they certainly cannot be expected to learn to read with any meaning. This point applies not only to children who come from a different language background, but also to youngsters who were born into the standard English-speaking family but who, for one reason or another, have not had sufficient experience communicating—and being communicated with—in their native language.

While Chapter 10 presents evidence and methods for working with children from other language or dialect backgrounds, the next two chapters will deal with the subject of readiness and its foundation in oral language development, a foundation essential for all children.

Chapter 2

What Is
Reading
Readiness?

In practice, reading readiness (often called "emergent literacy" these days) has been defined as everything from having a tea party to fussing with phonics. Most often it has consisted of generalized social and language activities.

While some argue that "readiness" cannot be taught, I contend that it is not educationally sound merely to sit around and wait for it to happen. Probably the best general statement on readiness was that of Carpenter (1961), who proposed that "readiness is somewhere between wanting to and having to." We might amend this to include "and being able to."

Certainly reading readiness is not a subject to be taught from 9:00 to 9:30 between socialization and nap, nor is it a stage of development that occurs at a specified age. *Reading readiness is a multifaceted continuum of cognitive and affective elements developed from birth to that stage (not a "go/no-go" point) when an individual has the skills, understandings, and attitudes necessary for reading.* In a broader sense, readiness is a continuously developing process that begins at birth and continues at ever higher cognitive levels until death, as each experience and strengthening of skill makes the individual ready for the next step.

Such a view recognizes reading readiness (emerging literacy) as a continuous developmental process beginning with abilities to perceive visually and auditorily and extending to the ability to function receptively and expressively in language. At whatever point more formal or intensive instruction merges with the natural informal development of the learner, that intervention must begin by identifying the present level of the learner's development and must result in placing that learner into appropriate experiences on the developmental continuum.

TRADITIONAL CONCERNS

Too often traditional misconceptions about reading readiness deprive children, even in kindergarten, of the experiences for which they are ready. Too often discussions of reading readiness present unsubstantiated beliefs that delay the kind of instruction from which many children could benefit. The following points, often considered as important reasons for delaying reading instruction in the kindergarten, need reexamination on the basis of existing evidence:

1. *Chronological age.* Many kindergarten teachers believe that the youngest child in the class is handicapped in terms of potential achievement.

2. *Mental age.* Many still believe that a child must attain a given mental age, usually six or six and a half, before being ready for reading instruction.

3. *Visual maturity.* Some contend that the five-year-old's eyes are not adequately developed physically for reading instruction.

4. *Language development.* Most often this point is interpreted as a need for additional vocabulary development prior to reading instruction.

5. *Experiences.* Children must have a variety of experiences in order to have established referents for the items about which they will read.

6. *Motivation.* The child must want to read before instruction in reading can begin successfully.

7. *Social development.* At age five, youngsters need to develop socially before being introduced into any formal activity such as reading.

8. *Visual discrimination.* Children need to be taught to see differences in shapes before they can be expected to notice differences in printed letters.

9. *Auditory discrimination.* Traditionally this has been interpreted to mean that children must be taught to hear differences in sounds before they can be expected to learn to read.

10. *Rhyming words.* Most kindergarten teachers—and the programs they use—provide for auditory drill on word endings, matching by rhyming sound.

In looking at some of these points, we might say, with Harste and others (1984): "Unless such constructs have a viable base in theory, one must seriously ask why hair color, shoe size, or other theoretically unrelated concepts are not also studied." But let's examine each of the foregoing points on the evidence that exists.

Chronological Age (CA)

Different states have different entrance requirements in terms of chronological age. When I was in Illinois, for example, children had to be five on or before December 1 to enter kindergarten. In that state, kindergarten teachers are quick to point out that they can "spot that November birthdate the minute the child walks into the room." In Ohio, children are older at each grade level since the entry month is September 30. There, kindergarten teachers claim they can "spot that September birthdate the minute the child walks into the room." If the date were moved up to March, I'm certain they would point to the "February birthdate." Yet research reveals little (Jansky and de Hirsch, 1972; Wolf, 1972) or no (Durkin, 1974–75) relationship between CA and achievement within any school age group.

All this is not to be considered a plea for early admission. It merely points to the fact that one cannot look to CA as an explanation for differences among children in a given age group. And that is what "grade level" is—nothing more than an age grouping. Furthermore, as will be discussed in greater detail in the next chapter, I would like to see such considerations as CA dismissed for another—and more important—reason: Its instructional implications are minimal. If CA were a major factor, what would be the implications: Make the child comfortable and *wait*! It seems to me that we, as educators, should look for factors that lead us to instruction.

Mental Age (MA)

The claim that a given mental age is necessary for beginning reading is based on a report by Morphett and Washburne (1931) from a study they did in 1928 in Winnetka, Illinois. While one might question details of the study, such as their definition of "satisfactory progress" as being the completion of thirteen progress steps and a knowledge of thirty-seven sight words by February of the first grade, the important point is that certainly methods, materials, teacher preparation, and children are different today from what they were in 1928 in Winnetka. Equally important, readiness does not relate to MA per se but is a function of method.

Finally, we need only look at the research correlating MA or IQ with reading achievement at the beginning levels of reading to recognize that there is far from a one-to-one correspondence since most studies at this level typically show a correlation of .30–.40, a predictive value about 10 percent better than chance. Besides, rather than avoid instruction with the child who is less advantaged, isn't this the one we should support even more through instruction?

Visual Maturity

Educators philosophically opposed to instruction of any kind in the kindergarten offered the argument in the 1960s that exposure to print would harm the eyes of five-year-olds because their eyes were not sufficiently mature to handle such fine detail. However, we have yet to find any evidence that exposure to print *at any age* can be harmful to a child's eyes. In contrast, there is evidence from a variety of sources, including two medical doctors (Eames, 1962; Shaw, 1964), indicating that exposure to print is *not* harmful. In fact, the former wrote:

> Children five years of age were found to have *more* accommodative power than at any subsequent age. The poorest *near* visual acuity found among the pupils studied was quite sufficient for reading the usual texts. (Eames, 1962, p. 432)

Only from anthropological studies can we find any connection between activities and visual changes. Those studies reveal that individuals in a reading society do tend to become nearsighted, while those in a hunting society tend to become farsighted. However, one would hardly say that the occupations have "ruined" the eyes.

Language Development

At any age, there is always a need for further language development. However, are there certain developmental activities in language that must be accomplished with all four- or five-year-olds prior to instruction in reading skills? Consideration of this point must be expanded beyond the mere concern for vocabulary development to include the expressive use of language, auditory discrimination, the production of sounds, and the use of the sentence patterns of the language.

Expressive language, of course, begins at birth. By age two, children typically have a vocabulary of about two hundred words and are speaking in at least two-word sentences. From the age of thirty to forty-two months, the average youngster experiences a rapid growth in vocabulary, culminating this period with an expressive vocabulary of about one thousand words (Menyuk, 1971).

By age five or six, it seems almost impossible to arrive at a reasonable estimate of the average listening vocabulary—approximations have ranged from thirteen thousand to as high as forty-eight thousand words. In fact, some estimates of receptive vocabulary for this age exceed other estimates of that vocabulary for adults! Certainly the receptive vocabulary of the average five-year-old is adequate for beginning reading instruction.

Furthermore, the acquisition of syntax—the rules for organizing words into sentences—is apparent in two-year-olds, who have already abstracted certain rules that are applied in the use of one- and two-word sentences (McNeil, 1970). This skill develops rapidly from about age three. By age five, it is clear from a variety of studies (for example, Hunt, 1965; Loban, 1963) that the typical five-year-old English-speaking child produces all the sentence patterns of the language. Loban indicated that one could not distinguish the kindergartener from the sixth grader in terms of basic sentence patterns used.

An important point in this development of syntax is that the type of error the preschool child makes moves from its beginning in omissions to substitutions, alterations, and finally to redundancy as the youngster experiments with the basic principles of English syntax. This sequence occurs as a result of normal preschool language experiences. In studies attempting to develop better control of syntax in young children, Menyuk (1971) reported that this acquisition seemed to be more than mere imitation. For example, one group of children was trained by having the teacher expand each child's original statement and then having the individual repeat the expanded statement; the other group had intensive verbal stimulation without imitation. Results indicated that increased verbal stimulation was better than an equal amount of time devoted to practice with expanded statements. (Chapter 3 will develop this point in much greater detail.)

The importance of verbal mediation has also been verified in other studies. Stein (1972) reported that four-year-olds reproduced only half as many actions from a simple nonverbal film as did seven-year-olds. However, when an adult verbally labeled the actions in the process of the silent film, the four-year-olds reproduced as many of the actions as the seven-year-olds.

This importance of human interaction and verbal mediation was clearly demonstrated by Moskowitz (1978), who reported on a child with normal hearing born to deaf parents who communicated in sign language. Because the child was asthmatic and confined to the house, unable to interact with speaking individuals, television was used to develop oral language. At three years of age, the child was fluent in signing but could neither speak nor understand English. Passive reception of the language is not sufficient.

In terms of the patterns of language development, however, a less traditional point ought to be made here. While typical four- and five-year-olds may have mastered the basic patterns of the oral language, they may not be familiar with the patterns of the printed language if they have not been read to at home. A transcript of spoken language will indicate very quickly that the oral mode represents a rambling, back-and-forth, fragmentary, self-interrupting kind of pattern. In contrast, the printed or literary language is a linear, direct kind of communication. We do things in speech that we would never consider doing in print. Hence, the child who has not been read to must be provided experience with the patterns of printed English in order to become familiar with those patterns as well as with the oral.

Finally, consideration must be given to oral language development in terms of phonology if a reading program is going to have youngsters working with phonics—with sounds in words. According to Templin (1957), all the single consonant sounds in English except *z* were produced correctly in initial position by 75 percent of four-year-olds. Since the production of sounds is more difficult than their auditory discrimination, one should expect no difficulty on the part of most four- or five-year-olds in the discrimination of those single consonant sounds in initial position.

In conclusion, it is readily apparent that the typical four- or five-year-old has adequate control of both vocabulary and syntax for that child to be introduced to reading instruction, if language development is the criterion. On the other hand, many children enter school who are—by definition—not "average." They may need additional language development prior to any kind of formal instruction in other skills. Their needs will be discussed in Chapter 3.

Experience

Concerns for providing experiences prior to any instruction in reading skills were based on the desire to be certain that children had referents for the things about which they would read. While this is an important consideration, the reality is that there are few children today who don't have adequate experiences to make the content of early reading materials meaningful to them. Even if informal programs were justified in kindergarten forty years ago, the backgrounds of children today are certainly different from that period. Increased mobility and social involvement of children have contributed to preschoolers' experience, just as television in general has contributed to their language development and *Sesame Street* in particular to their beginning reading skills. Obviously, those children who don't have pertinent experiences will require them. For most children, however, about all we can say is "What's new in the early levels of any reading program?"

Motivation

No one can argue with the importance of motivation; children should want to read by the time they are going to be taught how to read. However, this point seems somewhat overstated if one looks at reality. Often we may be doing more to unmotivate children with the delaying tactics practiced in some kindergartens and first grades. You need only ask children about to enter kindergarten why they are going to school. Their response usually is "to learn to read."

The social pressure, the prestige of being able to read, and the typical preschooler's fascination with the idea of words in print all indicate that the child *is* motivated to read if only we will take advantage of that motivation. In our culture, even the adult thinks nothing of joking about an inability in math with statements such as "I'm so poor in math, I can't even balance my checkbook." However, where does one find the adult who, even if it were true, would admit "I'm so poor in reading that I can hardly read the newspaper?"

To continue the preexisting motivation, of course, means to provide experiences that incorporate success. There is no better motivation for achievement than success each step of the way.

Social Development

Obviously there is a need for social development at any age. This does not imply that time must be taken to see that youngsters grow socially before they are prepared to develop reading skills. There is no evidence that children can develop socially only in a play situation. In fact, most of the social experiences of the preschool child have been in play situations. Nor is there evidence to suggest that a skill-oriented game will not provide as much social skill development as playing in the sandbox.

Visual Discrimination

Traditionally, activities in visual discrimination have been considered the formal part of reading readiness. The task was to teach children to see differences in pictures and in geometric forms. For example, children might be asked to look at a row of rabbits, one of which has only one ear, and to mark the one that is different. Such an activity has nothing to do with reading and is really an insult to the intelligence of a five-year-old who can already distinguish his own black cocker spaniel from that of a neighbor when the two dogs are playing down the street.

In one readiness program, children are asked to look at a row of mugs, one of which is turned in a different direction, and to mark the one that "is different," as if a mug becomes something different when it is turned. Worse, some teachers show children sets of triangles with one turned in a different direction for this same kind of activity. That is teaching children a misconception in math, since a triangle is a triangle, no matter how it is turned.

Besides, the ability to read has nothing to do with seeing the difference between one- and two-eared rabbits, mugs turned in different directions, or triangles. Gates demonstrated this point in his research in 1926, yet readiness programs persist in such time-wasting activities, even when common sense mitigates against them. Whoever reads pages of such symbols? Learning to read requires understanding that minor differences between letters can make a difference. It is pages of letters that children must learn to discriminate, because that is what they will be reading.

Some teachers use the "gross" kinds of discrimination activities with the excuse that they are teaching their children what they mean by "same" and "different." Yet one cannot ever teach the meaning of "same" or "different" in the abstract nor expect their meaning in one sense to carry over to another. A candy cane and a jelly bean are "the same" and they are "different"; a group of people can be considered "the same" and yet each person is "different."

Certainly such general instruction is of no value in terms of letters since what is the "same" or "different" in one sense is not true in another. For example, examine the following string of letters: a α a A $\mathcal{A}$. Any literate person would acknowledge that they are all the "same"; they are all a's. Yet b and d would be considered "different," even though they are obviously the same symbol merely turned around. Turning a mug doesn't change it; turning the letter b around does.

To look at this in another way—to a child, m, n, and h are all the same in that they are all hump-backed letters. However, in English, it makes a difference whether there is one hump or two. Furthermore, it even makes a difference if the stick is short or long.

Such discrimination is more than a matter of "seeing" the difference. The nonreader must realize what distinctions make a difference in letters. In other words, what has been called "visual discrimination" practice ought to be converted to practice in "letter-form discrimination" if it is to be part of an effective readiness program. When the young child looks at a dog, whether it is looking east or west, it is still the same dog; when the child looks at the printed letter, if it is turned one direction it is b, but turn that letter around and it is now a different letter. This is the kind of distinction a youngster needs to make to be successful in reading.

Auditory Discrimination

Traditionally, auditory discrimination activities have followed the same pattern of instruction in gross differences as visual discrimination activities, trying to teach children to distinguish differences that have nothing to do with reading, trying to teach them to hear the difference between the roar of a jet and the rumble of a truck, between the slamming of a door and the ringing of a bell.

Such activities are sheer nonsense for any four-year-old who can speak the language. These children can already hear a difference of one phoneme in words. Evidence on this point was very clear to me in 1965 during a summer spent evaluating Head Start Centers in the Midwest, from central-city to rural Appalachian areas. Because of my interest in beginning reading and auditory discrimination, I made it a practice in every center to ask various children, "What is your name?" If a child replied "Johnnie," I would say, "Oh, Tonnie?" After a response of "No, Johnnie," I would follow with "Oh, Bonnie?" "Oh, Connie?" and so on.

Without exception, not one child failed to correct me. Those "disadvantaged" four-year-olds were discriminating the difference of one phoneme in a word. On the other hand, it should be obvious that if the children had been asked, "What did I do to your name?" or "Did I change the beginning sound?" they would have been unable to understand or to verbalize an explanation about beginning sounds; in fact, they would not understand what was meant by "beginning sound." The point is that, barring physical impairment, the English-speaking child already discriminates the difference of one phoneme in a word.

It should be clear that any child who speaks the native language must hear differences of sounds in words, or communication with that individual would not be possible. How would a child know, without the ability to hear the difference of a single phoneme in words, whether a speaker is asking for "a bite from your bread" or "a mite from your head"? When asked to do so, the typical four-year old will bring the rock, as opposed to the lock or the sock, when those items are lying together on a table.

All this is not to say that the four-year-old could reply accurately if one asked whether two words began with the same sound or different sounds, any more than the Head Start children would have been able to verbalize what I did in changing the beginning sounds of their names. This point, the difficulty of helping children to understand what is meant by the beginning of a spoken word, will be discussed specifically in Chapter 4.

Rhyming Words

Work with rhyming words has been a tradition in kindergarten and is found in the reading readiness books of most basal reading programs. In working with a group of kindergarten youngsters who had been drilled on rhyming words, I became aware of what a handicap that was in getting them to recognize "the beginning" of spoken words and to identify whether pairs of words began with the same sound or different sounds; they insisted that "rock" and "sock" began with the same sound.

Since English is a language that is read from left to right, I wondered why kindergarten teachers, working with children who had not yet established this directionality, concentrated on the ends of words, a procedure that, at best, encourages confusion and, at worst, reversals. A search of the literature, from the present back to the 1890s, offered no research supporting the teaching of rhyming words. Apparently this practice is one of those traditions that have no basis in evidence.

On the other hand, I found where I believe the practice did begin. Edmund Huey, in his classic text *The Psychology and Pedagogy of Reading*, published in 1908, suggested that young children ought to have fun with the sounds of language, that they ought to enjoy listening to poems and jingles. Certainly I would not disagree with Huey, and apparently neither did William S. Gray, who included such activities in the original "Dick and Jane" readers. However, as too often happens in education, we somehow managed to turn a good idea into a drill on skill. Instead of enjoying the sounds of rhymes and jingles, children are now drilled on ending sounds. We need to put this activity back into the original perspective of Huey, letting prereaders enjoy listening to rhymes and jingles, having fun with the sounds of language, but without drilling them on the precise point of similarity and thereby setting them up for reversals.

In summary, evidence suggests that typical statements about reading readiness are irrelevant, delaying tactics that ought to be abandoned. They have been identified traditionally as some sort of official starting point for formal education, usually in the kindergarten, whereas reading readiness is actually a continuum that begins long before the start of formal education. By nursery school or kindergarten age, most children are well beyond the elements considered in the preceding list. In other words, instead of talking about reading readiness we ought to talk about emergent literacy: for some children this will be the prereading foundation in language (Chapter 3) and for many children by age five, the prereading decoding skills (Chapter 4).

TESTING FOR READING READINESS

Educators need to recognize readiness as a continuum in terms of evolving skill and experience. Then the task is to identify where youngsters are on this continuum—that is, to diagnose their needs—and to provide appropriate instruction to meet those needs. In contrast, those who view readiness as a *point* in development—and its teaching as a fixed block of content—are inclined to use readiness tests to measure whether or not a child has achieved the appropriate level, that is, whether or not the child is "ready" for instruction.

The tests are then most often used for grouping purposes, offering little or no diagnostic information.

Tests Need to Be Diagnostic

In order to be diagnostic, a test would have to measure factors that *cause* reading success or failure. In contrast, the typical reading readiness test is made up of a battery of items that have been found merely to correlate with future reading success, including tests of letter names, matching printed words, identifying picture names that begin and end with the same sound, and completing geometric shapes. Other such tests also include vocabulary measures and even simple numbers.

The basic problem with such tests is that they offer little help other than determination of the ranking of children; they are not diagnostic, so they fail to suggest to the teacher what must be done to help those children who score in the "not ready" category. For example, neither a knowledge of letter names nor the ability to copy geometric forms is necessary for success in reading, but those two skills represent the best subtests in terms of *correlation* on most readiness tests.

And "correlation" is the key word. Yet everyone learns in a first course in statistics that correlation does not imply a cause/effect relationship. There is a high correlation between the height of elementary children and their reading ability—sixth graders are taller than kindergarteners and they read better—but we don't stretch kids in order to make them better readers.

Readiness tests do a disservice since they are usually used to sort children. They are most often administered at the end of kindergarten or at the beginning of first grade and results used to place children in groups on the assumption that the test scores are good predictors of potential success for these children. Unfortunately, evidence suggests that not only is there lack of diagnostic value, but that even the predictive value of such tests is questionable for individual children. A collection of twenty-six studies has reported correlations ranging from .36 to .79, with an average predictive value about 15 percent better than chance (Hillerich, 1966b).

Probably the best statement on the matter was made by Silberberg and others (1968) when they correlated reading readiness test scores with reading achievement: "...a great saving in testing time could well stem from using only the Letters and Numbers subtest, or perhaps, by not testing reading readiness at all. In either case, the sacrifice in information would be minimal" (p. 218).

Since the late 1950s, as a result of the work of Durrell at Boston, educators have recognized that a simple test of letter names is as good a predictor of future reading success as any commercial readiness test, with correlations from .55 (Olson, 1957) to .67 (McHugh, 1962). However, as with so many items on readiness tests, this information is not diagnostic. As will be discussed in Chapter 4, a knowledge of the names of the letters is not needed in order to learn to read.

The important point is to quit using correlation in order to predict future success or failure in reading and to begin diagnosing youngsters' needs in order to prevent failure and to assure success. The danger with predictions is that they often become self-fulfilling prophecies. Some children are identified as "not ready" and are assigned to generalized kinds of activities, while those identified as "ready" are taught to read. When achievement in reading is tested, which group is likely to read better? How much does this policy help to continue even the modest correlation we now find between reading readiness scores and reading achievement scores?

The Self-fulfilling Prophecy

This point of the instructional determination of success or failure has never been better demonstrated than in a study by Fry (1965) that was designed to investigate whether or not reading readiness was a prerequisite to reading instruction. Subjects for the study were eight sections of entering first graders who were randomly assigned to "readiness" or "nonreadiness" groups. The former were provided readiness experiences, while the latter began immediately with preprimers of the basal program. When reading achievement was tested, the investigator found that the nonreadiness groups scored significantly higher in reading.

Behind these results are some interesting points, including the fact that one should never accept a researcher's conclusions without finding out how those conclusions were arrived at. Here is the background information: Reading achievement of pupils was tested in December of first grade with a word recognition test (words in isolation). At the time of testing, many of the "readiness" children were still "reading pictures"; they had not been exposed to print. It's little wonder that those who had an opportunity to see words in print recognized more words on the recognition test than did those who had never had such an opportunity! As Fry clearly pointed out, "Hopefully, it won't come as too much of a surprise to many educators that children learn to read if they are taught to read."

In effect, such findings suggest a point that has been even more clearly demonstrated in recent years: the importance of allocated time and time on task, also called academic-engaged time (Wiley and Harnischfeger, 1974; Gettinger and White, 1979; Denham and Lieberman, 1980). All these researchers seem to be finding that if children are given the opportunity to learn, they are more likely to do so. In fact, Gettinger and White reported that time on task was a greater contributor to achievement than was IQ!

KINDERGARTEN: A NATION DIVIDED

It would be most difficult, if not impossible, to make a general statement about kindergartens in this country beyond the fact that they began over a hundred years ago and were full-day programs. They were reduced to half-day as a result of a surfeit of children combined with shortages of teachers and facilities. Kindergartens today are as diverse as can be in terms of scheduled time as well as program content and expectations. Furthermore, in most school districts there is better articulation between elementary school and high school than there is between kindergarten and first grade. In fact, we might say that kindergarten has been the stepchild in the schools. When funds run low, what is one of the first programs considered for cutting? Even the designations "kindergarten" and "first" grade imply that kindergarten is no part of the graded sequence. Probably a major reason for the lack of articulation, however, is the fact that many principals feel uncomfortable at that level, so kindergarten teachers are pretty much left to do their own thing.

Nevertheless, we seem to be approaching a time when kindergarten will come into its own. While attendance usually is not mandatory for children, most do attend kindergarten. In fact, these days many attend nursery schools, although few of these are sponsored by school districts. In most school districts, children attend kindergarten for half a day, with one teacher responsible for both a morning and an afternoon group. However, at least nine states have a majority of school districts offering full-day kindergarten classes: Alabama, Arkansas, Florida, Georgia, Hawaii, Mississippi, New York, North Carolina, and Virginia. Furthermore, twenty-six states now finance full-day kindergarten (Humphrey, 1986).

While the increase in allocated time that comes with full-day kindergarten attendance provides the opportunity for greater accomplishment, what happens within that time is much more important. For example, most studies comparing the effectiveness of full-day with half-day programs indicate that the increased time results in significantly increased achievement (Humphrey, 1983). However, if the original half-day program is merely stretched out to fill a full day, there is usually no difference in achievement. Time helps, but program is vital.

Full-day/alternate-day kindergartens arose in the 1970s as a money-saving answer to fuel costs for buses. In contrast to the effectiveness of the full-day/everyday program, alternate-day programs usually result in no significant difference in achievement (Minnesota Department of Education, 1980), a finding to be expected since engaged time is the same as for half-day programs. Interestingly, a need for "naps" does not seem to be a factor in full-day programs.

Philosophical Differences

The 1960s witnessed the greatest outbreak of research in the area of kindergarten and reading readiness, with a resultant polarization on the question of early skills instruction. Professional articles ranged from "Harm Might Result" (Sheldon, 1963) to "They Should Have the Opportunity" (Durkin, 1963) and included the challenge "Dare We Evaluate Paradise?" (Hillerich, 1963).

While differences as extreme as those in the 1960s can still be found in some kindergarten situations, most have recognized the capabilities of five-year-olds, as well as the variations of background and abilities among them. Nevertheless, one still finds extremes of both the developmental school of thought and the cognitive.

Developmental Point of View

The developmental view, probably best exemplified by the Gesell Institute, goes back to the 1920s when Gesell initially exerted an influence. As a medical doctor, he was naturally interested in physical development and evolved his theory that failure in school was a result of pushing children into situations before they were developmentally ready. His followers today still see a major cause of failure in school as a matter of children being developmentally too young for the grade they are in (Ilg and others, 1978). In some school districts, as many as one-third of kindergarten-age children are sent back home for another year or, in some cases, assigned to a transition kindergarten, focusing on physical activities, that leads to two years in kindergarten. Usually the decision is based on a variety of Gesell Institute tests that—again—merely correlate with, but do not necessarily cause, future reading success or failure. In fact, as pointed out by Meisels (1987, p. 71), the Gesell test is based "on a set of tests with unknown validity and reliability, a theory that is outmoded and unsubstantiated, an unverified notion of developmental age, and a racially and ethnically narrow normative base."

While readily recognizing that some children come to kindergarten less "ready" than others in terms of their experiential background, language development, and so on, we certainly ought to question sending such children back home. If the home has done so little in the preceding years, why should school authorities expect more in another year? In fact, isn't the basis for early intervention the idea that the sooner we get such children, the more we can help them? And help them we can, as demonstrated by studies summarized by Chaille and others (1984). In contrast, the teacher or administrator who sends the child home for another year is, in effect, saying, "You can do a better job at home than we can at school." (Unfortunately, that might be true in a few of these instances!)

Others speak in dichotomies. Elkind (1981) talks about "the demise of the 'readiness' concept" in the shifting from the biological/physical (à la Gesell) to the intellectual. While his emotional appeals (Elkind, 1986) might attract some, we can still maintain that use of research and common sense can assure an appropriate and a balanced program of "readiness" for five-year-olds.

Piaget's stages of development are also referred to at times as a reason for not engaging in some cognitive development. Yet those stages were based on measures of children who had certain experiences up until the time of Piaget's testing. If the prior experiences of the subjects had been different, the "stages" would also change. In fact, Donaldson (1978), a student of Piaget, discovered that many of Piaget's findings were more a matter of the child trying to match the perceived expectations of the examiner than one of not being able to pass the test. For example, in the case of two sticks identified as equal, when the examiner asks the child to watch while moving one of the sticks and then asks if they are still the same, is it not reasonable that the child would consider the adult's admonition to "watch" as a significant point and therefore expect change in the result? Harste and others (1984) use the term "intentionality" in supporting the position that Piaget's findings often are a result of the language of the testing rather than a child's inability to perform the act.

Possibly more to the point, however, I find it most difficult to accept anyone's stages of development, as if humans were born with built-in cognitive clocks and could only make the next move when the time was right. As a teacher, I have to believe that prior experience determines what can be learned next; hence, the task is to determine what prerequisites to the desired learning are missing in this individual's background and then to provide those prerequisites.

Although more related to interest in language than to interest in children, there is much ado these days about metalinguistics—the ability to talk about language instead of learning to use it better. A number of educators seem to believe that "readiness" is a matter of having children verbalize what a word is (Yaden and Templeton, 1986). They feel that only after children demonstrate the ability to understand "word" are they ready to learn to read. However, even linguists cannot define "word" without reference to print. Hence, it should be obvious that understanding of "word" is a *result* of literacy; it is neither a *cause* nor a *prerequisite*.

Cognitive Point of View

In contrast to the delaying attitude at the developmentalist extreme, at the cognitive extreme one finds those who would move all program content down, and who would, in effect, turn kindergarten into a "little first grade." The danger here, of course, is in substituting workbooks and drill for the freedom of movement, experiences, and language development so needed by five-year-olds.

We might say, in fact, that the danger in either of the extremes lies in ignoring the most fundamental principle in education: children differ. Just as all first graders do not read at first grade level, so too all kindergarteners do not enter kindergarten as perfect little zeros in reading: Some are below zero and some well above. In fact, language assessment of 916 entering kindergarten children (Hillerich, 1978b) indicated a range in those children from a low of age two in language development to a high of age eight in reading ability—a six-year range in cognitive development among entering kindergarten children!

What Does Research Suggest?

As you might expect, practice lags behind the great amount of research that was reported in the 1960s on this topic. Even in 1964, when less evidence was available, Morrison (1964) reported the lag in practice as compared with the thinking of reading specialists: While 73 percent of 795 responding school districts did not allow kindergarteners to go beyond traditional reading readiness, 58 percent of the specialists surveyed felt that "formal reading instruction extending beyond readiness should be provided in the kindergarten."

A cursory examination of the research supporting and disclaiming the early introduction of basic skills might suggest that the evidence is mixed. However, a closer look provides some clarification. First of all, there were fewer studies discounting the importance of formal skills instruction in kindergarten or prekindergarten as compared with the number of those that found the early teaching of formal skills effective.

More important, a summary of this research (Hillerich, 1966a) clarified the difference between research studies that report no significant difference between formal and informal approaches and those studies that do report differences in favor of children who are taught formal skills in kindergarten or earlier. Studies reporting the latter finding, with or without a workbook, are usually dealing with specific reading skills, providing a definite decoding strategy, as opposed to the reading of pictures or instruction in irrelevant skills. In other words, if one does not want to teach specific reading skills, this can best be accomplished *without* a workbook. As the following studies demonstrate, however, if the desire is to teach a decoding strategy of specific skills, the workbook helps in the accomplishment of those skills.

Probably the largest study of this type was done by Brzeinski (1964), who randomly assigned 122 kindergarten classes to experimental or control groups. The experimental groups were taught the prereading skills of using oral context and consonant letter-sound associations to read printed words, while control groups participated in a regular informal kindergarten program. Figure 2-1 shows how the kindergarten groups were randomly assigned to a total of four treatment groups in first grade, with Group A serving as the control.

Results, measured by a reading achievement test at the end of first grade, indicated a significant difference between each of the groups. Highest was Group D, which had been taught the prereading skills in kindergarten and had a follow-up program that took advantage of that instruction; next highest was Group C, which had developed the skills in kindergarten—regardless of the reading program they had in first grade. Lowest of all was Group A, which had never received instruction in the specific skills as they were taught in kindergarten. In other words, the study clearly indicated that the formal teaching of the prereading skills in kindergarten was most effective, even if it was not followed up in first grade. While Brzeinski's study continued through sixth grade with findings still in favor of Group D, results along the way were contaminated with other factors.

Other studies support the effectiveness of such skills instruction in kindergarten, regardless of socioeconomic level (Wise, 1965), mental ability (Schoephoerster and others, 1966), or even chronological age (Wolf, 1972).

Hillerich (1965) reported a study involving twenty-two sections that were taught prereading skills in kindergarten. In this study, the previous year's children, who had been taught the prereading skills in first grade instead of in

Figure 2-1

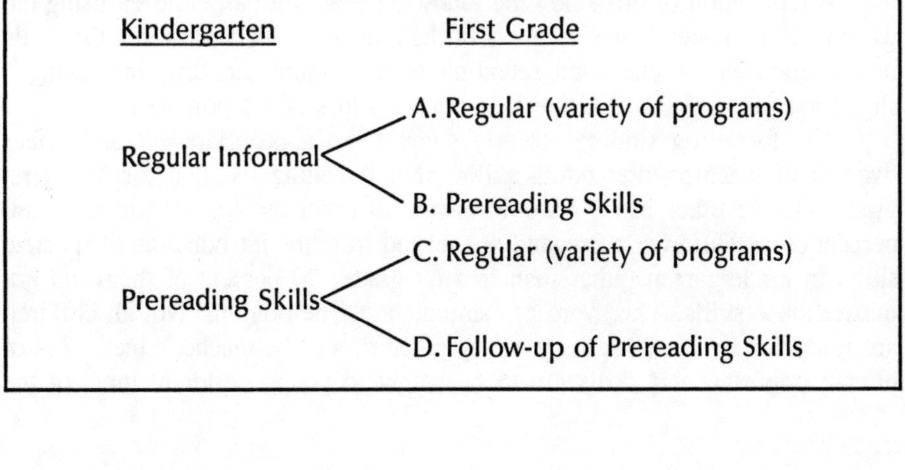

kindergarten, served as the comparison group, thereby controlling for program and teacher variables. The purposes were to identify whether or not:

1. kindergarten children could master the prereading skills requiring use of oral context and consonant letter-sound associations to read printed words,
2. this could be done more effectively with or without use of a workbook in kindergarten,
3. the skills would be retained over the summer,
4. the teaching of such skills in kindergarten would result in higher reading achievement at the end of first grade.

In answer to the first consideration, 70 percent of the kindergarten children mastered the skills at the end of the kindergarten year. Mastery was measured with an achievement test for the skills taught.

Half the sections were taught the skills with the aid of a workbook; the others were taught the same skills, but without the use of workbooks. The effectiveness of the workbook was clearly indicated in that 88 percent of the children using the workbook mastered the skills compared with only 50 percent of those who did not use workbooks.

The prereading skills achievement tests were repeated at the beginning of first grade before instruction or review took place in order to measure the degree of forgetting over the summer. The average loss was 2.6 points on the 58-item test. While statistically significant, such a loss could hardly be deemed of practical significance.

Reading skill was measured at the end of first grade. There was a significant difference in favor of children who had been taught the prereading skills in kindergarten, despite their slightly lower academic aptitude when compared with the control group. In fact, the difference in means on the reading achievement tests was 15 raw-score points.

A replication of this study the following year, with all children using the workbook, indicated that 83 percent of the kindergarteners mastered the skills in kindergarten. A check on retention over the summer, this time using a shortened survey form of the test, indicated a loss of 1.1 points.

The foregoing findings clearly suggest the appropriateness and effectiveness of teaching prereading skills, if not reading itself, before the first grade. On the other hand, I would hasten to point out that, while about 80 percent of the children in my study benefited from the introduction of specific skills in kindergarten rather than in first grade, 20 percent of them *did not* master those skills. This word of caution should be obvious: Not all children are ready for any given activity at any given time. The teacher's method is of utmost importance if skills are to be taught to young children; most of the teaching should take place through oral activity, physical movement, and games. A workbook may then be used to summarize the skill point of the activities.

There are educators who would group children and teach skills to some while not to others. We still lack the evidence and instruments to make those kinds of groupings with any degree of confidence. Hence, an exposure program in kindergarten or nursery school seems far more appropriate: All children have the opportunity to play the games and to participate in putting marks on workbook pictures; while many, if not most, will develop the skill intended, others can still take part and enjoy that participation with their peers. Those who do not master the skills must be retaught those skills at a later time. Although admittedly without solid research evidence for or against the point, I firmly believe that those children who have been pleasantly exposed to the skills, even though they haven't mastered them in kindergarten, are in a better position to master those same skills at a later time than they would be if they had never been exposed to them since I also believe that "the real variable then may be encounters rather than age" (Harste and others, 1984). This, of course, is in line with the point made elsewhere: The child who needs the most help ought to receive it as early as possible; that child should not be shunted aside to wait for that help.

KINDERGARTEN TODAY

Perhaps I'd better begin this section with a disclaimer of sorts. What I have been talking about for kindergarten and what I continue to deal with in this section is the "reading readiness" portion of the kindergarten. What is said is in no way intended to minimize the importance of the other kinds of activities that should make up a good kindergarten "day." The rhythms, art, puzzles, housekeeping corner, free play, and even snacks provide for important learning experiences in their own right. Reading readiness is only one of the many important activities for these children. Furthermore, in the good kindergarten, this "reading readiness" is not necessarily an unrelated block of time—much of it is incorporated into other activities as the teacher, for example, has youngsters organized for an activity on the basis of whose name begins like "Mary."

In fact, even the discussion of "formal" versus "informal" instruction should be clarified. Many people equate formal kindergarten programs with skills instruction and informal with lack of skills. The formal/informal distinction is more a matter of method, of how the teacher handles the class. I've seen many good kindergarten teachers who teach prereading skills, and their children are having a good time while learning. Unfortunately, I've also seen a few teachers who could turn a kindergarten party into the most formidable formal affair.

To continue, however, what do we find in kindergarten today?

Yes, research does have an impact. As a result of previous research, as well as observation of the needs and capabilities of youngsters today, most kindergarten teachers currently include some formal instruction in prereading skills, usually consonant letter-sound association, whether or not their adopted program provides for such instruction. In fact, the majority of kindergartens also make use of a workbook as part of their program. Furthermore, some now express a legitimate concern that there is too much workbook orientation for this age group.

Why must that "educational pendulum" swing to extremes? Yes, some have taken the cognitive-skills approach to the extreme of turning kindergartens into "little first grades." Conversely, with no evidence to negate research extending from the 1960s, others today (for example, Elkind, 1986; Fields and Hillstead, 1986) are echoes of the past, renewing emotional appeals in reactionary attempts to set kindergarten back to a caretaking endeavor.

Research has had an effect on publishers as well. No more do we find the readiness book devoted entirely to "reading" pictures. On the other hand, my analysis of readiness levels of the sixteen basal reading programs published in the 1980s revealed that many are far from pure in following the evidence on what is helpful and what is not. Yes, instructional time is precious and should not be wasted. Yet it is here that many basal reading programs, in their effort to appeal to everyone, sin so much by commission rather than by omission: They include many items that are irrelevant to skill or success in reading. Hence, it is here that the effective teacher must weed out the unimportant activities and develop those that are important.

Less than half of the sixteen readiness programs ultimately arrived at teaching consonant letter-sound associations, and most of those failed to present a specific decoding strategy. Most included such time-wasting fillers as gross auditory and gross visual discrimination, or even—in the case of four programs—sensory discrimination. Most of the programs did include some language activities, such as listening comprehension, following oral directions, sequencing, and expressive language. However, while most of them also incorporated work with color words and instructional language, very few provided for general vocabulary development. In contrast, some also had lessons in memory, occupations, and even body language.

From this one might conclude that "reading readiness" is anything a teacher does before reading instruction begins. However, evidence previously cited, including that of time on task, suggests that some activities are going to contribute more than others. Since instructional time is precious in school, let's not waste it on noncontributing activities. Instead, let's devote our energies to providing the foundation in readiness that leads to greater success in reading. That foundation—oral language development and the beginnings of print awareness—will be presented in Chapters 3 and 4.

Chapter 3

Prereading: Foundation in Oral Language Development

Nowhere are the language arts more obviously interrelated than in the case of oral language skill as a prerequisite for success in either reading or writing. The act of reading or writing involves not only the ability to think in the language, but it requires the ability to manipulate the sounds of words, and to understand and use the spoken language.

Chapter 2, which discussed the process called readiness, pointed out the great amount of language expertise already possessed by the typical preschooler at age four or five and presented some of the negatives, the "housecleaning" chores so necessary if instructional time is to be used wisely at the beginning levels. It is the purpose of this chapter to analyze the oral language needs of the preschool child and to discuss ways of developing specific aspects of language mastery in the child who needs these kinds of skills.

This chapter will deal, item by item, with those skills and understandings that are most often developed in the home in the preschool years. If they are not developed when the child enters a more formal school situation, whether prekindergarten or kindergarten, they are the point at which the teacher must start, regardless of the child's age. While the specifics are given in an approximate sequence, there is no solid evidence to indicate that this is the necessary or only sequence; most often each of these items is developed at various stages of sophistication while other elements are being initiated or further developed.

EARLY IDENTIFICATION

For some years, one of the educational slogans at the nursery and kindergarten level has been "kindergarten screening" or "early identification." Some educators have become seriously concerned about the kinds of activities engaged in under this banner. Too often early identification has been little more than early labeling, a labeling that can result in early assignment of some children to failure.

To be more explicit, what too often happens in early identification programs is that a battery of tests is put together consisting of various activities that correlate with reading success or failure. These activities may be anything from the ability to copy geometric forms to the ability to walk a balance beam. Investigators then test kindergarten children with these activities, classify those children according to the results of the testing, and then give a reading achievement test at the end of first grade to verify the self-fulfilling prophecy that they established: Children who scored low on the items that correlated with reading success were indeed the ones who were not successful in reading. And so the investigators congratulate themselves on having successfully predicted reading failure.

As reported in Chapter 2, Fry (1965) demonstrated how well this classification for failure can work. Children do "learn to read if they are taught to read," and they will not learn to read if we deprive them of the opportunity to engage with print.

It is not the task of educators, any more than it is the task of parents, to *predict* reading failure; the task is to *prevent* that failure. Prevention requires more than merely testing with items that correlate with reading success or failure; it entails testing diagnostically—and with items that *cause* success or failure—to discover what the youngster needs or doesn't need, and it must include follow-up of that diagnostic testing with instruction in the areas of weakness in order to assure success. Fortunately, even some state agencies are expressing concern about predicting and assigning to failure:

> The central administration and building level administrators in local school districts should...limit prescreening of kindergarten children to the identification of handicapping conditions and/or gaining information about the learning needs of incoming students. (Nebraska State Board of Education, 1984)

FACTORS OFTEN CONSIDERED
IN EARLY IDENTIFICATION

Researchers (de Hirsch and others, 1966) investigated a battery of tests and later (Jansky and de Hirsch, 1972) compiled an excellent summary of factors related to reading failure. While their study was a correlational one and involved only fifty-three children, they administered a total of thirty-seven tests to those children and correlated the results with reading, spelling, and writing achievement at the end of second grade. In their report they summarized evidence on the various factors often considered in early identification. Most helpful is the direction their summary should give educators in terms of recognizing that reading failure is not something to blame on the child. It is time for us as educators to look to ourselves and what we're doing or not doing in order to explain why a youngster is or is not successful in reading.

Socioeconomic Status

Jansky and de Hirsch pointed out that, according to the evidence, socioeconomic status was not a significant factor in reading success or failure. Although some research refutes this claim, the point is an important one to make in terms of our attitudes. Too often low socioeconomic status has been used as an excuse for not teaching. Furthermore, it is not the low socioeconomic status that causes failure, even in studies that report such; it is the factors that often, *but not always*, are associated with low socioeconomic status—such as poor nutrition, lack of books in the home, not being read to in the preschool years—that are likely causes of reading failure. But by translating to these latter terms, we can do something about them; they are diagnostic in contrast to low socioeconomic status, a factor that most of us don't have the financial wherewithal to change.

Neurological Problems

These same investigators also reported that while a few children do have serious neurological deficits, the incidence of such deficits was so small that they did not stand out as a significant cause of reading failure.

Emotional Problems

While emotional problems may be a factor among some children, this has been a most difficult area to investigate. General evidence suggests that research has not identified which came first, the emotional problem or the reading problem. Although one can aggravate the other, I suggest that success in reading through appropriate instruction in skills certainly will not intensify a preexisting emotional problem. Conversely, lack of success in reading will most likely aggravate the problem. To put it another way, existence of emotional problems indicates the need for additional help with those problems, but it does not suggest that appropriate reading instruction be avoided.

Reading Readiness Tests

As discussed in Chapter 2, the traditional standardized reading readiness tests have been a way of life with kindergarten teachers for many years. Unfortunately, while they are a tradition, their use for individual children has very little justification since predictive values run only about 10 percent better than chance. Furthermore, they offer no diagnostic information since the slight predictive value they have is based only on correlation.

Teacher Judgment

Teacher judgment was reported by Jansky and de Hirsch to be a reliable indicator or predictor of reading success or failure. I would certainly verify that point from my experience working with kindergarten teachers. The problem here is that such judgment tends to be global rather than diagnostic; teachers need to back up their judgment with an organized checklist, much as an airline pilot—no matter how experienced—uses a checklist for every take-off and landing.

Of the thirty-seven tests administered in the de Hirsch studies, most correlated significantly with reading success or failure. However, statistical "significance" merely means that if the study were repeated with the same procedures and type of population, the investigator would most likely get the same results. It does not necessarily mean that the correlation is either practically significant nor dependable in terms of accuracy of prediction. Furthermore, of all the correlations with reading success, the highest was only .55, which means—in terms of forecasting efficiency—that it was only about 16 percent better than chance.

Five Best Predictors

The five best predictors from the de Hirsch study included tests of letter names, picture names, word matching, items from the *Bender Motor Gestalt Test,* and sentence memory. Considering these individually, one might identify only the ability to name pictures of common objects and sentence memory as subtests that have diagnostic value. Certainly the ability to function in language in terms of vocabulary and general familiarity with the language is essential if one is to be successful in learning to read.

Word matching, which has to do with the visual discrimination of words, relates to reading success if one considers that a child may not have had experience with print and does not notice the fine differences that distinguish one letter from another. Such an identified deficit should lead to instruction in letter-form discrimination, as will be discussed in Chapter 4.

In contrast, the high correlation between knowledge of letter names and reading success has been known for years (Durrell and others, 1958); however, one does not need to know the names of the letters in order to learn to read. Likewise, the copying of geometric shapes, such as those included in the *Bender Gestalt,* has been an element in most reading readiness tests since they were developed. Here too there is no evidence that the ability to copy geometric forms is necessary in order to learn to read. In fact, there is considerable evidence that training in visual motor skills contributes nothing to reading success (Cohen, 1969; Hammill and McNutt, 1981; Jensen and King, 1970).

A DIAGNOSTIC APPROACH TO EARLY IDENTIFICATION

As educators, we should be eager to move from the prediction of failure to the determination of needs and the avoidance of failure. In order to do this, we must take a diagnostic approach to early identification. We should try to discover what essential background, experiences, and skills children have and what they don't have, and to provide the ones they need so they can be successful in future reading activities. Hence, we need to consider what the necessary elements are for success in reading.

The act of reading involves the ability to function in the language, that is, to think in the language, an ability we might refer to at the prereading stage as listening comprehension. In order to comprehend oral language, children must have a certain meaningful vocabulary and control over the syntax of the language. This, in turn, presumes auditory discrimination ability, that is, the ability to hear differences in the sounds in words. In addition, it should be obvious that the act of reading involves printed symbols, so visual discrimination of letters and words is necessary. In order for youngsters to be successful, certain physical conditions are also important, despite the fact that research does not point to physical problems as significant causes of reading disability. Nevertheless, care should be taken that youngsters have adequate vision, auditory acuity, and a general physical health that will enable them to devote their energies to the task.

These prerequisites must exist in children who are going to be introduced to basic reading skills; for those who lack them, the prerequisites themselves must be supplied. A lack or a deficit in these areas is not a signal to avoid instruction, to wait, or to assign children to failure; it is a signal to provide even more intensified efforts at instruction so that such children will be given the background they lack. As will be explained later in this chapter, providing this background has been demonstrated to result in greater reading success by the end of first grade.

Specifically, a diagnostic approach to early identification should include a battery of tests to identify each child's development in terms of language skills arranged in a hierarchy. Despite an absence of research on this point, we might argue that using a language element receptively is easier than using that same element expressively. Hence, the following hierarchy suggests one kind of reasonable progression of language skills:

Receptive Skills	Expressive Skills
Auditory discrimination	
Instructional language	
Following oral directions	
Listening comprehension	Sequencing
Recalling sequence of events	Basic vocabulary
Using oral context	Expressive language

Let's examine each of these language skills in order of testing (Hillerich and Johnson, 1986) and in terms of what each consists of and how each can be diagnosed and further developed. The importance of these skills and techniques was verified in a study of 916 beginning kindergarteners and will be discussed later in this chapter.

Auditory Discrimination: Diagnosing

Authorities are in agreement that auditory discrimination is essential in learning to read. We can go even further and say that auditory discrimination is absolutely essential if one is to understand the spoken language. After all, how would an individual know if one were asking for silk or milk unless that person could discriminate the difference of one phoneme in those two words? While much has been made of auditory discrimination and its lack among children who are not successful in reading, there is a serious question as to whether it is an inability to discriminate auditorially or an inability to follow the test directions that causes a child to score poorly on an auditory discrimination test.

Those who disagree with this point often base their position on experiences with the Wepman Auditory Discrimination Test. That test is partially a test of auditory memory rather than just of auditory discrimination. Furthermore, young children have a difficult time understanding what is meant by "same" and "different" as applied to spoken words. In fact, comparisons of results on the Wepman and PDQ (Hillerich, 1974a)—the latter using picture pairs—indicated that five-year-olds made as many as ten times the number of errors *on the same sound contrasts* when using the Wepman.

At this point, it should be obvious that children learn their native language by engaging in it, by being communicated with, and by communicating, by listening, and by speaking. They are not born with language competence, nor does anyone sit down to drill them, sound by sound, on the sounds of language. They listen and imitate, and at age two they may not imitate very accurately. However, as indicated in Chapter 2, by age three they are beginning to do a fairly good job, and by age four most children demonstrate their competence, not only by their understanding but by their ability to reproduce and to communicate back the appropriate sounds of language.

Any parent or teacher who has doubts about a child's ability to discriminate language sounds can test that ability by using sets of pictures that differ by initial sound, to check each of the initial consonant contrasts. Directions to the child are: "Here are some pictures. I'll tell you the names of two; then I'll ask you to point to one of them. You point to the one I say" (Hillerich, 1974). Pairs of pictures might include: pan/man, bat/hat, dish/fish, rug/jug, sun/gun, yarn/barn, mouse/house, socks/fox, goat/boat, rock/lock, mail/nail, time/dime, wing/ring, bear/pear, dollar/collar, tie/pie, van/fan. Obviously the child who consistently points to the requested picture can hear a difference of one phoneme in a word.

While endings and vowel sounds can be tested as just described, if your view of reading is like mine, you will test only for initial consonant sounds since reading instruction will begin with such sounds rather than with vowels. Furthermore, vowel sounds—especially simple vowels such as in *pit, pet, pat, pot, put, putt*—are the most difficult to discriminate, and some, such as *pin/ pen*, are not distinguished at all in certain dialects. Barring the dialect problem, however, one is hard pressed to find even a four-year-old who can't bring the pin or the pen, depending upon which is requested. In other words, very few children will be identified who have difficulty with auditory discrimination. In fact, such children would probably be identified without the formal testing, if teachers were aware of the problem, since they will be children who come from a different language background and therefore do not have some of the sounds of English in their repertoire; speakers do not "hear" language sounds that are not significant in their own language.

Auditory Discrimination: Teaching

When there is a doubt, activities such as the following can be used for further practice in auditory discrimination:

1. Provide the child with a lot of oral language experience, talking about anything and everything, as well as taking walks, trips, and so on, so that child has more to talk about and to listen to.

2. Read nursery rhymes to the youngster and talk about them.

3. Collect pictures and miscall the names of some of them. For example, hold up a picture of a ball and ask, "Is this a call?" or "Is this a tall?"

4. Play a game of funny questions: "Do you eat Jell-O or yellow?" or "Do you sleep in a red or a bed?" Often four-year-olds will begin to participate by making up funny questions themselves.

5. Collect pictures whose names represent minimal sound contrasts, such as used in the testing, whether that be the initial consonant, vowel, or final phoneme. Then put a pair of pictures on the table and ask the child for one of the two; for example, from the pair wing and ring, ask for the wing.

6. Use objects instead of pictures to represent minimal contrasts, such as a rock, sock, lock.

7. Read a story such as "Henny Penny." Then have children make other combination words that differ only by the beginning sound, following the pattern of Henny Penny and Ducky Lucky. Children can also make these alliterative names from common objects found around the house: nickle pickle, fake cake, bare chair, and so on.

8. At a slightly more advanced level, have youngsters collect all the pictures they can find whose names have the same beginning sound. They might even paste these on a scrapbook page. For example, cut out a picture of moon or monkey and paste it at the top of the page. Have the children then name other pictures and compare the beginning sounds to decide which ones begin with the sound heard at the beginning of "moon" or "monkey."

9. Have children engage in a treasure hunt. This is the same kind of activity suggested in number 8, but they will collect all the little toys or objects they can find whose names begin with the same sound.

10. Use children's names to play "Going to Boston." If Mary is going to Boston, she may take only objects such as marbles, mirror, and so on. Jack may take only jumpers, jacks, jewelry, and so on.

It is important not to confuse immature speech with problems of auditory discrimination. For example, I have tested a considerable number of four- and five-year-olds who exhibited immature speech. Yet those youngsters, who would say "wing" for both wing and ring, could very clearly distinguish which was being asked for. In other words, immature speech is usually an expressive problem; it doesn't indicate a receptive one.

Instructional Language: Diagnosing

One step further in assessing the ability of children to function effectively in the language is the need for them to understand the instructional language teachers use in school: *in, on, under, first, next, last,* color words, and any other major words you as a teacher might use initially.

Incidentally, we are talking about criterion-referenced testing, which means that the teacher is free to add, delete, or modify items being assessed. For example, if color words are not essential to communication in your class early in the year, you might omit that particular item from your assessment. Conversely, if you are going to ask your kindergarten children to "elucidate" on everything, you'd better check to see that they understand the meaning of that instructional term.

Diagnosis can be accomplished by using a block and a shoe box for the placement words and pictures of colored objects for the color words. Youngsters may be told to place the block "in," "on," and so on; they may be asked to point to a particular color in the pictures.

Instructional Language: Teaching

Once more the test implies the kind of instruction needed. Children who have difficulty with placement words should be given practice with them; those who have difficulty remembering the names of colors can engage in the following activities dealing with colors:

1. Us a shoe box and block. Give directions to various children to put the block "in," "on," and so on.
2. Use a truck and blocks for the same kind of activity.
3. Play treasure hunt, where youngsters are to find objects that are "blue," "red," and so on.
4. Give children each a sheet of paper on which a square has been drawn. Have them use a crayon to put an X "under" the square; "in" the square; "beside" the square, and so on. This can be made more complex by having them put a "red" square "in" the box.
5. Consider movement as an important part of a young child's life. If a packing crate or large furniture box is available, a child can be the object, calling out "I am in the box," or "I am on the box."

Following Oral Directions: Diagnosing

Certainly the child who cannot understand and follow oral directions will have difficulty in any school task. Assessment of this skill is a matter of giving simple one-, two-, and three-step oral directions. You may begin by giving a simple one-step direction such as "Please close the door." Move on to a two-step direction and, if the child is successful here, to three steps, such as "Open the door, touch the window, and move the book from the desk to that chair."

Following Oral Directions: Teaching

This is one aspect of listening comprehension, but it is an easy one for most children since it deals with the spoken language that they are more familiar with. Begin where each child is, with one-, two-, or three-step directions, as follows:

1. Give simple one-step directions such as "Touch your nose," "Stand up," and so on.
2. Play "Simon Says."
3. Give a series of directions that involve body movement.
4. Play "Grocery Store" and have the child get one or more items.
5. Use the outdoors for more strenuous body movement directions, if weather permits.
6. Interrelate the language activities. Directions, for example, can involve expressive as well as receptive language. The child may follow an oral direction and then have practice in giving directions to peers.
7. Have children make or draw items as you give oral directions to "fold," "draw," "cut," and so on.

Listening Comprehension: Diagnosing

Children who, from their very earliest experiences, are involved in an active interchange with peers and adults usually develop quite adequately in the area of listening comprehension. On the other hand, the youngster who has been deprived of active participation in the language will need considerable experience to develop the ability to comprehend in the oral language. Furthermore, the experience of some children may have been limited to conversational—informal—language. As discussed in Chapter 2, such children, if they've never been read to, may be very proficient in the oral language and still have difficulty in understanding printed language. Skill may be assessed by reading a simple paragraph-story to the child and asking what it was about. Check off the memories (important items) that the child recalls.

Listening Comprehension: Teaching

1. Read to the child and discuss the story *for fun*. In such reading, the discussion should never become a quiz to find out if children

understood everything; rather, it should be a discussion to encourage active participation, using questions beginning "Would you have...?" "Why do you think...?" "Do you think...?"

2. Make up some "Who am I?" or "What am I?" riddles for the child to answer. "I am planted in the ground. I have a long trunk and wear leaves in the summer. What am I?"

3. At a more advanced level, you might read a three- or four-sentence story to the child and ask what it was about. Then reread it, changing a major situation or event. Have the child tell what was different.

4. Have children listen to a story and then draw a picture of their interpretations of that story.

It should be apparent at this point that the purpose for diagnosing these language skills is to enable the teacher to individualize instruction in the kindergarten or nursery school. I've certainly spent enough time with kindergarten children to realize they are not noted for their independent work habits. However, the kindergarten teacher with twenty-five or more children can still individualize by having a parent, senior citizen, or older student in the school come to the class and read to the small group who need extra experience in this language area. The only thing the reader needs to understand is that the story should be read and then discussed for fun—not as a quiz. For example, if *The Cat in the Hat* is read to the small group, discussion should not deal with "How many bad things did the cat do?" or "What color was the cat's hat?" It might begin with "If that cat came to your house, what would you do?"

Story records can also be used, and the child may draw a picture in reaction to the story listened to. Although not as effective as a live performance followed by discussion, stories recorded on tape by volunteers can also be used for children to listen to a short story and then make a picture of their interpretation of that story.

As part of the research study to develop this kind of diagnostic approach (Hillerich, 1978b), a parent survey asked the amount of time parents spent per week in reading to their children. It was in those schools where the parents admitted to doing very little reading to their children that the youngsters did poorly on the listening comprehension subtest. Is this any surprise? What has been said, from time immemorial, when parents asked how best to prepare children for school? Read to them!

The testing is certainly not to suggest that only children who have difficulty with this assessment need to be read to! *All* students should be read to—daily, at least—at all levels of schooling! However, there will be some who are identified as needing two or three times as much experience in listening to the patterns of printed English. These are the ones who must be taken aside and provided the extra experience that they missed in preschool years.

Sequencing: Diagnosing

Awareness of a sequence of events can be assessed in at least two ways. In one method, have the child recall the order in which events occurred in the story read; in the second method, have the child arrange, in order, three or four related pictures to tell a story. The first method saves time in the assessment, and children seem to do as well—or as poorly—on either. However, young children, even if they do recall a story sequence, have a tendency to begin retelling by starting with the point that appealed most to them. When this happens, allow the child to finish. Then ask "What happened first?" ... "What happened next?"

Sequencing: Teaching

The ability to recall or to identify a sequence of events is a more sophisticated skill in the area of language comprehension. In the study of 916 beginning kindergarten children, some were identified who didn't seem even to be aware that there was a sequence to anything they did. Thus, for such children, experiences need to begin at a very basic level: Children are more likely to recall a sequence of events that actually happened to them than they are to recall a sequence from a story read to them. Hence, the first items suggested in the following list are ones that deal with children's direct experiences:

1. Help pupils become aware of natural sequences in daily activities: They eat breakfast before they eat lunch, and lunch before dinner; they get up in the morning, and then they eat breakfast; they turn on the water faucet before the water comes out.

2. Discuss the sequence of events when youngsters go for a short trip, even to the grocery store. Ask them: "What did you do first?"..."What next?" The point here is not to recall every detail that took place but to report the recalled items in the proper sequence.

3. Involve children in sequencing by taking slides or pictures of the group on a field trip or engaged in some activity that has a sequence to it. Then have them arrange three or four of the pictures in the proper sequence.

4. Read a short story or nursery rhyme to the youngsters. Then have them recall what happened first, what happened next, and so on.

5. Make some simple item with your students, such as peanut butter sandwiches. Then discuss with them the steps taken, from the making to the eating of the sandwiches.

6. Use sequence sets of pictures that are available commercially for nursery schools and kindergartens. When these are used, the sets should be limited to four to six cards. To include a greater number is to make the mechanics more difficult than the skill you are trying to develop.

7. Create homemade sets of sequence pictures from old picture books or magazines. Always accept any justifiable sequencing of pictures.

Expressive Language: Diagnosing

There are many ways of getting a sample of an individual's oral language. Comparisons of various techniques, from retelling a story read to them to telling a story from a sequence of picture cards, and from engaging in informal conversation to using a "feely box," indicate that the most accurate measure comes from informal conversation. However, this is a very time-consuming technique in large-group assessment. If the purpose is, as discussed here, to identify the child who has difficulty in this area, a satisfactory and time-saving method is to use the sequence cards. After the youngster has suggested the sequence in which the cards should be placed, turn on the tape recorder and ask that child to tell you the story about the pictures.

The easiest and best single measure of sophistication in language, oral or written, is a count of the number of words used per T-unit (Hunt, 1965; Loban, 1976). A T-unit (minimal terminal unit) is an independent clause with all of its subordinate clauses and modifiers. Essentially a T-unit is the same as a sentence except that a compound sentence is more than one T-unit. The measure of words per sentence is *not* a good measure of sophistication since one would say that average kindergarteners speak in about 150-word sentences because they string sentence after sentence together with *and*.

To measure words per T-unit, you need not transcribe the language samples; merely listen to the tape twice: first to count the total number of words used, then the number of T-units. Divide the total number of words by the number of T-units counted. Repetitions (garbles or mazes) are not included since they would provide an artificially inflated word count.

Any effort to provide norms would put us back into the business of ranking children. However, so that you have some idea of what to expect, typical five-year-olds speak in five words per T-unit (Hillerich, 1978b; Loban, 1976; Templin, 1957). Incidentally, six- and seven-year-olds also speak in the same number of words as their age, six and seven words per T-unit. Based on these studies, it would seem that any five-year-old using fewer than four words per T-unit is in serious need of additional language development.

Teachers who do not want to evaluate in terms of T-units can at least listen carefully to the way in which the youngster speaks rather than be impressed with a torrent of words. Although kindergarten children rarely speak in complex sentences, they do normally use prepositional phrases. Hence, since these are usually three-word expressions, such children will typically be beyond four words per T-unit. In contrast, the child who speaks in sentences such as "Me go" is certainly in need of further language development.

Expressive Language: Teaching

The child who cannot function satisfactorily at the oral level is not likely to be able to function in beginning reading. The lack of oral language development by its very nature also implies the kinds of activities that the youngster needs: Experiences in talking and any experiences that will stimulate talking are going to contribute to oral language development. Of course, there are at least two necessary elements to this activity. First, the child must have something to talk about; second, that child must have someone who is willing and able to listen.

Returning for a moment to individualization, even the teacher who refuses to group in kindergarten can benefit from advance knowledge about which youngsters need oral language development. For example, during the show-and-tell period, who gets most of the experience in talking? Of course, it is the child who is already very verbal. With advance information, that teacher can be certain the identified youngsters also talk every time.

Following are some examples of experiences that can stimulate a child to use oral language:

1. Take children for a short walk for a specific purpose: "To see how many sounds we can hear," "...colors we can see," "...shapes we can see."

2. Encourage youngsters to tell about their paintings or drawings.

3. Keep children talking during sharing time. Break them into small groups so that more get chances to talk within the time period. Volunteers are handy here as additional "ears."

4. As another way to get additional "ears," teach youngsters how to use the tape recorder. Then place the recorder in a private spot and let children know that, when you are too busy to listen, they can talk into it, and you will listen to their message when you get the time.

5. Use a grab bag of pictures or objects. Children may reach in, pull out a picture or object, and tell a story about it. For reluctant or reticent youngsters, you might participate or "go first" in this game.

6. Use puppets as a good way to get a shy child to talk. In fact, I recall a nursery school experience when I was checking oral language development of four-year-olds. Inadvertently, I was sent a little three-

year-old and thought I had my first refusal. When I asked this little girl to tell me the story about some pictures, I got nothing more than a smile. Fortunately, I noticed she was carrying a stuffed Garfield toy. After several wordless smiles, I suggested that if she didn't want to tell me the story, perhaps Garfield would. What a story Garfield told!

7. At a more advanced level, have youngsters listen while a short story is read aloud. Then the reader can suggest a changed event in the story and ask the children what they think would have happened "if." For example, in the story of Goldilocks, what might have happened if the bears had been home when Goldilocks first arrived?

8. Have children "read" stories from wordless picture books.

Basic Vocabulary: Diagnosing

Present pictures of common objects that a kindergartener is expected to recognize and have the child name the pictures. While we can't even guess the precise words or number of words necessary for success in beginning reading, the child who has no name for chair, shoe, cow, wagon, and so on, is going to be in dire straits trying to learn to read.

Basic Vocabulary: Teaching

While general expressive language development is a top priority in that youngsters must be able to use the normal patterns of their language, they must also have a certain basic vocabulary of common words that they can understand and use. The most effective way of developing vocabulary related to common objects is to provide direct personal experiences with those objects. However, as discussed previously, that experience must include verbal mediation, without which a thousand experiences with that thing we sit on will not provide "chair" in the child's vocabulary.

1. Personal experience with real objects is usually the most meaningful kind of vocabulary development. Take the youngsters on field trips, walks, and so on, always using the names of items seen.

2. When direct experience is not possible, pictures offer a viable alternative.

3. Sometimes vocabulary deficits are in a particular area: foods, wild animals, furniture, clothing, vehicles, domestic animals. In such cases, focus on the neglected area by using charts or large posters dealing with that topic and discussing with children the various items.

4. You can visit the zoo or any other place that might make for additional vocabulary development.

5. At a more sophisticated level, you might play an add-on game, where an object such as a ball is held up. One child will use the name of the object in a sentence: "That is a ball." The next child will add another word to say something about the ball: "That is a red ball." The next child will continue with another word: "That is a big red ball."

Categorizing: Diagnosing

While it is difficult to find research documenting the need for ability to categorize or classify in order to be able to read, it seems only fair that we check and develop this ability before we ask children to perform a more advanced task using it. And we do ask them to use it when we ask them about "same" or "different," including the question of whether or not two words begin with the same sound.

Diagnosing can be done with the same pictures used in the vocabulary assessment. With several picture cards in the same category, such as pictures of dog, horse, cat, frog, ask how these are all alike. The child who can reply that they are all animals obviously has the ability to categorize.

Categorizing: Teaching

This is one of the more difficult tasks for a five-year-old, yet it can be developed through many varied and enjoyable activities. The point is to provide experiences like the following that enable a child to understand that things can be sorted by rules we make up or that others give us:

1. You might begin at a simple level by providing three or four pictures, one of which is not in the same category as the others: a picture of cow, dog, sweater, and cat. Ask which picture does not belong with the others and why it does not belong.

2. Common materials can be used for further practice in sorting: blocks of various sizes and colors, bottle caps, buttons, pictures, seeds, leaves, marbles, rocks, stamps, and so on. They can be sorted into piles by size, color texture, use, or whatever. The learning experience to be achieved here—but not necessarily verbalized—is that sorting is a matter of making certain rules and then following them. For example, one might have six items, and those items might be grouped by color into two piles of three items each. By changing the rules and deciding to group by size, the child can reclassify those same items into different groups.

3. You can place three or four pictures together and ask how they are all alike or why they are all together: animals, foods, clothing, "things we ride in," and so on.

Using Oral Context: Diagnosing

Most four-year-olds, if they have learned to speak their native language, are already intuitively using oral context. It is not uncommon for such youngsters to supply a missing word when being read to if the person doing the reading omits a word or fails to complete a sentence. These children expect what we say to make sense and they anticipate upcoming words much as adults do. Nevertheless, there are a few youngsters who enter kindergarten having had so little experience with language that they cannot use oral context to anticipate a missing word.

To assess this ability, begin by explaining:

> "I'm going to say something, but I won't finish it. You finish what I start to say. Tell me what word would make sense to finish what I say. For example, I might say it is so hot, I want a drink of cold _____. What do you think I was going to say? [If the child hesitates too long, help to clarify what you mean.] Could it be milk? I want a drink of cold milk. What else might it be? Yes, it could be water, tea, soda, or anything we drink, couldn't it?" (Hillerich, 1974)

Using Oral Context: Teaching

As in the case of the other skills, instructional activities are implied by the testing. The following suggestions are again arranged in some sequence of difficulty.

1. Begin with broad kinds of context, such as "At the zoo, Kari likes to watch the _____."

2. Use action pictures. Begin the description but leave out a key word: "The boy was running, but now he _____."

3. Gradually make the context more limiting: "My brother wrote a letter with his new _____."

4. As you read to youngsters, you might want to leave out an important word once in a while to allow them to tell what the word should be.

It should be readily apparent that, although we can talk about and diagnose each of these language skills separately, any effort to provide practice would result in great overlap and interrelation, simultaneous use of the skills.

One cannot use vocabulary without using expressive language, and often one cannot demonstrate listening comprehension without also understanding vocabulary and using expressive language. Nevertheless, it seems important to assess specifically so that one of the underlying elements of language development is not overlooked. For example, perhaps the child who seems limited in expressive language is so because of a limited vocabulary. Encouraging that child to speak without further development of vocabulary is going to be fruitless if not frustrating.

THE RESEARCH SUPPORT

The foregoing battery of language tests was piloted with 153 entering kindergarten children in an effort to verify the test items and to consolidate them to shorten testing time. Pilot tests were revised and, with the help of a grant from the Edyth Bush Charitable Foundation, were administered to 916 entering kindergarten children in three school districts. The population ranged from a fairly affluent suburban area to a blue-collar community to a transient area.

The project was designed, first of all, to test kindergarten children diagnostically the week before school started, then to provide a more individualized kindergarten program based on the results of the diagnostic testing. The effectiveness of this procedure was to be evaluated at the end of first grade in terms of the reading achievement of these children compared with control groups in the same three school districts that did not experience the early diagnostic procedure (Hillerich, 1978b).

Probably even more important than the results of testing was the effect of this approach on the kindergarten program in these schools, as reported by the teachers and observed by me. To begin with, others might question introducing five-year-olds to school through a testing procedure. This certainly presented no problem since the kinds of tests described were nonthreatening and success was ensured: They were tests at which no four- or five-year-old could "fail" in their own eyes. Furthermore, children had the personal attention of their teacher on a one-to-one basis, as compared with the more typical introduction to school where twenty-five children come en masse, one or two begin crying, and chaos sets in. Kindergarten teachers reported that this was the most pleasant introduction they had ever provided for entering kindergarten children and that they would like to continue the procedure whether or not it contributed to reading success.

The testing itself was much less involved that it might sound and took only fifteen minutes per child. Naturally, this kind of testing must be done on an individual basis since I know of no way anyone can get an accurate measure of a five-year-old in a group situation. To be most beneficial, the testing should be done before children actually begin that first full day of class. Unfortunately, few schools can afford to hire kindergarten teachers a week before school begins. However, in states where it is legal, kindergarteners come on an individually scheduled basis, twenty minutes apart, for the first week while the teacher does the diagnosing. And it is the kindergarten teacher who should do the testing, not only to enable the child to become more comfortable with that teacher but also because it is the teacher who will benefit most from personal insights gained from the testing.

As others had stated in the pilot, kindergarten teachers in this study reported that it was enlightening to see the great deal of language development among most of the children and to discover that a few children came to school with so much less than they had assumed every four- or five-year-old had accomplished: The range extended from a few whose oral language was equivalent to that of a two-year-old to others reading at third grade level—a range of six years at the beginning of kindergarten!

Norms were not the goal in this testing. The test was criterion-referenced with the intent to discover whether or not each child could perform adequately in the language. We ought to be less concerned about what percentage of children can or cannot perform such activities and more concerned about whether or not the child at hand can perform them. Therefore, a norm-referenced test would be inappropriate. In fact, as others have pointed out, with four- and five-year-olds, variation is the norm. However, so that you might know what to expect from a typical group, Figure 3-1 indicates averages from the diagnostic testing of the 916 entering kindergarten children.

Figure 3–1

Results of Language Testing in Three School Districts (N = 916)		
Subtest	Possible Score	Average Score
Auditory Discrimination	39	37.2
Following Oral Directions	12	10.9
Instructional Language	13	11.6
Listening Comprehension	6	4.1
Sequencing	100%	48%
Expressive Language (Words/T-unit)	—	5.2
Basic Vocabulary	36	31.2
Categorizing	6	3.9
Using Oral Context	7	6.6

As shown in Figure 3-1, auditory discrimination was certainly not a problem with most children, nor was the understanding of instructional language, the ability to follow oral directions, or even the ability to use oral context. The oral language development, 5.2 words per T-unit, was about the same as found in other research, thereby also verifying that the research group was representative of typical kindergarteners. In fact, additional reports from a variety of schools that have used the published version of the test *(Ready Steps,* Hillerich and Johnson, 1986) verify findings from this research that three subtests identify the most children in a typical school: sequencing, listening comprehension, and categorizing. Of course, the number of children having difficulty with listening comprehension will vary with school communities, depending upon the amount youngsters have been read to in the preschool years.

Armed with this kind of information about each child, kindergarten teachers in the research study were prepared to carry on a more individualized program, making use of the activities suggested in the early part of this chapter for those children who needed experience in certain areas. As a result, when these children were tested for reading achievement at the end of first grade and compared with 881 in the control group, there was a significant difference in reading achievement in favor of the treatment group. In fact, using a reading achievement test score that demarked the lowest third of the control group, we found that this score cut off only 22 percent of the treatment group: We literally pushed up the bottom of the curve for our treatment group.

Not only has the effectiveness of this kind of diagnosis been verified (Chaney, 1979), but the technique for developing oral language skill is clearly supported in other research. In fact, from over two hundred citations dealing with the relationship between oral language and reading achievement, Hillerich (1984), eliminated studies dealing with dialect, ITPA (Illinois Test of Psycholinguistic Abilities), and those where success was measured only with a readiness test, to find eighty-seven dealing with typical youngsters. From the experimental studies, the picture was very clear. The best way to develop skill in oral language that contributes to reading success is not through intensive drill, sentence repetition, and the like. It is through using language in meaningful situations as a means of communication. In fact, within this category of language development through the meaningful use of language, the research summary supported the following three specific programs that proved effective:

1. Teacher-developed immersion in oral language, that is, classroom programs where the teacher set out deliberately to immerse children in meaningful use of oral language

2. The *Peabody Language Development Kit* (American Guidance Service)

3. *Ready Steps* (Houghton Mifflin)

The *Peabody* and *Ready Steps* provide materials (posters, records, wordless picture books, puppets, and so on) to entice children into meaningful use of the language.

INTEGRATING THE LANGUAGE ARTS

Even at this basic level there is an interrelationship between and among the language arts if one sees language as a tool for communication rather than as an accumulation of noises or symbols. As already demonstrated, research and common sense support the relationship between skill in the oral language and success in reading.

More specifically, experience in listening to stories makes a contribution from several standpoints. First, it provides experience in hearing the patterns of printed English, which are quite different from those of the oral language. Second, through discussion of the stories heard, children begin to develop those thinking skills that are actually the same skills that we call "reading comprehension skills" when used in the act of reading (Follman and Lowe, 1973). Third, listening to stories acquaints children with story grammar, the elements—including characters, plot, resolution—that make up what we call "story" as opposed to exposition or argument. This topic will be discussed further in Chapter 7 and is of current interest to researchers in their efforts to improve reading comprehension (Rand, 1984).

At a more basic level, letter-form discrimination is enhanced through tracing and copying the letter forms. In so doing, children are forced to pay attention to the detail that distinguishes one letter from another. Also, as demonstrated from research with i/t/a—where writing was encouraged and therefore improved—writing experience brings another sense to bear in the learning, and therefore increases that learning.

Even experience with expressive language—just talking about things— makes a contribution to future skill in writing. As pointed out by Moffett and Wagner (1983), writing itself can be broken down to two elements: composing and transcribing. For example, if a business person dictates a letter and the secretary takes it down and types it for the former's signature, who "wrote" that letter? The business person composed it; the secretary transcribed it. Hence, oral—or at least, mental—composition is essential to the writing process, whether or not one does the transcribing. Experience in oral composing contributes to greater expertise at the writing stage (Blazer, 1984).

Chapter 4

Prereading: Foundation in Decoding Skills

Once individuals demonstrate the ability to function in the language, as suggested in Chapter 3, they are ready to take the next step toward reading success no matter whether they are six years old, five years old, or fifty-five years old. Also, whether one wants to refer to these skills as more advanced "reading readiness," "prereading," or "beginning reading skills," some must be developed prior to others; they have a necessary sequence. Others are interchangeable.

THE SEQUENCE OF SKILLS

Since previous skill development was strictly oral, if children are to engage in pencil-and-paper activities, we must provide some transitional instruction as a first step: The child who can follow oral directions in terms of body movement may not be able to follow directions while doing the doubly complex task of marking a paper as directed. It also makes sense to begin with the use of oral context since this is such an easy and natural activity for youngsters. Work on letter-form discrimination and listening for beginning sounds can be interchanged since neither is dependent upon the other, although the former is much easier for children. Obviously, consonant letter-sound association follows and presumes the ability to discriminate letter forms and to understand "beginning sound." These skills culminate in the ability to use oral context along with initial consonant letter-sound associations to read printed words.

Left-to-right orientation can be a continuing process and will be discussed in the section devoted to it. Recognition of high-frequency words can be conducted along with the other activities shortly after children have developed some of the letter-sound associations.

TRANSITIONAL ACTIVITIES

The vocabulary that teachers use as part of their instructional language—"in," "on," "under," and so on—was discussed in the previous chapter, and suggestions were made for its development at the oral level. Nevertheless, the child who can demonstrate an understanding of "on" may not follow the direction to take a pencil and put an X on a picture. Several more complications are included in the latter direction. Hence, children should be given some preliminary instruction through demonstration and then some practice in following the kinds of pencil-and-paper directions they will be getting as part of subsequent instruction.

These activities should make use of pictures or letters that are familiar to children so that lack of recognition is not a handicap. Next, an individual direction should be demonstrated by the teacher and children given an opportunity to practice it. Such direction might be to "put a line under," "put a circle around," or "put an X on." These directions can also include demonstration and practice of how to "draw a line from" one picture to another.

Handling books—learning "front," "back," "top," and "bottom"—is also an important transitional skill if youngsters are going to be using a workbook of any kind to develop the prereading skills. If they are to find objects in colored boxes, provide some preliminary practice with pictures your children easily recognize: Have them find the picture in "the green box" or "the red box" before they are asked to do this in connection with some more advanced skill.

COMPREHENDING STORIES

While listening comprehension was a skill discussed in the previous chapter as important for initial diagnosis of entering kindergarten children, the purpose here is more sophisticated. Rather than merely being concerned with the child's ability to make general sense out of a story read by an adult, now the task is to develop the "reading comprehension skills."

These skills and methods for developing them in actual reading will be discussed thoroughly in Chapters 7 and 8, so specifics of method need not be presented here. Suffice it to say here that all the reading comprehension skills are actually thinking skills applied in reading and therefore can be developed as well at the listening level as in actual reading. Hence, now the task is to range through the various comprehension skills and to teach children how to use them through demonstration and practice.

USING ORAL CONTEXT

This skill is an excellent one with which to begin at the four- or five-year-old level since children who speak and understand their native language already intuitively use oral context as they listen and anticipate words that would make sense. The previous chapter offered suggestions for checking on and providing practice in the intuitive ability to use oral context. Hence, the purpose here is not to *teach* children to use oral context. The twofold purpose is as follows:

1. to make them consciously aware of this intuitive ability to use the sense of other spoken words in order to supply a missing word, and

2. to make them aware that more than one word can make sense if only context is used.

Thus, this twofold purpose prepares youngsters to use printed context in reading, and it makes them aware that they need more than context to be certain of the precise word intended. Consequently, it lays the foundation to help them avoid becoming merely context "guessers" or, at the other extreme, it helps them avoid becoming letter-by-letter "sounder-outers" of words.

Development of this awareness may begin by merely saying to your youngsters that you are going to tell them something but will stop before you finish. They are to tell you what word they think you were going to say. For example, "I bought some————at the grocery store." Children may supply any word that makes sense. Be certain to use sentences where the missing word is not always at the end since children need to realize that stronger context often comes after the missing (or unfamiliar) word; they should get into the habit of continuing on beyond a strange word in order to get additional context instead of stopping every time they come to an unfamiliar word.

After a little practice, children in the group might make up sentences for classmates to complete. In doing so, they should understand that others need not supply the exact word so long as the words suggested make sense in the context. Also, as you read a story to your pupils, pause once in a while before reading a word that is in strong context. Let children supply the word they think you were about to read. Naturally, you would not want to do this so often that they lose their interest in the story.

While such practice will undoubtedly increase the vocabularies of some of your youngsters, this is not the prime purpose for practice in using oral context. It is usually better to elicit only a few words before going on to the next sentence; there is no need to try to pull from children all possible words that would make sense in a given context.

DISCRIMINATING LETTER FORMS

It is most important that you be aware of *what* must be taught under this heading. The purpose in dealing with letter forms is to teach children to pay enough attention to the detail of those letters so as to distinguish *b* from *d, m* from *n,* and so on. The primary purpose is not to teach the letter names, although most children will know them anyhow, and you certainly will want to use letter names as you talk about the letters.

We have known for many years that there is a high correlation between knowledge of letter names and future success in reading. In fact, correlations are as high as those found between commercial readiness tests and reading achievement, ranging from .52 to .69 (Durrell and others, 1958; de Hirsch and others, 1966; Hillerich, 1966b).

Because of the high correlations, some educators have jumped to the conclusion that letter names need to be drilled upon. However, correlation does not necessarily imply a cause/effect relationship, as most educators realize (Hillerich, 1976–77). A variety of studies have verified the fact that children can learn letter names and that such knowledge correlates with reading achievement, but they also report that such knowledge does not increase reading achievement at the end of first grade (Jenkins and others, 1972; Samuels, 1972; Silverberg and others, 1972). In fact, Muehl (1962) found that too much stress on letter names became a handicap in reading: Children so drilled tended to go through an intermediate step of naming the first letter of a word before beginning to say it. And it is not the letter name but the letter sound that must be learned in order to be successful in reading.

Since half the consonant names in English do not begin with the sounds those consonants usually represent, using the letter name would be a distraction from the beginning sound. Letter names such as "bee" (*bat, ball*) or "dee" (*dog, dipper*) are fine, but what does "aitch" have to do with *house* or *hat?* Of course, "double you" is worst of all, having nothing to do with *water, wagon,* or *wind.* In fact, I recall an inner-city kindergartener, as we discussed several letters on the board, pointing to *w* and suggesting that it was not a "double U" but a "double V."

As suggested elsewhere (Hillerich, 1966b), the high correlation between knowledge of letter names and reading success is undoubtedly no more than a demonstration of the past experience and ability of the child—experience or exposure to print and the ability to retain some of the learnings from that experience.

The task of learning to discriminate letter forms is not one of learning letter names, nor is it one of learning to *see* differences in letters. It is one of attending to the fine detail that differentiates one letter from another. This would include noting points such as the extra hump that distinguishes *m* from *n*, the stick length for *h* and *n*, or the mere change of direction that distinguishes *b* from *d* and *p* from *q*. Of course, in the process of providing practice in discriminating letter forms, it is only sensible to use the names of letters referred to.

Work on letter-form discrimination should be handled in cycles to provide for variety and, even more important, to enable learners to get to application of the skills as soon as possible so they can see what these skills have to do with really reading. In other words, a group of just a few letters should be developed through each skill stage: discriminating letter forms, identifying beginning sounds, associating consonant letters and sounds, using oral context and initial consonant sounds to read printed words.

There is no need to develop—at least at this beginning stage—letter-sound association for vowels (what sound would be taught?) or for *x* or *z* (no primary word begins with *x; *zoo is the only likely *z* word, and children learn this word early.) Furthermore, *q* is best delayed until a word is met beginning with that letter, and the digraphs—as the last elements to be added in speech— are also best delayed until children actually meet words beginning with those letters in their reading.

Of the eighteen remaining single consonants, with which do we begin and in what sequence should they be taught? Based on the research, one might justify a number of different sequences. For example, the following sequence is based on frequency of use in initial position, as dictated by the 3,455 most frequently used words (Hillerich, 1978a) and ignores sound values of the letters:

1. s, c, b, p, t, d,
2. f, a, m, r, e, w,
3. h, l, g, i, n, o,
4. u, v, j, k, y, q.

On the other hand, since frequency of use and frequency of error are unrelated (Cohn, 1976), one might look at sequences in order of difficulty. Even here, however, there are choices to be made. For example, Nicholson (1957) reported an order in terms of the ability to name lowercase letters:

1. o, s, c, i, p, y,
2. k, m, w, e, a, n,
3. r, t, j, v, u, f,
4. b, h, g, d, l, q.

Since we are ultimately concerned with the development of letter-sound associations, perhaps Nicholson's sequence based on the ability to give sounds for the lowercase letters should be used:

1. s, o, t, k, p,
2. m, j, b, n, c,
3. g, a, h, r, v,
4. f, e, d, i, l,
5. w, u, y.

In the absence of clear research evidence, one might be free to select whatever set of letters is preferred and to begin instruction in letter-form discrimination. However, any sequence for teaching should be based on a combination of factors: (1) discriminability and demonstrability of the sounds are important in the early stages of reading; (2) ease of learning, as reported by Nicholson, ought to be considered; and (3) frequency of use is important if children are to apply their skills. Finally, while letter-sound associations usually are not developed for vowels, the vowels are letters and therefore must be included in letter-form discrimination activities. Also, so that children get an easy and successful start, only a few letters should make up the initial set.

Additional considerations, such as the desire to include a letter whose sound is not to be taught in each set and the desire to teach *c* and *k* together because they represent the same sound, lead to a likely sequence such as the following:

1. s, m,
2. t, p, n,
3. c, k, r,
4. b, j, o,
5. f, g, i,
6. h, d, a, x,
7. w, v, e, q,
8. l, y, u, z.

Taking the first cycle of letters, *s* and *m*, the easiest level in work on letter-form discrimination is to use simple one-to-one correspondence. Put these two letters in a row in the pocket chart. Then, in a row below this sequence, transpose the same letters. Point to the first letter in each row and ask if they are the same or different. Then have a child rearrange the cards so the second row is identical to the first.

With extra letter cards or by writing letters on the board, put *s* (or *m*) before a row of two or three letters where only one is the same as the stimulus letter. Have children identify the letter in the row that is just like the first letter.

Such activities can be followed with individual work for those who need more practice. On a scrap of newspaper, print with a felt marker whatever letter the youngster is to work on. With crayon or pencil, the student is to find and mark all of the examples of that letter. The size of newspaper type is not a problem. Large type is used in beginning reading material to fill space, not because youngsters can't "see" smaller type: Two or three words in small print on a page would get lost in white space; a full page of small print would take six months for a beginner to complete.

The emphasis in letter-form discrimination should be on lowercase letters, since these are most frequently encountered at the beginnings of words. At this point, however, children should also have experience with the capital forms of the letters by engaging in activities that require matching the lowercase with the capital form of the same letter.

Following are some additional activities to use with preschool or kindergarten children to provide additional practice in letter-form discrimination, using whatever sets of letters you are working on:

- *Bingo*. Play bingo or lotto, where each player has a card with letters in the squares instead of numbers. You may use lowercase matching to lowercase, or capital to lowercase. When playing this game, don't merely call out the letter name; this is a visual skill, so hold the letter card up to allow children to see the shape as they match it on their own cards.

- *Matching Letters*. Write the letters on the chalkboard, mixing both capital and lowercase forms. Have individual children connect the lowercase letters with their capital forms.

- *Finding Letters*. Use word game sets, such as Scrabble, to have the child find all copies of a given letter form.

- *Race*. Two children, each with a small set of letter cards, stand side by side some distance away from the teacher. The teacher will hold up letters one at a time. The first child to show the new letter takes one step toward the teacher. The winner is the first one to reach the teacher.

- *Fruit Basket*. Children form a circle with one child in the middle. Each has a card with one capital or lowercase letter on it. Duplicate letters are used. When the leader in the center holds up two letters, children with those letters change seats while the leader tries to get one of their seats. The one left standing calls the next letter.

• *Letter Rhythms.* Children sit in a circle, each with a letter card. There are two cards for each letter. As the music is played, cards are passed around the circle in time to the music. When the music stops, the teacher calls on one pupil to stand and show the card. The child who has the same letter also stands. Anyone who misses, sits in the center. If a second child misses, the first one may reenter the circle.

• *Make-Believe Stream.* A "stream" goes through the middle of a large circle. Letter cards are used for stepping-stones and placed across the stream. A child names the letters before stepping on them and tries to get across the steam without falling in or miscalling a letter.

• *Go Fish.* After four or five letters have been introduced, give children a bowl in which they can "fish" for their letter of the day. Let them find matching letters hidden in the room.

• *Writing Experience.* This experience can help in letter-form discrimination. For example, a good culminating activity with a given set of letters is to gather the children around an easel or chalkboard. Write the lowercase form of one of the letters studied, for example, *m*. With a box of colored chalk or crayons nearby, ask individual children to come up and make a "green letter m," a "red letter m," and so on. When all have had a turn and it appears they have noticed the detail of that letter's formation, a final activity might be to distribute a duplicated sheet on which there may be six to nine opportunities to practice the formation of the letter, as shown in Figure 4-1.

The purpose of this activity is not to teach handwriting; it is to be certain that, with a kinesthetic approach, children are paying attention to the detail of the letter forms under consideration. If this stage—the formation of letters—is to take place in nursery school or kindergarten, that teacher should have a copy of the manuscript style used in first grade, so children learn to form the letters in the same manner as the adopted handwriting program suggests.

IDENTIFYING BEGINNING SOUNDS

As documented in Chapters 2 and 3, children who already speak their native language do not need to be taught to hear differences in sounds. Conversely, they do need to be taught what is meant by "the beginning" of a spoken word. In fact, we know that most preschool children don't even understand what a "word" is, much less what the beginning of it is. In the act

Figure 4-1

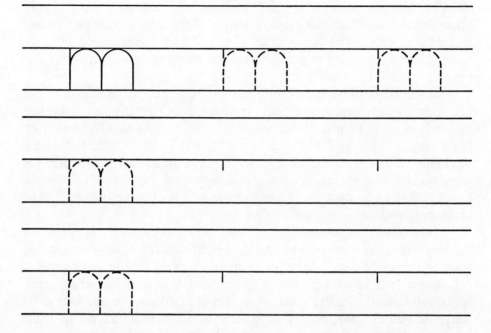

of saying a sentence, we run words together and may have longer breaks between two syllables in a word than between some sets of words: "She's a nice person" might be said "Shesanice per son." The whole sentence might even seem to a preschool child, like one glob of sound and be interpreted as one word. A nonreader certainly has no reason to think of spoken words as having beginnings and endings, and—unlike the adult—the child may not have had the advantage of seeing words pointed out in print, where it's easy for you or me to identify a "word" as a special collection of letters separated from other collections of letters by extra space. In fact, even linguists have not been able to satisfactorily define "word" in terms of speech alone.

The primary purpose of instruction in this skill is to teach children what is meant by "the beginning" of a spoken word. A secondary purpose is to provide practice in classifying words by their beginning sounds. To say that there is no need to teach children to *hear* beginning sounds in no way implies that teaching them what is meant by the beginning of a spoken word is an easy task; it is a very difficult one, but it is made easier when we understand what that task is.

You might begin to clarify the meaning of "beginning sound" by holding up a picture of a common object that everyone can recognize, such as a house. Hold it up and say, "Is this a picture of mouse?" Children will correct with

"No, house." "Is it bouse?" After several changes and corrections, ask children, "Do you know what I did? I changed the beginning sound. I said 'mouse' and 'bouse' but the name is house." Then take another picture and repeat the process. After changing the names of a few pictures, you will find some children beginning to get the idea, and they can then change names of pictures for others in the class.

Incidentally, always make certain children recognize the pictures used and call them by the name you expect. It is not a fair criticism of published materials to say that a picture can be called by different names. There are very few pictures that can be called by only one name in English, so the name must be clarified if that particular name is significant to the activity, as it certainly is when working with beginning sounds. I once made the mistake with kindergarteners of holding up a picture of a hammer and asking "Is this bammer?" The children agreed that it was because you *bam* with it!

This technique of changing picture names does work. However, in working with kindergarteners to find better techniques to clarify "beginning sound," I recently discovered a direct approach to be even more effective. I collected a page of pictures whose names all began with the same sound, specifically "seal," "sock," and so on. On the first day, the children and I talked through the entire page, item by item, to decide with each picture name whether it began with the same sound as "seal." Then the children used a crayon to draw a line under each picture whose name began with that sound—in this case, every picture on the page.

On the next day, we did the same with a page of pictures whose names began with the sound heard at the beginning of "monster," "moon," and so on. However, on the third day, I warned children that I was going to trick them. I had another page of pictures, most of whose names began like "sock," but including a few distractors such as "tiger." On the fourth day, we completed another "trick" page, where most picture names began with the same sound as "monster."

This procedure—swamping children in one beginning sound, then in a second for contrast—seemed better than any I had attempted, since even the poorest was able to complete a paper independently by the fourth day. Of course, other kinds of activities, including the first mentioned and those upcoming, are also helpful in clarifying this most difficult understanding.

Incidentally, some teachers might justifiably question the use of one sound and then immediate work with a second sound before the first is "mastered." The reason for doing this is that children need a second sound for contrast; it helps them to understand the portion of the word referred to. Furthermore, in working with comparisons, such as *sun/bun,* do not assume that you are dealing with rhyming words: Attention is on the beginning—the part that changes—not on the rhyming portion.

The three following points should be kept in mind as you work with children on "beginning sound":

1. When naming pictures, drop the article before the words to be classified. Don't say "Is this a picture of a house?" Say "Is this a picture of house?" By dropping the article, you make the initial sound stand out in crisp clarity; using the article muddies that initial sound. Furthermore, if you drop the article, children will do likewise.

2. Be careful of your instructional language and be sure that you say what you mean. Teachers have been heard to ask children if "monster" and "moon" *sound alike* when they obviously mean "begin with the same sound" or "sound alike at the beginning."

3. Consonant sounds should never be pronounced in isolation. Any attempt to pronounce /m/ in isolation will result in "muh." Refer to that consonant sound as "the sound you hear at the beginning of monster." Of course, after the letter sound has been taught as the next skill, you can also refer to a consonant sound as "the sound *m* stands for." Furthermore, you might clarify for children who are having difficulty in this area by exaggerating the initial sound as you pronounce the name, another reason that *s* is a good beginning letter, or you may show the formation of the beginning sound in the mouth, a technique useful in the case of /m/.

In working with beginning sounds, you will use words that begin with the sounds of the consonant letters already developed in letter-form discrimination, in this case *m* and *s*. Children, of course, are not aware of this fact, since with them you are talking only about sounds, without reference to letters at this point.

Once children begin to get the idea of what is meant by "the beginning" of a spoken word through the previous demonstrations, move on to activities involving the set of beginning sounds you are going to work with. Further clarification of "beginning" sound will come as children participate in classifying words according to beginning sound. One of the easiest activities is to start with two sounds, the sound heard at the beginning of "sock" and of "monster." Put a picture of sock at the beginning of one row in the pocket chart and a picture of monster in the next. Mix about six picture cards, three for each of the two sounds, and have the children name a picture and decide if its name begins like "sock" or like "monster." Do this by having the selected child say the name of the picture you hold and then the name of each stimulus picture with which to pair the beginning sounds. The selected picture may be placed by the child beside the stimulus picture that has the same beginning sound. The names of the stimulus picture and the newly placed picture should be repeated by the group as a check and for further auditory practice. In fact, since this is an auditory skill, children need to say and hear, over and over again.

Other activities may then follow, where the group will concentrate on one of the beginning sounds at a time. For example, take a set of four picture cards, three with names beginning with the same sound and one with a name that does not. As you put the four pictures in the pocket chart, say their names: "sock," "sun," "house," "sign." Have youngsters identify which names do not begin with the same sound as the others. Continue with additional sets of pictures.

In working with pupils on beginning sounds, it is important to truly note sound and not spelling. For example, the child who says "circus" begins with the same sound as "sun" is correct. Any such matching should be complimented. On the other hand, there is no point in deliberately providing matching words or pictures whose names are spelled differently at the beginning.

Along this same line, although we always accept and compliment the child's statement that "truck" and "tree" begin with the same sound as "tooth," we should try to avoid suggesting names that begin with consonant clusters since the second sound comes so close that it may interfere with the clarity of the initial sound.

In all the following activities, children should say the names of the pictures or objects they are using. This auditory experience is essential in helping to clarify the meaning of "beginning sound" and in providing practice in listening for the different sounds. Activities are arranged in approximate order of difficulty, recognizing that it is easier to identify pictures or objects whose names begin with a given sound than it is to think up or to draw the appropriate pictures.

- *Changing Names.* While working with a given beginning sound, have all the children change their names to conform to that sound. If the sound is that heard at the beginning of "sock," children's names become Sob for Bob, Sed for Ted, and Seth for Beth.

- *Treasure Hunt.* Have children see how many objects they can find in the room whose names begin with the sound heard at the beginning of "sock."

- *Treasure Hunt, Variation.* Place picture cards in various parts of the room. Divide children into teams with a captain for each. Each captain receives an envelope with a picture on it, and the teams hunt for objects whose names begin with the same sound as the name of the picture on their envelope. The captain checks to see that objects are matched correctly.

- *Sound Page.* Give each child a sheet of newsprint with a picture of sock at the top. Using old magazines, have youngsters cut out and paste on the page all the pictures they can find whose names begin with the sound heard at the beginning of "sock." As they progress to various sounds, they may do a sound page for each, collecting the pages into their own individual sound books. (The first or second time you do this, you may want to do it as a group, using a sheet of easel paper for the sound page.)

• *Picture Match.* Make three large cards, each with a picture whose name begins with one of the consonant sounds being studied. Given twelve smaller picture cards, four for each sound, children are to match the four smaller cards with each large card.

• *Beginning Sound Lotto.* Paste six pictures on 8″ × 11″ tagboard. Have each child match other pictures to the large card by beginning sound. The winner is the first to cover all six pictures.

• *Fish.* Deal five picture cards to each child. Place the remainder of the deck in a center pile. The first player asks another player, "Do you have a picture card whose name begins like————?" (Names picture card in hand.) If a pair is made with the other player's card, the first player gets another turn; if not, the first player draws a card from the pile and the next player has a turn. The winner is the first to match all cards.

• *Concentration.* Picture cards are placed face down on the table and players alternate turning up any two cards. If a match is made (same beginning sound), the set of cards is kept by the player and that player continues until no match is made. The winner is the player with the most cards when all are gone.

• *Racing Game.* Divide the class into two teams. Place two small boxes in the front of the room, each labeled with a different picture. Small objects and/or pictures are scattered around the room. Each team finds all the pictures or objects whose names begin with the same sound as the name of the picture on their box. The winning team is the one with the most correct items in the box at the end of the period of time.

• *Magic Sound.* Pictures of objects whose names begin with various initial consonant sounds are distributed. The teacher (or child) calls out for all pictures whose names begin like————. Those who have appropriate pictures take turns saying the name of their picture and skipping around the room.

• *Name Game.* Spread pictures on the floor, one for each child, and say, "Find a picture whose name begins with the same sound as your name."

• *Name Game, Variation 1.* Ask each child to point to all things in the room with names that begin with the same sound as the child's first or last name.

• *Name Game, Variation 2*. Have children form a circle. They are to say their names individually and then name an object whose name begins with the same sound.

• *Knock, Knock*. One child is "it" and covers eyes while another stands behind "it" and says, "Someone's knocking at your door. My name begins like———." If "it" guesses correctly, he or she stays for another turn; if not, the one who knocked becomes "it."

• *Animal Party*. Mickey Monkey, Sally Seal, and so on, all find gifts (pictures) whose names begin with the same sound as their names.

• *Going Fishing*. Make construction paper fish that are about five inches long. Paste a picture whose name begins with a consonant sound on each fish. Put a paper clip on each and place them in a cardboard "pond." Make a fishing pole of string and a magnet. Children "fish," and when they catch a fish, they say, "I caught a fish whose name begins like——— (another word beginning with the same sound)." If correct, the fish is caught; if not, the fish must be thrown back.

• *Sound Relay*. Place pictures whose names begin with several different consonant sounds on the floor. Line the children up in three or more rows as relay teams. Say, "I'm looking for a picture whose name begins with the same sound as———." The first child in each row runs to get the picture. The winner is the team with the most cards.

• *Magic Castle*. Pass pictures around a circle while music is playing. When the music stops, say, "If you have a picture whose name begins like———, you may come to my magic castle."

• *Train Ride*. Line up chairs as a train. Play as "Magic Castle" above.

• *Sound Hunt*. Pass out big pictures, two for each sound. Each child finds a partner with a picture whose name begins like the name of his or her picture.

• *Musical Pictures*. Hang large magazine pictures (one for each of the consonant sounds under consideration) around the walls. As music plays, children skip around the room. When the music stops, each child names a word that begins like the name of the picture he or she is standing beside.

• *Sound Chairs*. Play like musical chairs, except use words instead of music. When a word with the predetermined beginning sound is mentioned, children try to get a chair.

• *Sound Bingo*. Use cards with pictures instead of letters in the squares. The caller will pull out a picture and call its name as players cover the picture whose name begins with the same sound.

• *Grocery Store*. Distribute pictures of items found in a grocery store. All children are clerks and use their desks as counters. A designated "shopper" goes from desk to desk asking for all things whose names begin with a certain sound. If the shopper fails to take all appropriate pictures and the clerk notices, the clerk becomes the shopper.

• *Sound Dominoes*. Make dominoes with pictures on each end. Play like regular dominoes, matching pictures by beginning sound.

• *Clock*. Make a large clock face with slots for picture cards instead of numbers on the face. Insert picture cards and attach one movable hand. When the hand is set at a picture, ask a child to give a word that begins with the same sound as the name of the picture.

• *Follow the Leader.* Distribute a picture card to each child and have them form a circle. Select two leaders, each of whom has a different beginning sound on the picture card. Each leader seeks another person whose picture card has the same beginning sound, and that person helps the leader find others with the same beginning sound on their picture cards.

• *Drawing a Sound Page*. Instead of making a sound page by cutting out pictures, have children—individually or as a group—draw pictures whose names begin with a particular sound.

• *Drawing a Sound Page, Variation*. Provide a context sentence and have students draw pictures whose names begin with the same sound and would make sense in the context given. For example: "Draw all things Carol got at the grocery store whose names begin with the same sound as her name."

• *Thinking of Things*. Give a key word and have children take turns thinking of things whose names begin with the same sound. When no more words can be thought of, the last successful player gets to name a new key word.

• *Going to Boston*. Showing a picture card, one player says, "I'm going to Boston and I'm taking something that begins with the sound you hear at the beginning of (show picture)." Any child who guesses correctly takes another card and is "it."

ASSOCIATING CONSONANT LETTERS AND SOUNDS

While knowledge of letter names is not a prerequisite to being able to read, knowledge of the sounds those letters represent certainly is. One need not know that the name of a particular letter is "double you," but that individual must know it stands for the sound heard at the beginning of *wagon* or *wind* in order to read a word such as *water.*

The teaching goal for activities related to associating consonant letters and sounds is to establish with children an immediate response to an initial consonant letter in terms of the sound that letter usually represents. There is no way to "explain" why the letter *s*, for example, stands for the sound that it does; it is just that English speakers agree on this point, and the sooner children agree, the sooner they will learn to read.

There are many different ways in which various reading programs attempt to develop this letter-sound association. In one approach—a "See, Hear, Associate" method used in "sight" programs—pupils learn some words such as *man, mop, met.* Then they are asked to look at those words to SEE that they all begin with the same letter; they say the words to HEAR that they all begin with the same sound; they are then told to remember that this letter stands for the sound they hear at the beginning of *man, mop, met.* Such children are at a disadvantage because there is no reason, no rationale, and no device to help them remember this abstract idea. At the other extreme, youngsters are merely drilled and drilled on the notion that *s* "says suh," *m* "says muh," and so on.

To overcome both the ineffectiveness of the former—a "shotgun" approach—and the danger to comprehension of the latter with its isolation of consonant sounds, a few educators have introduced the use of mnemonic devices to help nonreaders remember the sound each consonant letter represents. The following three types of mnemonic devices have been found for individual consonant sounds in various reading programs:

1. A letter and beside it a picture unrelated to the letter shape but whose name begins with the sound that letter represents; for example, a picture of sun beside the letter *s,*

2. A letter superimposed on a pictured object, where the letter sound is what the pictured object might utter; for example, *m* superimposed on the humps of a camel eating ice cream and saying "mmmm,"

3. A letter superimposed on a picture whose name begins with the sound that letter represents; for example, *s* superimposed on a picture of sock that follows the shape of the letter (see Figure 4-2).

The first device, where the picture does not relate to the shape of the letter, is not helpful in recalling letter-sound associations (Marsh and Desberg, 1978). Nor is it effective to take the twice-removed tack of superimposing a letter form on a pictured object and have the sound be what the pictured object might utter, such as *m* superimposed on the humps of a camel eating ice cream while saying "mmmm" (Coleman and Morris, 1978). The strength of a key-picture device lies in the direct correspondence between letter shape, picture shape, and beginning sound of the picture name as related to the letter sound. In comparisons with the variety of mnemonic devices just described, Ehri and

Figure 4-2

others (1984) demonstrated the effectiveness of the type of key picture shown in Figure 4-2 and the ineffectiveness of the other types.

The effective key picture technique, where the picture follows the shape of the letter, has been widely used with adults for many years by Laubach (1947) in his world literacy campaign. The importance of the picture following the configuration of the letter was demonstrated by comparisons of different key pictures with 120 beginning kindergarten children (Hillerich, 1966b). These children were tested at the beginning of kindergarten with seventeen pairs of key pictures in the hope of identifying what kinds of key pictures were most effective: novel pictures or common ones, those that followed the configuration of the letter or those that did not. Children were shown the key pictures in random order and asked, "What is this a picture of?" They were then merely told the name of the letter while the examiner traced that letter with his own finger.

A week to two weeks later, the same children were retested by being shown just a letter card and asked, "What picture does this remind you of?" While results gave support to the importance of the picture's following the configuration of the letter, the most interesting result was the ability of most children to recall a majority of the key pictures from the letter stimulus after being merely exposed, with no instruction whatsoever.

From this study we might conclude that the particular kind of picture may not be important, but the use of a key picture is effective in helping children recall a key word. Use of key pictures, of course, requires consistency in the choice of pictures among teachers working with a given child. It isn't so important what picture is chosen for each letter, but if different teachers use different pictures, the effectiveness is lost. The pictures are no longer key pictures but merely different reminders of a beginning sound.

Common sense as well as research supports this approach. Suppose you were to learn to read with a different alphabet that included the following letters:

Even with practice, you would undoubtedly have difficulty remembering that the first is called "em" and stands for the sound at the beginning of *man* and *moon;* the second is "en" and stands for the sound at the beginning of *noon* and *note;* and the third is "double you" and represents the sound at the beginning of *wagon* and *wind.* However, with little or no practice at all, you would have no difficulty remembering the key word if you saw the following key pictures of man, note, and wagon:

Of course, you can spell. If you couldn't and you saw ──○ at the beginning of a word, you might recall that the word begins like "wagon," but you probably would not remember the name of the letter. However, which is necessary for success in reading, knowing that the word begins with the same sound as "wagon" or knowing that the name of the first letter is "double you"?

The sets of letters to be used for letter-sound association should be the same consonants as were used in letter-form discrimination and in working with beginning sound. Begin by showing youngsters a key picture card, such as sock with *s* superimposed. Ask children to say the name of the picture and write the name on the board to demonstrate that the word *sock* begins with the letter *s.* Then point out that the key picture will help them remember, when they see a word beginning with *s,* that the word will begin with the same sound as "sock."

After a key picture has been introduced, it is a good idea to keep it displayed in the room as a reference so that children who need a reminder can check it.

Following the introduction of a key picture, the same kinds of activities can be used to establish letter-sound associations that were conducted with beginning sounds. The only difference is that the stimulus becomes a letter rather than a picture name. For example, children working on beginning sounds may have made a sound page where they collected pictures whose names began with the sound they heard at the beginning of the word "sock." A picture of sock was put at the top of the sound page as a reminder for the sound. Now, for letter-sound association, children will collect pictures whose names begin with the sound for which the letter *s* stands. The letter *s* now becomes the reminder at the top of the page.

In addition to adaptations of activities suggested under "Identifying Beginning Sounds," the following may be used:

- *Collect the Alphabet.* Show children an alphabet card. Whoever can name the key picture for that letter gets to keep the card.(Reinforce immediately by showing the key card).

- *Matching.* Paste pictures on a flat board. Provide small letter cards. The child draws a letter card from the pile and places it on the matching picture, for example, *s* on sailboat.

- *Clothespin Matching.* Use a pizza board or make a large cardboard circle and divide it into eight or ten sections with a picture in each section. Also prepare the same number of spring-type clothespins with a letter on each. The child is to match each clothespin with its proper picture. (This may be made self-checking by using matching symbols or color codes on the backs of the clothespins and the board.)

- *Electric Matching.* Make a game board with pictures down the right side and letters down the left. Put an electric contact beside each letter and picture and connect appropriate letters and pictures on the back with copper wire. Set up a battery with a small light bulb and wires to be used as connectors between letter and picture. When the child touches the wires to the proper picture and letter combination, the light will go on.

- *Yarn Board.* Make a board as in the previous activity, but put a hole beside each picture. Attach a piece of colored yarn permanently beside each letter. Children can thread the yarn through the hole beside the proper picture. Color coding on the back enables self-checking.

- *Spinner Bingo.* Make bingo cards with pictures on them and a spinner with letters instead of numbers. Children spin the spinner and cover the picture whose name begins with the sound for which the letter stands.

- *A la Chutes and Ladders.* Make a trail-type game board such as is used in "Chutes and Ladders" but have each square contain a picture. Use alphabet dice. Children move to the next square that has a picture whose name begins with the sound represented by the letter rolled.

- *Puzzle.* Use rectangular tagboards about 3″ × 6″. Paste a picture at one end and a letter at the other end of each. Cut each diagonally to form two-piece puzzles. Color code or mark the backs for self-checking. (NOTE:

All puzzles should be cut exactly the same to avoid having children match appropriate pieces merely by physical fit.)

• *Relay.* Put four letter cards in a vertical column on the left side in each of two pocket charts. Distribute picture cards, one to each child. Divide the youngsters into two teams. The first player on each team puts a picture card in the proper row with the letter card. The first team to place all cards correctly wins the relay.

• *Choo Choo.* Line children up in two rows to form trains. The teacher is the engineer and holds up a letter card. The first player in the line (engine) answers with the key picture word. That child then goes to the end to be the caboose and the next player is the engine.

• *Spinner.* Make a spinner with slots for letter cards. Put letter cards in and spin the needle. Call on a child to give the key picture and a word that begins with the sound for which that letter stands.

• *Teacher Says.* The teacher gives a picture card to each child in a circle, saying, "All those whose picture name begins with the sound this letter stands for (hold up letter card) may hop (skip, jump, and so on)."

• *Golf.* Divide a pizza board or large cardboard circle into sections. In each section, paste one picture and put letters around the edge, with a small hole beside each letter. Children may put golf tees into the hole beside the one letter of the four that stands for the sound the picture name begins with. Again, self-checking is possible through marking the correct hole on the reverse side.

Incidental Practice

Of course, much practice can be incidental after initial instruction with a key picture. For example, "All those whose names begin with the sound this letter stands for (hold up letter card) may (get in line first, go outside, get a drink, and so on)."

USING ORAL CONTEXT AND INITIAL
CONSONANT SOUNDS TO READ PRINTED WORDS

Once letter-sound associations are developed for a set of consonants, such as *s* and *m*, children can be told that now, with your help, they will be able to read some words. Develop sentences that provide good context and write on the board one of the important words that you will leave out when you say the sentence. Clarify where the beginning of the printed word is by pointing to or underlining the first letter of that word. Then review with children how they are going to figure out what that printed word is: They will use the sense of the words you say and the sound they know that first letter stands for.

After *n* has been taught, you might write the word *nail* on the board and tell children that you will say something but will leave out this word. Then say: "Mother needed a _____ to hang the picture on the wall." They should be able to use the sense of the other words you say—the context—along with the sound they know that first letter stands for in order to read the word.

Another important point to make with children has to do again with metacognition, that is, helping them *know how they know.* After they read the word *nail,* ask how they know the word isn't "hammer." (Hammer makes sense, but it does not begin with the sound *n* stands for.) Then ask how they know the word isn't "nest." ("Nest" begins with the sound *n* stands for, but it doesn't make sense.)

At this beginning stage, it is also important to be careful about the context and words selected. Be certain the word on the board is the only one that makes sense and begins with the sound the first letter represents. For example, it would be unfair to children at this stage of their skill development to put the word *house* on the board and say, "It started to rain, so we decided to go into Johnny's _____." In such a case, *house* or *home* could make sense and begin with the same letter.

Following are a few examples that might be used with children. The word to be written on the board for each sentence has been underlined:

m At night you can see the <u>moon</u> in the sky. Rosa always drinks <u>milk</u> for breakfast. At the zoo, we saw a <u>monkey</u> hanging by his tail.

s Before lunch, I wash my hands with <u>soap</u> and water. That boat doesn't have a motor. It has a <u>sail</u>. Will you please <u>sit</u> down and be quiet?

LEFT-TO-RIGHT ORIENTATION

Although some educators go to great lengths to help children learn the terms *left* and *right,* such knowledge is not needed for reading: These terms are merely labels. What is necessary for success in reading is the understanding and habit of starting "here" (the left side) and going "this way" (toward the right side of the page).

Children will begin to develop this habit if they use worksheets or workbooks as part of their work on the previously discussed skills. Even without workbooks or worksheets, left-to-right orientation can begin very early. The adult, sitting side by side with a child—or using a big book—and reading to that child, has the perfect opportunity to begin left-to-right orientation by running a finger along the lines being read. This will lead the child to follow from left to right.

In working with groups of children, teachers might gain a similar advantage by putting some stories on transparencies. When the transparency is projected overhead, a finger can trace along the lines being read, and children will follow on the screen.

This use of stories on transparencies has another advantage once children have developed letter-sound associations for some of the consonants and have been given some initial practice in using those associations along with oral context. In the process of reading from a big book or a projected story, stop once in a while at a word in good context and have the children use their skill to read the word. For example, in reading the fable "The Wind and the Sun," you might tell youngsters you'll let them read a word when you point to it: "Once upon a time the wind and the sun were talking. 'I am stronger than you are,' the wind said to the *s*——." Since children know the sound *s* stands for and there is good context, they should be able to read the word *sun*.

In doing this reading, pupils get a chance to apply their skills and can gain a sense of accomplishment. However, stories should not be interrupted so often that enjoyment of the story is destroyed.

Left-to-right orientation may also be developed through the use of experience charts. While I have reservations about the language experience approach as a total reading program, these charts can be used effectively to demonstrate several points about reading. First, they demonstrate that the printed form of language is the same language children have been speaking: In a sense, it is "talk written down." Second, the production and use of these charts demonstrate left-to-right movement. By having youngsters dictate their story while you write it on a chart, you demonstrate both of these points very effectively.

More important, as mentioned previously, composing is one element in written expression and is an act that is practiced by the children as they dictate their experience stories. They not only develop expressive language, but they also learn how to compose—a necessary skill for any type of writing. If the composing goes beyond mere recall of an experience and gets into "stories" themselves, youngsters will also be developing an awareness of story grammar—the essential elements that make up a piece of writing that we call "story." Such an awareness provides an important portion of context—expectation of elements that make up a "story."

As you work with the experience charts, read them back to the children for changes or additions. You might also suggest to beginning readers that you will save their charts until a future time when they might like to look back and read about some of the things they did early in the year.

RECOGNIZING HIGH-FREQUENCY WORDS

The act of reading, even at the very beginning, is not one of merely making noises for printed symbols any more than it is, at the other extreme, a matter of merely learning words. Initially, the act of reading is one of learning the two-pronged skill of using context and consonant-sound associations. Even so, we must recognize that the individual who has completely mastered this dual skill developed thus far cannot be handed even the most simple book and be expected to read it. That individual usually has no recognition vocabulary, hence no printed context to use in unlocking unfamiliar words; all the words are unfamiliar in their printed form.

This "recognition vocabulary," sometimes referred to as a "sight vocabulary," consists of those words in print that are known or recognized instantaneously, without recourse to any analysis, phonic or contextual. "Word recognition" may be contrasted with "word identification," which is a process whereby the reader determines what a word is through analysis, that is, through use of skills such as context, phonics, or structural analysis.

Although we acknowledge here that some words must be recognized instantly if a reader is to have any printed context, we must also point out that very few words are worth learning for their own sakes. In fact, Horn (1926) found that just three words accounted for 10 percent of all words written by adults. Hillerich (1978a) reported that those same three words (*I, and, the*) accounted for 11 percent of the 380,342 words written by elementary school children. The ten most frequently used words in either of these studies accounted for at least 25 percent of all words written by children or adults. This means that the child who recognizes those ten words instantly will automatically recognize a fourth of all the words in any book in English, from *The Cat in the Hat* to *Gone With the Wind*.

The best way to develop this recognition is through exposure to words in a variety of meaningful contexts, whether that language is oral or printed. Hence, rather than take the first ten of the most frequently used words, we should be a little more selective in order to do something meaningful with those words. Examine the first preprimer of your adopted reading program to determine what are the most frequently used six to ten words. In addition, if the following are not among those found, I would also include *the, a, is, was, in, on*.

Now you have a collection of a dozen or so high-frequency words that will account for at least 20 percent of the words your children will meet in print.

Introduce your pupils to a few of these high-frequency words after they have completed one or two cycles of letters and then continue activities with these words simultaneously as you pick up another cycle of letters. Introduce the words in meaningful context, just as you have read stories to children from transparencies. For example, you might put the words *the, is,* and *in* into separate sentences on a transparency: "The cat is not on the box. It is in the box." Tell the children you will read the sentence twice. The first time you read it, you will skip the underlined word and you want them to figure out what it is by using the sense of the other words and the sound the first letter stands for. Then the second time you read the sentence, they are to read the underlined word.

By now, the reason for the choice of high-frequency words should be clear. By also introducing *a* and *was,* additional options are provided for rebus sentences, as *a* is substituted for *the* and *was* for *is.*

In the case of a word beginning with a vowel, such as *in,* you will have to tell them that this word begins like "it" and "if." Nevertheless, I believe it is important that every word be introduced in this fashion so that children understand, from the very beginning, that you will not be the "great giver of words"; they will have to figure out their own words. Of course, if the high-frequency word you are introducing begins with a consonant sound that has been taught, you need merely remind children of the skill they are to use in figuring out the word.

Each word should be introduced and read in the sentence several times. Once two or three words have been introduced, such as *the, is,* and *in,* you can put those word cards in a pocket chart with picture cards to make rebus sentences for children to read: For example:

The (picture of a girl) is in the (picture of a house).

Point out to pupils that they can read the whole sentence. Have several do so. Then change the sentence by changing one of the picture cards and have the new sentence read. Invite youngsters to select picture cards to make new sentences for others to read. Very soon kindergarteners will make sentences with boys in tigers, monkeys in hats, and elephants in jars. They think they are playing great jokes, but in reality they are doing exactly what you want: They are getting practice in reading the high-frequency words in meaningful contexts. And it is these "meaningless" words, such as *the,* that are difficult for children to recall; they can see *brontosaurus* or *tyrannosaurus* once and remember, but *the* seems to take a thousand exposures for some children.

For youngsters who can form letters, these simple rebus sentences can be transformed into questions merely by moving *is* to the beginning of the group of words. Then, by introducing the word *not* on the board, have children write answers in reply to questions written in rebus form. Also encourage them to write rebus sentences of their own in which they draw pictures for nouns—or even for the action verbs. As we learned from research with i/t/a, writing experience reinforces that recognition vocabulary as it brings another sense to bear on the learning. The more ways children use a word, the more likely they are to remember that word.

Furthermore, with a few high-frequency words, your youngsters are freer to indulge in writing for its own sake. They can write rebus stories, making pictures for the words they can't spell. As they learn some of the consonant letter sounds, they might like to write the first letter of some words and draw a line to represent the balance of the word. Incidentally, this technique is beneficial at later stages of development: Young writers should get into the habit of using this device of a few letters and a line—or in some manner identifying words about whose spelling they are uncertain—so they don't use a phonetic misspelling and then, in proofreading, forget that they were uncertain about that word.

Chapter 5

Extending the Decoding Skills

The typical child who has experienced the prereading skills in or before kindergarten will be ready by about the end of kindergarten or the beginning of first grade to make use of these skills in reading book materials. Of course, there will be some pupils entering first grade who are well beyond this level and others who have not yet mastered the necessary prereading skills, even though they may have been exposed to them.

Children who have progressed up to this point in their skill development have the essential foundation for reading. They have gained the following skills and understandings:

1. Adequacy in oral language, including both sentence patterns and vocabulary,

2. Awareness of their ability to use oral context to anticipate a word,

3. Ability to discriminate differences between letter forms,

4. Understanding of what is meant by "the beginning" of a spoken word,

5. Experience in classifying spoken words according to beginning sounds,

6. Association of consonant letters with the sounds those letters usually represent at the beginning of a word,

7. Ability to apply the skill of using oral context along with the consonant-sound association for the first letter of a printed word in order to read that word,

8. Familiarity with the patterns of the literary language from having been read to,

9. Interest and enjoyment in stories from having been read to,

10. Experience with certain high-frequency words, enabling instant recognition of those printed words.

The remaining task in increasing decoding ability is to strengthen and extend these skills and to increase interest in reading. The key to reading success for any child is the enjoyable application of what skill is possessed, the gradual and successful adding on of additional skills, and legitimate praise and documentation of each small step of progress. We must remember that, while instruction is an important means of advancing these skills, experience in actually reading is equally essential: Children also learn to read *by reading*.

INTRODUCING NEW WORDS

Most basal reading programs suggest that new words be introduced in context, especially at the primary level. However, the way a new word is introduced varies and reveals much about the philosophy of reading espoused by the program and by the teacher using it.

Word introduction, properly conducted, is one of the most important elements in the teaching of beginning reading. Obviously, if the teacher sees reading as making noises for print, then there is no need for word introductions at all; children merely learn the letter-sound correspondences and make appropriate sounds for each of the symbols. However, even with such programs, we owe it to children to clarify the application of the skills we have been teaching, that is, to remind them of what they are to do when they come to an unfamiliar word. Even here, I would precede the children's reading by asking, "When you come to a new word, how are you going to figure it out?" And in such a program, I would expect them to indicate that they will "sound it out."

Until children have an adequate recognition vocabulary to provide printed context for them to use, new words may be introduced in oral context. However, printed context—where all words except the new one are familiar—should be used as soon as possible since this is the form in which youngsters will meet printed words.

Most reading programs—and therefore most teachers—introduce new words in a fashion that does a disservice to children (Hillerich, 1986). Let's examine three different examples, taken from three major basal reading programs, to see the difference in implication by the manner in which new words are introduced. Notice that all of them suggest that the word—*box*, in our examples—be introduced in some sort of context.

Example 1. The teacher writes *box* on the chalkboard and says, "Boys and girls, here is a new word from the story we will read today. It names something that can be square or round. It usually has a lid, and we put things in it. Mother might put a gift in it to send in the mail. What is it?"

Example 2. The teacher says, "How many of you keep your toys in something?" Then the teacher writes *box* on the board and asks if anyone can read the new word. After some bright youngster recognizes it, the teacher begins to discuss the word: "Yes, what is the word again? (point) What kinds of boxes do you know? What do you use a box for? Let's read the word again. (point) What are boxes made of? What is the word? (point)"

Example 3. The teacher writes the sentence "Erin keeps her toys in a box." Underlining *box,* she says, "Boys and girls, here is one of our new words. How are you going to figure it out?" The teacher will expect the pupils to say that they will use the sense of the other words, the sound they know the first letter stands for, and—if necessary—the sound the final letter stands for. If this kind of response is not forthcoming, the teacher might like to clarify pupils' metacognitive understanding by following up their response of the correct word by asking, "How did you know the word was not *chest*?" (*Chest* does not begin with the sound *b* stands for.) "How did you know the word was not *bug*?" (*Bug* does not make sense.)

In examining these three word introduction patterns, one might say of the first that it implies preparation for participation in quiz shows. The second presents the word, expects someone to tell the rest of the class what it is, and then proceeds to teach the word, building associations by talking about the word and strengthening its memory by constantly calling pupils back to look at and say that word. As you can see, in neither of the first two examples are pupils being taught anything about how to decode words independently. They are being made to rely on the teacher as the great "giver of words." Is it any wonder that, in many classrooms, when children come to a word they don't know, they immediately wave a hand to the teacher with a comment such as "We haven't had this word yet" or "What did you say this word is?"

The third example demonstrates how new words ought to be introduced in any classroom, regardless of the type of program the teacher is using. In this latter case, children are not being *taught* the word; they are being reminded of what they are to do in order to *figure out* any new word. They are being made independent of the teacher and are put on their own to use the skills they have been learning. In fact, children who do not remember the word when they meet it in the reading selection have an advantage because they get another opportunity to practice the skills that we are trying to teach.

This purpose for introducing new words is a direct answer to one of the few valid criticisms of reading instruction: Too often, in classroom or clinic, we do a great job of teaching skills, but the poor child never finds out what these skills have to do with reading any book—*application* of skill is neglected.

Not only is application—the decoding strategy—demonstrated through this word introduction technique, the technique also eliminates the necessity for introducing every new word from a selection. The skill can be reviewed using only a few of the new words, but this kind of word introduction needs to be continued until children are independently applying the skill that is being taught, extending from the use of context and initial consonants to clusters, final consonants, and affixes. Some students may demonstrate this independence by the end of first grade; others, not until third grade. Even if youngsters appear to use the skill consistently at the end of first grade, it is usually wise to introduce new words again at the beginning of second and third grades just as a reminder or review.

Of course, by late third grade, after they have been taught to use a dictionary for meaning, the independent skill is no longer one of using context and phonics. Now students will be expected—and should be reminded through the word introduction technique—to use context and the dictionary when they meet a word that they do not know.

EXTENDING CONSONANT-SOUND ASSOCIATION SKILLS

One task now is to reinforce the single consonant-sound associations taught previously through use of key pictures. To a large extent, this is best done through wide reading. However, an additional technique often used is that of consonant substitution. Write on the chalkboard a word children know, such as *can.* Have them read the word and say, "Watch what I'm going to do." (Erase *c* and substitute *t.*) "You know the sound *t* stands for. What is the word now?" Repetition of this procedure enables testing or practice of initial consonant sounds. This is not a means, as some misunderstand, of practicing the phonogram *-an,* since that is only a constant in the process; that which changes is the item being practiced.

While consonant substitution will serve as a test or as a review of consonant-sound associations, it is not designed to teach children what to do when they come to an unfamiliar word; a reader does not look at a strange word and substitute consonant sounds to convert the strange word into one that is known.

Youngsters will also need to use their knowledge of letter-sound associations for consonants in positions other than the initial one. Use in final position is developed before use of these associations in medial positions.

Children seem to make the transfer from using sound associations in initial position to their use in other positions easily. One way to provide initial practice in using ending sounds is to use oral context in which two words both make sense and begin with the same sound but have different endings, for example, "Mother was making soup in a big _____." Then put on the board the initial letter *p*. Possible words to be elicited are *pot* and *pan*. Now finish printing the word *pot* and have children identify whether the printed word is *pot* or *pan* by reminding them that they know the sound *t* stands for. They should be able to use that knowledge to decide if the printed word is *pot* or *pan*.

Consonant Digraphs and Clusters

The consonant digraphs *ch, sh,* and *th* should be taught through demonstration and practice as words beginning with those elements are met in actual reading. The digraph *wh*, representing /hw/ *(wheel)*, need not be taught as a separate element in the beginning stages of reading, since even most adults pronounce that combination of sounds as only /w/, thereby making *wheel* and *we'll* homophones.

In the same manner as the first three digraphs, youngsters should be introduced to others as they meet them. Most common are:

gn = /n/ : gnash, gnat, gnaw, gnu, gnome
kn = /n/ : know, knew, known, knee, knife, knock
ph = /f/ : pheasant, phone, phonic, photo, physical
wh = /h/ : who, whose, whole, whom
wr = /r/ : write, wrote, written, wrap, wreck, wrong, wring

In contrast to digraphs, which are combinations of letters representing a single sound, clusters ("blends") are combinations of letters that continue to represent their usual individual sounds but have those sounds running very closely together. Hence, these are not new elements to be taught. In most cases, it is sufficient merely to call attention to the fact that these are letters whose sounds we know.

Children need this attention to clusters as they are met in reading. The most common are *bl, cl, pl, sp,* and *br, dr, fr, gr, pr, st, tr.* Additional clusters include *fl, gl, sc, sk, sm, sq, str, tw, thr,* and *cr, scr, sl, sn, spr, sw.*

Blending

While the reading of consonant clusters merely requires use of two or three known consonant-sound associations, some children will still have difficulty with them. On the other hand, unless the beginning reader has been taught to pronounce consonant sounds in isolation, there is no need to teach that child to "blend" those sounds together. In learning to speak, no child has ever had difficulty in blending the sounds of language in order to form words. Only the child who has used an artificial means of learning to read—isolating the sounds in words—may have a problem in getting those sounds back together so they sound like words.

We must avoid isolated sounding of consonants if we are to avoid more serious problems in reading. With those few children who need help in identifying the two or three consonants in a cluster, use a blending technique, such as the following, that produces no distortion.

First, we must recognize that it is the final consonant, not the initial one, that controls the sound value of a single vowel in a one-syllable word: Given the endings -*an* or -*all*, the reader expects the vowel sounds to be those in *can* or *call*, regardless of the initial consonant or cluster to be used. On the other hand, given the beginning *ba-* or *be-*, there is no way to know the vowel sound: in the first it might be the sound in *bat, babe, ball, bar,* and so on; in the latter it might be *bell, berth,* or *bey.*

By using ending phonograms, we can control the sound value of the vowel and use a pronounceable unit that may be added to in order to produce new words using clusters that we want to review. Either write a phonogram on the board or use the technique of consonant substitution: write *lay* and have pupils read the word. Add *p* and have them use their sound association for *p* to read the new word. Or you might write -*ain*, add *r* and have them read *rain*, add *t* (*train*), and add *s* (*strain*).

Following are a few examples of words to be used with consonant substitution to provide this reverse kind of blending:

> low: blow, flow, glow, slow
>
> ring: bring, spring, string
>
> lay: clay, play, slay
>
> lock: block, clock, flock
>
> rain: drain, grain, sprain, strain, train
>
> ray: pray, spray, stray, tray
>
> led: bled, fled, sled

The following phonograms may also be used for this purpose:

> /a/: -ack, -ad, -am, -an, -ap, -ash, -at
>
> /e/: -ell, -en, -est, -et
>
> /i/: -ick, -ill, -in, -ing, -ink, -it
>
> /o/: -ock, -op, -ot

/u/: -uck, -ug, -ump, -un, -unk

/ā/: -ail, -ain, -ake, -ame, -ate, -ay

/ē/: -eat, -eed

/ī/: -ice, -ide, -ight, -ine

/ō/: -oke, -ore, -old

/ô/: -all, -aw

/ä/: -ar

/ů/: -ook

Inflected Endings

Inflected endings should be presented and discussed as they are met in children's reading matter. Children who have dealt with the *-ing* phonogram should have no difficulty in recognizing that as a pronounceable unit at the end of a word.

Plural and past markers *(-s, -es, -d, -ed)* should be taught as meaning units rather than as elements of phonics. There is no point in trying to teach young children the three different sounds a plural marker or past marker has at the end of English words: /z/ *plays,* /s/ *tops,* and /əz/ *bushes* or /t/ *tossed,* /d/ *happened,* and /əd/ *hunted.* The English-speaking child who has been taught to recognize the meaning of these—indicating "more than one" or "it happened in the past"—will automatically pronounce the ending correctly. In fact, most educated adults are not even aware of the three sounds for these markers.

Incidentally, while I continue to believe we need to teach these endings as meaning units, we cannot even be assured that the resulting words will be recognized. The conventional wisdom has been that anyone who has been taught these endings—at least by second grade—will recognize the inflected form of any word for which the base is known: Anyone who recognizes *play* will also recognize *played, plays,* and *playing.* With fifty-four average fourth graders and fifty-six poor readers at grades six through nine, tested individually on fifteen sets of regularly inflected words, Hillerich (1981) found recognition extremely erratic: Students might recognize one form but not other forms. The only pattern of recognition was that they tended to recognize the more frequently used forms, whether inflected or not.

WORD RECOGNITION

One of the major tasks in teaching reading is to provide lots of experience in reading: Children learn to read by reading. There is no better way to expand a recognition vocabulary than through experiencing words over and over in a variety of meaningful contexts (Hillerich, 1980b), and the expansion of this recognition vocabulary is one of the principal tasks for the beginning reader.

While there may be a place for enjoyable word games, there is no place for isolated flash card drills with beginning readers. First of all, it is easier to recognize words in context than it is in isolation: Junior high students, reading third-grade material, missed three times as many of the same words in isolation as they did in context (Hillerich, 1980a).

Furthermore, there are very few words so important that they are worth teaching for themselves. We quickly reach a point of diminishing returns if we try to teach reading strictly as a word-learning process. Hillerich (1978a), in a count of 380,342 words used by children in writing, found that the most frequently used word—*I*—was used 16,178 times; the one-hundredth word— still relatively high in frequency—was used only 647 times. If we are merely trying to teach specific words, any one of another hundred could be just about as important as the one-hundredth word. In fact, the first hundred words account for 48 to 61 percent of all words in English print; the next hundred expand the percentage by only 6 to 11 percent; the third hundred add 4 to 5 percent.

To put this another way, Nagy and Anderson (1982) analyzed vocabulary encountered by students in grades three through nine and reported:

> Our findings indicate that even the most ruthlessly systematic direct vocabulary instruction could neither account for a significant propor- tion of all the words children actually learn, nor cover more than a modest proportion of the words they will encounter in school reading materials. (Nagy and Anderson, 1982, Abstract)

Writing

As previously mentioned, writing experience is another way to increase this recognition vocabulary as kindergarten or first-grade youngsters move from the limited vocabulary of rebus sentences to labeling pictures or writing sentences based on stories read. You may also encourage them to write their own little stories in response to pictures from greeting cards or magazine pictures. Any and every idea, occasion, or object should be used as a jumping off point for creative writing.

Have students use phonograms—word endings such as *-an, -ock, -ing*, and so on—to make rhyming couplets and jingles. In fact, they might like to make a collection of words generated from the different phonograms they can locate, keeping the list in their language logs.

That language log—a notebook of any format you choose—should be maintained by every student, from kindergarten throughout schooling. Initially, in addition to phonograms, other interesting words or phrases, and pieces of writing, it may include a simple spelling dictionary, listing frequently used words, merely alphabetized by first letter.

Research indicates that teachers at this level should not be concerned about formal spelling (Hillerich, 1985); provide the spellings for your children and recognize that the basic job is one of encouraging them to write and to enjoy writing. In fact, when they don't know how to spell a word, have them merely put down a few consonant letters, draw a line, and continue with whatever they are writing. When they finish, they will remember what the word was that they intended and—*if* they are concerned—you can show them the correct spelling for them to fill in.

How do we deal with older children, those beyond first or second grade, who are having difficulty with reading? We know they have been exposed to important—that is, frequently used—words in meaningful contexts hundreds of times. Yet these students need intensive work in word recognition in order to instantly recognize these words.

One way to provide that work is again through writing experience. Have these older students use a basic word list to rewrite favorite stories at an easier level for younger readers. Or they may enjoy using such a word list to write their own original stories or poems for lower grades. In any event, the question arises: What word list should be used to assure that these youngsters will be learning the most important words?

Of course, you might question the use of *any* word list. The assumed purpose of a word list is to expose children to the "most important," that is, the most frequently used words. However, if students are reading English material, how can they avoid being exposed to the most frequently used words? By definition, the "most frequently used words" are the words that must be used most often in any English communication.

However, for checking, testing, or just for added insurance, many teachers like to have a basic word list. The Dolch (1939) basic sight vocabulary of 220 words has been a standby, despite the fact that criticism of that list as outdated arose in the late 1960s. Hillerich (1974), in the development of the "Starter Words," felt that it was not outdated—how do *the* or *was* become outdated?—but that it was inappropriate.

The Starter Words

Like most basic word lists, the Dolch list was made from basal readers that are made from word lists that are made from basal readers. . . . To avoid this circular "tail chasing" and to find out what the "real world" of vocabulary is like, Hillerich (1974) began with the following four most recent counts of natural writing, where there was no control over vocabulary:

1. Carroll and others (1971) tabulated 5,088,721 words from 1,045 school materials, grades three through nine.

2. Hillerich (1978) tabulated 380,342 words used by children, grades one through six, in creative writing.

3. Kucera and Francis (1967) tabulated 1,014,232 words from fifteen categories of adult printed material.

4. Rinsland (1945) tabulated 6,012,359 words used by children, grades one through eight, in writing.

A composite of the 500 most frequently used words in each of these studies resulted in a total of 995 words. From this collection, Hillerich selected only those words that were common to all four lists and within the first 300 in frequency. Just 190 words met these criteria. These 190 words were then compared against the different lists in an effort to explain differences among word lists.

Differences did not seem to be a result of datedness; differences among the word lists seemed clearly to reflect the source of the list. Unique words—those not on any of the other three—within the first 500 on the Kucera/Francis list read like a businessperson's glossary: *board, business, department, economic, federal,* and so on. The source of the Carroll study is easily recognizable by its unique words: *check, explain, list, mark, correct,* and of course, *slowly, quickly,* and *carefully.* In checking against the Dolch, which deliberately omitted nouns—a peculiar decision if one wants all frequently used words—Hillerich found that 43 of the 190 words were not on the Dolch 220; conversely, 62 of the Dolch words were not even among the most frequently used 240 words from the composite. While not dated, the Dolch words reflect the preprimer words of the 1930s and 1940s materials from which they came: color words, *funny, laugh, jump,* and so on.

Which list is more appropriate or more helpful? One way to answer that question is to evaluate the percentage of running words in different studies accounted for with each list, as shown in Figure 5-1.

Figure 5-1

	Hillerich 190 words	Dolch 220 words
Hillerich (children's writing)	70.0%	67.5%
Rinsland (children's writing)	67.5%	65.6%
Kucera and Francis (adult print)	53.2%	51.7%
Carroll and others (textbooks, grades 3–9)	56.9%	55.3%

Figure 5-1 reveals that the Starter Words provide about 2 percent more coverage in running words, regardless of the kind of material checked against, in spite of there being thirty fewer starter words as compared with the Dolch words. Incidentally, this table also shows that fewer different words were used by children in writing than were used in adult printed material, or even in school materials.

Originally the 190 words were asterisked in publication with the next most frequent 50 words included. The additional 50 words represented those included if one accepted commonality within the first 500 instead of 300 on the composite list of four studies. However, further analysis (Hillerich, 1973) revealed that these 50 words accounted for only about 2 percent more coverage in the four studies and, therefore, were not worth adding.

In using any basic word list, it is helpful to know what might be expected of typical children. The starter words have been administered as a word recognition test to over a thousand children, grades one through three, in a variety of school districts during January of the school year. Figure 5-2 lists the results, indicating the words known by the typical first grader (50 percent) with a plus sign.

One of the most interesting facts revealed in Figure 5-2 is the pattern of words known by first graders. The left column—the most frequently used words—has the most plus signs, with each successive column having fewer, again suggesting that the more frequently an individual is exposed to a word, the more likely that person is to recognize the word.

THE ROLE OF ORAL READING

Oral reading requires more than merely silent reading out loud. Because the oral reader must be concerned about items such as pronunciation, enunciation, phrasing, stress, and so on, some of the reader's energy is eroded from comprehension. Too much oral reading will produce slow, plodding readers—poor readers who believe "reading" is a matter of "knowing the words."

The oral reading skills are "taught" through demonstration and practice. You can demonstrate the effect of different emphases in reading a passage, discuss it with students, and have them attempt to read the section as they believe it should be read.

Furthermore, no one should be expected to read materials orally that have not been read silently. This statement even applies to reading the three words that might be on the page of that first preprimer. The only exception to this statement is in the case of an oral reading test. Even the adult does not usually relish reading material orally without first having the opportunity to look that material over in advance.

Figure 5-2

The 190 Starred Starter Words in Order of Frequency of Use from Four Original Lists*

Midyear Norms, based on individual recognition testing in eight school districts:

+ = Grade 1 (N=344)—118 words were known by 50% or more of pupils

Grade 2 (N=329)—all words were known by 75%, except 9 words marked "(2)"

Grade 3 (N=357)—all words were known by 90%, except 12 words marked "(3)"

In order of frequency of use, words 1 through 125 are on this page; words 126 through 190 continue on the next page.

+ the	+ when	+ if	+ how	+ good
+ and	+ all	+ some	+ down	well
+ a	+ this	about	+ back	came
+ to	+ she	+ by	+ just	new
+ of	+ there	+ him	+ year	+ school
+ in	+ not	+ or	+ little	+ too
+ it	+ his	+ can	+ make	been (3)
+ is	+ as	+ me	+ who	think
+ was	were (2,3)	+ your	after	+ home
+ I	would	+ an	people	+ house
+ he	+ so	+ day	+ come	+ play
+ you	+ my	their	+ no	+ old
+ that	+ out	other	because	long
+ for	+ from	+ very	first	+ where
+ on	+ up	could (2,3)	+ more	only
+ they	+ will	+ has	many	much
+ with	+ do	+ look	know (3)	+ us
+ have	+ said	+ get	made	+ take
+ are	+ then	+ now	thing	+ name
+ had	what	+ see	+ went	+ here
+ we	+ like	our (3)	+ man	+ say
+ be	her (3)	+ two	want	+ got
+ one	+ go	+ into	+ way	around
+ but	+ them	+ did	+ work	any
+ at	+ time	+ over	which	use (3)

Figure 5-2 (Continued)

place	than	thought (2,3)	once	left
+ put	three	last	+ something	white
+ boy	found	+ away	+ room	+ let
water	these (2)	each	must	world (2)
also (2)	saw	never	didn't	under
before	find	while (2,3)	always	same
+ off	+ tell	+ took	+ car	kind (3)
through (2,3)	+ help	+ men	told	+ keep
right	every (3)	+ next	why	+ am
+ ask	again	+ may	small	best
most	another (2)	+ Mr.	children	better
should	+ big	+ give	still	+ soon
don't	night	+ show	head	+ four

Source: "Starter Words" © 1973, by Robert L. Hillerich. Permission is granted for teachers to reproduce for use in their classes.

Moreover, all oral reading ought to be purposeful, and it is not a very good purpose for me to read orally merely because the teacher says it is my turn! Round-robin reading ought to be outlawed from our schools. In contrast, good purposes for oral reading include the desire to inform, to entertain, or merely to share some enjoyable information. Hence, the most appropriate vehicle for oral reading is usually a library book since the others don't have copies themselves. At other times, oral reading might result from the time-saving effort to prove a point in a discussion, or a group of students might like to dramatize a story they have read.

Another important purpose for oral reading at the beginning level is to relate the printed word to the spoken language those youngsters have been using for years. Beginning readers need the ear contact—they need the reinforcement of hearing the words pronounced. Hence, the first grade teacher can easily be forgiven for running out of strong purposes for reading that same sentence after the tenth time. However, much of a good beginning reading material is in the form of conversation, so a dozen different children can be asked to read the same sentence the way they think the character said it.

READING TO CHILDREN

It is questionable whether there is ever a time that individuals are either too young or too old to be read to. Certainly, there is no such time at the elementary school level.

First of all, as pointed out in Chapter 3, it is important to read to young children in order to acquaint them with the patterns of the literary or printed language. Once you have selected a story appropriate to the interest level of the group, the reading ought to be done without paraphrasing. It does no harm for children to hear a word now and then that is outside their listening vocabularies. They can follow and enjoy the story, and talking down to them often detracts from that enjoyment.

A second purpose for reading to children is to increase their interest in reading. Before children have learned to read, this might be done with books of all kinds, from the nonsense of Dr. Seuss to the humorous solutions to problems faced by Frances in the Hoban books. Large picture books, including Caldecott Award winners and runners-up, not only make excellent reading to youngsters but they also provide the picture books for children themselves to "read." These books are seldom actually read by children other than for pictures since the reading level is such that by the time youngsters can read them, they will not; by then the books have too much the format of a "baby" book.

As children begin reading, some of the beginning-to-read books can be read to them and made available for them to read independently. Reading a book to children only increases their desire to read it themselves. Good sources of beginning-to-read books are the Follett "Beginning-to-Read" and "JUST Beginning-to-Read" books, Harper and Row "I Can Read," Random House "Beginner Books," and Childrens Press "Start-Off Stories" and "Rookie Readers." Nor should Mother Goose and poetry, factual books and picture dictionaries, be forgotten at this level.

Another purpose for reading to children is to begin the development of the reading comprehension skills that will be discussed in Chapters 7 and 8. When a story is read to youngsters, depending upon the length, it may be discussed part by part or in total. The discussion should be aimed primarily at increasing enjoyment of the story, but it is also an opportunity for the teacher to range through various comprehension skills at the listening/speaking level. Such practice in the use of these skills at an oral level paves the way for the use of these skills in actual reading.

TEACHING ABOUT VOWELS

In English we have five vowel letters plus the semi-vowels *y* and *w* to represent the fifteen "vowel sounds" usually identified in a dictionary. Reading teachers have traditionally referred to these sounds as "long," "short," and "neither long nor short."

Because this terminology is not descriptive, the 1970s witnessed a concerted effort to get teachers to change to more appropriate terms, based on the linguistic principle that all vowel sounds fall into two categories, depending upon whether they are single phonemes or combinations.

A phoneme is the smallest sound unit that distinguishes one language sound from another. For example, *bit* and *pit* are minimal pairs in English, differing by only one phoneme, the initial /b/ and /p/. Likewise, *pin* and *pen* differ by only the vowel phonemes /i/ and /e/.

The two classifications of the vowel sounds are "simple" and "complex," also referred to as "checked" (or "tense") and "glided" (or "lax"). Any of these sets is linguistically honest: Simple vowel sounds are made up of a single phoneme, such as /i/ in *sit;* complex vowel sounds are made up of more than one phoneme, such as /ī/ in *site,* formed from the simple phonemes /i/ plus /y/.

Figure 5-3 shows the "fifteen vowel sounds" according to the position in which each is formed in the mouth. Complex vowel sounds are placed in the position where they originate, with the combinations of phonemes that make them up indicated in parentheses, showing that they all glide to a /y/ (up and forward) or a /w/ (up and back) conclusion.

Facts About Phonics for Vowels

While some basal reading programs and many teachers still attempt to teach generalizations about the sound-symbol correspondences for vowels, the evidence is very clear. A spate of reports in the 1960s began with Clymer (1963), who found that forty-five phonic and structural rules were agreed upon in the teacher guides of four basal reading programs at the primary level. Of the forty-five rules, twenty-four dealt with vowels.

Clymer then applied the rules to the contents of the pupil books *used to teach those very rules* and found that only six of the twenty-four vowel rules were true as often as seventy-five percent of the time. In fact, one of the

Figure 5-3

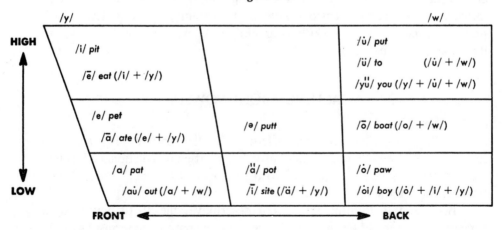

common rules, "When two vowels go walking, the first does the talking," was true only 45 percent of the time: A child who faithfully applied that rule would be wrong more often than right.

Following are the six rules, with Clymer's numbers, found to be true at least 75 percent of the time:

5. The *r* gives the preceding vowel a sound that is neither long nor short *(horn)*. 78%

8. Words having double *e* usually have the long *e* sound *(seem)*. 98%

10. In *ay* the *y* is silent and gives *a* its long sound *(play)*. 78%

16. When *y* is the final letter in a word, it usually has a vowel sound *(dry)*. 84%

19. When *a* is followed by *r* and the final *e,* we expect to hear the sound heard in *care (dare)*. 90%

44. When there is one *e* in a word that ends in a consonant, the *e* usually has a short sound *(leg)*. 76%

As shown, three of these six rules barely reached the 75 percent criterion, and of the six, two are of very doubtful value: Rule 5 merely tells what a sound is *not,* and rule 16 provides a choice of all fifteen vowel sounds!

Others verified Clymer's findings with vocabularies beyond the primary level (Bailey, 1967; Emans, 1967). Some felt it was the lack of specificity of existing rules that presented the problem, so they attempted to improve on instruction by proliferating very specific rules, resulting in generalizations that were true most of the time but that applied to so few words they were not worth teaching.

The largest study of the relationship between letter and sound was done by Hanna and others (1966). They programmed a computer for over three hundred rules, including those for position of the sound in a word, and examined seventeen thousand English words to determine whether the computer could use the rules to spell the sounds correctly. They reported that the English language is 84 percent "regular" in its sound-symbol relationships, and therefore one can teach rules. However, this finding is based on several questionable factors.

First of all, three hundred rules are more than any student can be "programmed" for. Furthermore, the computer was programmed for the eight most frequent spellings of the schwa sound—the sound at the beginning of *about*—a sound that represents 25 percent of all vowel sounds in English and one that is spelled at least twenty-two different ways. With such programming, it was not too difficult for the computer, when asked to spell the schwa sound spelled *o,* to reply *o*.

Finally, the 84 percent was the result of input of the seventeen thousand words phoneme by phoneme. Since two out of three phonemes in English are consonants, and consonants tend to be fairly regularly spelled, this too assisted the high percentage of regularity.

In contrast to this finding, when the seventeen thousand words were fed into the computer as whole words, the computer was able to spell with only 49.8 percent accuracy. And youngsters are asked to spell and to read *whole words*, not phonemes. Not many teachers would compliment a child for spelling *stop* as *stap* by saying, "Great Johnny. You are 75 percent correct; you got three phonemes out of four."

So that you, as reader and teacher, may draw your own conclusions from the Hanna study, Figure 5-4 presents the data about vowels from that study, merely combining into one sound those, such as schwa, that were artificially subdivided to make the computer's task easier. The proportion of individual letter-sound correspondences are essentially the same as those found in Dewey (1970) and Hillerich (1982).

Across the top of Figure 5-4 are the fifteen vowel sounds identified in a dictionary; alphabetically down the left column are the spellings of those sounds. The table can be used to check generalizations from either a spelling or a reading standpoint. Numerals in the boxes represent the number of words where a given sound was represented by given letters. To use the table for reading, begin with a letter and go across to check the various sounds that letter represents. For example, *a* stands for the vowel sound in *pin* in 4 words; in *elf* in 158 words, and so on. Only about 42 percent of the time does that letter represent the vowel sound in *bat*, yet this generalization forms the basis for some "linguistic" programs. This exemplifies the fact that linguists approach language from an oral—spelling—viewpoint. From that standpoint, to spell the vowel sound in *bat*, we begin with the sound and find that it is spelled *a* in about 98 percent of the words.

Effectiveness of Teaching Vowel Rules to Children

Examination of the nature of the English language answers only part of the question about the value of teaching vowel generalizations. What happens to children's reading ability if the generalizations are taught?

On this point, more has been reported on the lack of effectiveness in teaching such rules for spelling (Hillerich, 1982) than has been done in reading. However, the evidence that does exist indicates that children who are taught vowel rules read no better—in fact, usually not as well—as those not taught about vowels (Hardy, 1972; Ibeling, 1961).

Figure 5-4

Key Word	pin	elf	bat	top	saw	foot	cup	ape	eel	kite	boat	oil	owl	moon	few
Sound	/ĭ/	/ĕ/	/ă/	/ŏ/	/ô/	/ů/	/ə/	/ā/	/ē/	/ī/	/ō/	/ôĭ/	/aů/	/ů/	/yů/
Spelling															
a	4	158	4192	80	683		1606	1002							
a-e	187	51	147		34		3	790							
ae		1							5						
ah					4										
ai	15	50	1				9	208							
ai-e		3						18		1					
aigh								4							
ao					2										
au					150		1				3				
au-e					9			1			2				
augh					12										
aw					75										
aw-e					2										
ay	1	1						131		3					
ay-e								1							
e	69	3320			5		2742	16	1765						
e-e	28	113					143	6	62						

Figure 5-4 (Continued)

Key Word	pin	elf	bat	top	saw	foot	cup	ape	eel	kite	boat	oil	owl	moon	few
Sound	/i/	/e/	/a/	/ä/	/ô/	/ù/	/ə/	/ā/	/ē/	/ī/	/ō/	/ôi/	/aù/	/ü/	/yü/
Spelling															
ea	50	152			18		32	14	245						
ea-e	1	1					2		30						
eau											6				5
ee	42								249						
ee-e									9						
ei	13	6					2	14	16	6					
ei-e								2	6						
eigh								18		3					
eo		3					10		2						
et								9							
eu						1	6							4	28
eu-e															1
ew											3			22	38
ew-e															1
ey	40	1						14	6	1					1

Key Word	pin	elf	bat	top	saw	foot	cup	ape	eel	kite	boat	oil	owl	moon	few
Sound	/i/	/e/	/a/	/ä/	/ö/	/ü/	/ə/	/ā/	/ē/	/ī/	/ō/	/öi/	/aü/	/ü/	/yü/
Spelling															
ey-e										7					
eou							8								
i	5349														
i-e	339						1459		38	554					
ia							7		44	555					
ia-e	3						2								
ie	43	4					22		33	26					
ie-e	4						4		23						
ieu															4
iew															6
igh										88					
o	1			1558	435	17	2044				1876			37	
o-e				20	21		48				370			12	
oa					9						127				
oa-e											3				
oe									5		13			4	
oh											4				
oi												92			
oi-e							2					8			

107

Figure 5-4 (Continued)

Key Word	pin	elf	bat	top	saw	foot	cup	ape	eel	kite	boat	oil	owl	moon	few
Sound	/i/	/e/	/a/	/ä/	/ȯ/	/u̇/	/ə/	/ā/	/ē/	/ī/	/ō/	/ȯi/	/au̇/	/ü/	/yü/
Spelling															
oo						114	7				9			173	
oo-e														12	
ou						25	388				29		227	29	
ou-e							1				10		54	3	
ough					15						8		4	2	
ow				4							124		119		
ow-e											1		2		
oy										1		48			
oy-e												1			
u	3	2				200	1743							93	814
u-e	3					11	60							34	256
ue														16	27
uo														2	
ui	16													6	8
ui-e														4	
uy										3					
y	1801						29			211					
y-e	1									23					

108

After finding that first graders who were taught nothing about vowels achieved higher in reading than those who were taught vowel rules (Hillerich, 1967), Hillerich (1970) investigated the value of teaching vowel generalizations to second graders who had not learned about them in first grade. In this study, six classes participated in three treatments, with the same reading program adapted to all three. Two classes were taught the vowel generalizations just as the teacher's guide directed. The second treatment used the same program but stopped short of developing a generalization about vowel sounds; children worked only at the hearing level, identifying a vowel sound and then finding other words with the same sound but never attempting to generalize that a given letter or letters represented a certain vowel sound. The third treatment group was taught absolutely nothing about vowels in second grade.

Reading achievement, tested by standardized test at the end of grade two, indicated that the highest in achievement were the groups that were not taught rules but that had identified given vowel sounds and found other words with the same sound—a heavy auditory approach. Next highest were the groups who were taught nothing about vowels in either first or second grade. Lowest were the groups who were taught the vowel rules the way they are taught in reading programs, including the usual wording of "sometimes, but not always," "usually," and so on.

In summary to this point, we find that neither analysis of the language nor of the effectiveness of teaching vowel generalizations to children supports the practice of teaching those generalizations. In fact, the teaching of some of these rules, through a contrived vocabulary that forces some "truth" at the time, is dangerous from another viewpoint: Youngsters initially exposed to regularity in symbol-sound correspondence seem to develop a "mind-set" for regularity and, when meeting the natural language, have more difficulty than those exposed to the natural "irregularities" of English from the beginning (Levin and Watson, 1963; Williams, 1968; Ackerman, 1973).

What Can Be Taught About Vowels: The "Exploration" Method

While it is certainly better to ignore the vowels than it is to teach the fallible and misleading rules, apparently some attention to vowels is even more effective than ignoring them. In fact, experience has shown that kindergarteners who read at second or third grade level without having had instruction, given a test of nonsense syllables using a variety of vowel representations, can read them as well as can second or third graders. In other words, good readers may not be able to verbalize rules—may not even have been taught them—but through experience they gain an intuitive grasp of the sounds those letters represent. Such an understanding may be much more beneficial than verbalizing rules, and it is just such an understanding that seems to have taken place in the treatment group that worked with vowels at the hearing level.

Specifically, the first step is to clarify with children the vowel sound under consideration, for example, the "sound you hear at the beginning of *ape*." In fact, vowel sounds can be pronounced in isolation, so you might also want to say "the sound /ā/." You may continue by saying three words and having pupils identify which two of the three have that vowel sound: "angel, at, ate." Once youngsters understand what sound is under consideration, have them return to a page from their reader that has been read and discussed, asking them to reread the page and to make a list of all the words they can find that have the /ā/ sound.

After pupils have completed their lists, ask for the words and put the total list on the chalkboard. Then sort the words according to their spelling:

/ā/ as in ape

<u>a</u>	<u>ai</u>	<u>a-e</u>	<u>aigh</u>
able	aim	bake	straight
lazy	paint	age	
	chain		

Once your students begin to get the idea—and particularly in later grades—suggest that they use library books or other printed material to find additional words with the same sound. A day or so later, bring the group together to share the words they have found. In making a composite listing on the board, the class may find the original chart expanded to something like this:

/ā/ as in ape

<u>a</u>	<u>ai</u>	<u>a–e</u>	<u>aigh</u>	<u>ai–e</u>
able	aim	bake	straight	raise
lazy	paint	age		
April	chain	ate		
	rain			

<u>eigh</u>	<u>ay</u>	<u>ey</u>	<u>ea</u>
eight	play	they	break
weigh	day		

Your pupils may also like to reverse the process, finding words with *a* and sorting them according to the sounds represented by that letter.

Such experience has several benefits. First, obviously no generalization may be drawn other than the fact that /ā/ is spelled in a variety of ways or a variety of letters may represent that vowel sound. Second, this kind of approach is truly a discovery method: It doesn't "stack the deck" with a few preselected items that will force children to the generalization we want them to learn; it opens the door to the whole world of language. Third, this approach has its own built-in adaptation to individual differences. Every child can participate: The bright child will collect fifty words and fifteen different spellings; the slower one will collect fifteen words and five different spellings. All can benefit from the ensuing discussion of the findings. Finally, this kind of activity has implications for future use of a dictionary, as will be discussed in Chapter 6.

Teachers may adapt this exploration method to any reading program without danger of violating the philosophy of that program. If your program suggests teaching a vowel rule—and most do—instead of teaching it blindly, announce that rule to your youngsters: "Here is a rule we are supposed to learn. I wonder if it is any good. Collect all of the words you can find that would fit under the rule, and let's see how often the rule is true." If the generalization is effective, children will remember it far better for having become involved in this exploration; if it is not, I don't believe you want them to learn it anyhow.

STRUCTURAL ANALYSIS

Syllable rules as well as some prefixes and suffixes are usually taught at the primary level in both reading and spelling programs. There is a great deal of question about the value of the former; the latter is very limited in its scope at the early reading levels but gains value in middle grades, where we will discuss it in connection with study skills.

Syllabication

It is helpful for children to be taught something about compound words: that there are certain longer words that are made up of two shorter familiar words, and the meaning of the longer word is usually related to the meanings of the two familiar words. This can be done by examining a few examples, such as *campfire, snowman,* and so on and having youngsters find other compound words. Some teachers even like to have primary children make literal pictures of the two base words—a head and a light—and then of the compound—a headlight.

This kind of experience with compound words is as close as anyone should get to having youngsters find "little words in big words." Such a practice will mislead much more often than it helps. Following is a quick check of a few basic words that gives some indication of the problem:

name = am	another = a not her	because = be use
down = own	find = in	came = am
good = go	head = he ad	house = ho use

After learning something about compound words, youngsters can also be made aware of the fact that longer words can be pronounced in "chunks" or syllables. This is helpful so that when they come to a multisyllable word they don't attempt to pronounce it all in one chunk and choke on it. The practice is easily accomplished by exaggerating the separation of syllables, such as "hap-e-ness" and asking how many parts they hear. With additional spoken words, students might clap their hands or in some manner indicate the number of chunks they hear.

Beyond these points, little can be taught about syllables that is helpful in reading. Of course, basal readers don't stop here. They have teachers teaching about the point of syllable division in words, including at least the VCCV and VCV rules.

In the former, youngsters are taught that when they see two consonants between two vowels, they are to divide between the two consonants unless they are a cluster or digraph, in which case they never divide but apply the VCV rule. Using the VCCV rule, one divides the word *yellow* between the two *l*'s. This is the rule for dividing a word at the end of a line—a writing convention— and has nothing whatsoever to do with reading, where one is converting, actually or mentally, to speech. In reading, if any syllable division is used, it should be the pronunciation syllabication, and the pronunciation is indicated as /yel-ō/; there is no /l/ in the final syllable.

Actually, however, it takes a well-trained ear to distinguish in normal speech whether the speaker is saying "yel–low," "ye–lo," or "yel–o." And who really cares anyhow? As the linguist Wardhaugh (1966) indicated, "Syllabication has no 'truth' value." It is a writing convention, where polysyllabic words may be divided either phonologically, morphologically, visually, or typographically.

To make matters even worse—that is, to continue to waste precious instructional time—most teachers continue with the VCV rule: "When you see a single consonant between two vowels, try the long sound of the vowel before that consonant and divide before the first consonant following that vowel; if that doesn't sound like a word you know, try the short sound of the vowel and divide after the first consonant following that vowel." Of course, if neither sounds "like a word you know," you are on your own! How is anyone expected to pay attention to meaning with rules like that cluttering up the mind? Basically, however, I defy you—even with that rule in front of you—to divide the word *patum* properly. There is no way you can decide how to divide that word until you know how it is pronounced. And if you know how it is pronounced, why would you want to divide it! The rule represents after-the-fact reasoning.

Research on the contribution of syllable division to the reading achievement of students is also consistent with common sense: Students taught syllable division read no better than those not taught the rules (Marzano and others, 1976; Canney and Schreiner, 1976–77; Cunningham and others, 1981).

In contrast, apparently children can benefit not only from an awareness of "chunking," but also from an awareness of certain common syllables. As they meet some of the more frequently used syllables, call their attention to the syllable and its pronunciation in the known word. Then have them find other words with the same syllable. While this contributes nothing to meaning, it does provide a quick pronounceable chunk to get pupils off and running on other words. One common syllable is the final consonant *-le,* as in *table, candle, turtle,* and so on. Other common syllables to become aware of are:

com-	-able	-est	-ly	-tion
dis-	-ance (-ence)	-ment	-ing	-tive
in-	-dom	-ful	-ness	-ous
mis-	-er	-less		

Affixation

Teaching youngsters to recognize for pronunciation and meaning certain prefixes and suffixes has value at the primary level. We should teach for meaning, however, only those prefixes and suffixes that are frequently used and consistent in meaning. With such criteria, very few prefixes and suffixes, beyond the inflected endings, will be taught at the primary level.

Gibson (1972) reported a study of the prefixes and suffixes found in a list of over two thousand frequently used words. Of the prefixes, she found only *un-* and *dis-* used frequently enough and consistent enough in meaning that they should be taught. This list might be expanded, in keeping with practice of basal reading programs, to include *in-, pre-, re-,* and *mis-.* Even with such a limited list, one could argue about *in-* and *dis-. In-* assimilates. How does one recognize *in-* spelled *il-, im-,* and *ir-?* Deighton (1959) pointed out that *dis-* has six different meanings and therefore should not be taught.

In terms of suffixes other than the plural and past markers, Gibson found only *-less* and *-ful* to be frequently used and consistent in meaning. This is not to say that the more sophisticated affixes and combining forms cannot be useful at upper elementary and middle school levels, where students meet technical vocabulary in the content areas. (See Chapter 8.)

Gibson also investigated an interesting point: Assuming a youngster has been drilled that *pre-* is a prefix meaning "before," how does that student interpret the unfamiliar word *preach*—"the ache that comes before"? She found that there are ten times as many of these anomalous prefixes as there are real ones. The implication is that we must be careful, when we teach the use of prefixes, that we teach children to begin by making certain there is a base word following the assumed prefix. Otherwise, children will be misled about ten times for every time they are helped.

Usually the best way to approach the few prefixes and suffixes mentioned as worth teaching is to do so by starting with the words children meet in their reading. Then have them produce other words in their writing that use the affixes introduced in the reading.

Chapter 6

Expanding Vocabulary Through Reading and Writing

Anyone who hopes to function effectively in a language must have some control over the vocabulary of that language. Certainly knowledge of the meanings of most words in a selection is necessary for understanding that selection. Hence, one of the tasks of every individual is to constantly expand vocabularies, whether that person is a primary child, an advanced student, or an adult. Given the tremendous size of the English lexicon—over 500,000 base words—it is doubtful that anyone ever masters all the words. Nor is such complete mastery even necessary. Furthermore, as pointed out by Nagy and Anderson (1984), we could not possibly teach deliberately even a fraction of the words learned by elementary school children.

It is here that writing experience stands out as a primary means for skill development that enhances communication, receptive and expressive. For it is here that the experience of writing not only adds another sense but provides active thought and searching for appropriate words, as well as experience aimed at giving students control over the patterns in which those words can be used to persuade or influence a reader. I am convinced that this latter experience—having engaged in the manipulation themselves—is the best method for having students understand how a writer is trying to manipulate them.

To continue the point made initially, just ten words account for 25 percent of all words in English print. Hence, depending upon whether one considers adult print (Kucera and Francis, 1967) or that of children (Hillerich, 1978a), we rapidly reach a point of diminishing returns when teaching words. The five hundred most frequently used words account for from 64 percent to 85 percent of all words in print; the first one thousand 69 percent to 87 percent; and the first twenty-five hundred from 79 percent to 95 percent.

Of course, as shown in Figure 6-1, we have a variety of vocabularies. The smallest, discussed in Chapter 4, is the *recognition* or "sight" vocabulary, those words known instantly and without benefit of context, phonics, or any other tool. This is a receptive vocabulary, usually referred to only in connection with reading.

Next largest is the *expressive* vocabulary, used in speaking and writing, while the largest is the *receptive*, used in listening and reading. The relative size of the speaking and writing vocabularies will depend upon the education and experience of the user. Obviously, a primary child's speaking vocabulary exceeds the writing vocabulary, whereas an educated adult's writing vocabulary may exceed the speaking because of the time to consider word choices and

Figure 6-1

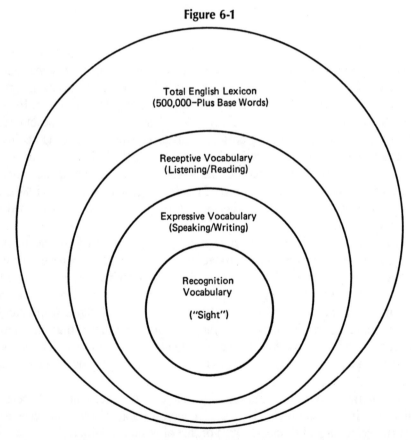

Source: Robert L. Hillerich, *Teaching Children to Write, K–8* (Englewood Cliffs, NJ: Prentice-Hall, Inc., 1985), p. 81.

access to a thesaurus or other tool, not to mention the fact that writing tends to be more formal than speech. Likewise, for similar reasons the reading vocabulary of educated adults tends to surpass the listening since time allows more effective use of context and tools such as a dictionary.

Looking at Figure 6-1 from the reverse direction also provides the pattern in which words usually come into an individual's vocabulary. They usually enter through the receptive mode. With some additional experience they are added to the expressive lexicon, and ultimately they are so familiar that they become part of that automatic recognition vocabulary.

What then are the best means for developing vocabulary? As shown in Figure 6-2, they fall into two categories: skills that are generalizable and those that are not.

Generalizable skills are those that extend beyond the word or words taught. For example, beginning reading skills such as the use of context and phonics generalize beyond the words used to teach those skills: The new word *water* might be introduced in context to demonstrate how to figure out that word with no concern about whether or not the word itself is remembered. This skill generalizes to determination of many other words. In contrast, there are times when we want to teach a specific word. Such teaching is nongeneralizable since the fact that one teaches the word *parget* will certainly not carry over to the understanding of any other word in the language.

While generalizable instruction and nongeneralizable instruction both have a place, most concern in the area of vocabulary development ought to be on one aspect of the latter: the general expansion of vocabulary with no specific word in mind. Nevertheless, there are times when specific words need to be taught, usually in preparation for reading in a content area where knowledge of the word is essential for understanding the selection.

In terms of generalizable instruction, we have already discussed a major tool for word identification: use of context and phonics. However, when words are met that are outside the receptor's listening/speaking vocabulary, use of

Figure 6-2

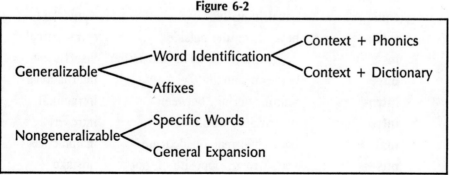

phonics is supplanted by use of a dictionary along with context. Dictionary skills will be discussed later in this chapter. Knowledge of affixes—prefixes and suffixes—also generalizes since knowing that *un-* reverses the meaning of *cover* or *tie* should help me figure out the meaning of *unlock*. Let's examine instruction in this area before continuing with nongeneralizable techniques.

GENERALIZABLE INSTRUCTION: AFFIXES

A few basic prefixes and suffixes were suggested in Chapter 5 for primary children. However, as students get more heavily into the content areas, additional affixes may be helpful. Even here, however, the number is limited if we accept Deighton's (1959) criteria that no affix should be taught unless it is frequently used and consistent in meaning.

Following are lists of those items, based on Deighton, that are possibly worth some instruction by upper elementary or middle school level. Such instruction is not effective through dictionary drill or through memorizing a list. Begin when a word containing one of the affixes is met in reading material. Have students check the meaning and then find other words with the same affix. You might even have them collect such items in their language logs for future discussion.

Prefixes

Of sixty-eight common prefixes, only these are useful in terms of frequency and relatively invariant meaning:

Prefix	Meaning(s)	Example
anti-	opposed to, against	anticommunist
apo-	from, detached, formed from	apology
circum-	around, about	circumscribe
equi-	equal, equally	equidistant
extra-	beyond, on the outside	extracurricular
in-	not, in, into, or as an intensifier	insufficient
inter-	between, among	international
intra-	within, during, between	intramural
intro-	in, inward, within	introvert
mal-	bad, abnormal, inadequate	malpractice
mis-	bad, wrong, opposite of, not	mistake

non-	not, absence of	nondistinctive
over-	exceeding, surpassing	overanxious
pre-	before, in front of	predate
re-	again	recall
syn-	with, at the same time	synonym

Suffixes

Most suffixes indicate part of speech rather than meaning. However, the following noun suffixes can be useful by middle grades and above:

Suffix	Meaning(s)	Example
-ana	collected items concerning	Americana
-archy	rule, government	monarchy
-ard, -art	one associated with a characteristic	dullard, braggart
-aster	one that is inferior or not genuine	criticaster
-chrome	colored thing or matter	heterochrome
-cide	killer, killing	pesticide
-fer	one that bears	conifer
-fication	making, production	electrification
-gram	drawing, writing, record	telegram
-graph	something written or instrument for	telegraph
-graphy	writing in a manner or on a subject	oceanography
-ics	study, knowledge, skill, practice	electronics
-itis	malady from or proneness to	televisionitis
-latry	worship	idolatry
-meter	instrument or means for measurement	barometer
-metry	art, process, or science of measuring	chronometry
-logy	doctrine, theory, science	sociology
-phore	carrier	gametophore

Adjective Suffixes

-able, -ible	capable of, liable to	perishable, collectible
-est	superlative form	biggest
-ferous	bearing, producing	coniferous
-fic	making, causing	horrific
-fold	multiplied by, times	threefold
-form	in the form/shape of	cuneiform
-ful	having much, tending to	helpful
-genous	producing, yielding, originating from	homogenous
-ic	related to	allergic
-less	without, unable to act or be acted on	dauntless
-like	resembling or characteristic of	ladylike
-most	most toward	headmost
-ose	full of, having the qualities of	verbose
-ous	full of or having the qualities of	poisonous
-wards	in the direction of	backwards
-wise	in the manner/direction of, in regard to	slantwise

Eight noun endings indicate agent: *-eer, -ess, -grapher, -ier, -ster, -ist, -stress, -trix.* Six endings are used as diminutives: *-ule, -cle, -cule, -ock, -kin, -let.*

The following noun suffixes shed no light on meaning but may be of value as common syllables (to aid in identification of base words) or from a writing viewpoint: *-acity, -ance, -action, -ence, -dom, -ery, -hood, -ism, -mony, -ment, -ness, -tion, -ty, -tude, -ship.*

Combining Forms

According to Deighton, the following lead to understanding of two hundred English words:

anthropo-	auto-	biblio-	bio-	centro-
cosmo-	heter-	homo-	hydro-	iso-
lith-	micro-	mono-	neuro-	omni-

pan-	penta-	phil-	phono-	photo-
pneumo-	poly-	proto-	pseudo-	tele-
uni-				

A few items included above, such as *inter-* and *pre-*, were not listed by Deighton because they have half a dozen meanings. However, I believe they are worth instruction since all meanings relate to a general meaning: The former generally implies "between" and the latter, "before." Noticeably missing from the list are some prefixes often taught in reading programs, such as *de-*, *sub-*, *trans-*, and *pro-*, each of which has half a dozen meanings, or *com-*, which has lost its meaning in most English words.

NONGENERALIZABLE INSTRUCTION: SPECIFIC WORDS

Seldom are we concerned with the teaching of specific words. However, there are times when advance knowledge of the meaning of a word is essential for comprehension of material. This is most often the case in reading in the content areas where technical or abstract words are not clearly enough explained. The basic method for such teaching is one of building from known to unknown, finding examples and relating to other words, of fitting those new words into the schemata or mental blueprints of students by associating meanings for the word. Following are a few of the ways this can be done.

The Frayer model (Peters, 1975–76) is useful in teaching a specific word. It includes four clarifying techniques:

1. State the relevant attributes (a *gnu* is a type of antelope; it has horns).
2. State irrelevant attributes (the size of the horns is irrelevant).
3. Use nonexamples (a *gnu* is not a fish or a bird).
4. Place in a hierarchy (size: elephant, *gnu,* fox).

A similar technique is the mnemonic keyword method (Pressley and others, 1982), which is particularly forceful when combined with context (McDaniel and Pressley, 1984). This technique has been successful as low as grade two and transfers to use in new situations after appropriate instruction and practice. For example, to remember the meaning of the word *caterwaul,* pupils can associate the *wail* of a *cat* on a *wall.* A picture is helpful with younger children, whereas older pupils can merely visualize the situation.

The mnemonic keyword device is usually used to assist in paired associate training, where two related items are to be recalled. For example, remembering the capital of Ohio can be assisted by visualizing (Christopher) *Columbus* on the *high* seas.

Webbing, also called semantic mapping or semantic networking, is another device used to build meaning for a specific word. The word *feline* can be clarified through the various interrelationships shown in the semantic map in Figure 6-3.

Students can also be helped to develop meanings for words by examining them from a variety of views, as demonstrated here with the word *parget.*

Use:	The bricklayer decided to *parget* the wall.
Definition:	to cover with plaster
Synonym:	plaster
Antonym:	panel
Class:	wall coverings
Example:	kitchen wall

Figure 6-3

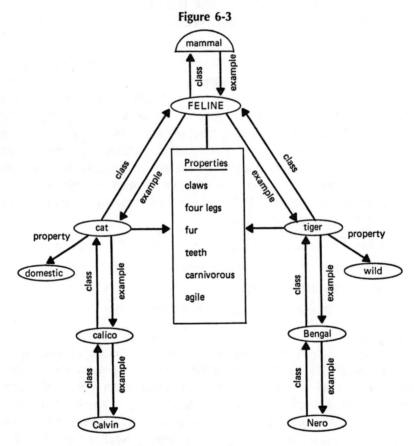

Source: Robert L. Hillerich, *Teaching Children to Write, K-8* (Englewood Cliffs, NJ; Prentice-Hall, Inc., 1985) p. 88.

NONGENERALIZABLE INSTRUCTION:
NONSPECIFIC WORDS

In most cases, the concern for vocabulary development is in this category where the desire is merely to expand every student's meaning vocabulary with no specific word in mind. There are some activities, however, that overlap the two categories, that can be helpful in the case of specific or nonspecific development.

Classification Activities

Have students classify words. For younger pupils, such classifications may be little more than simple collections of words relating to the senses: smells, sounds, sights. More mature students may classify under abstract headings, such as *democratic* versus *undemocratic* or *positive* versus *negative*. These kinds of classification activities may also take the form of deletion exercises, where sets of four or five words are provided and students are to decide which of the words in each set does not belong.

In developing any of these kinds of activities, a language log is essential. This is nothing more than a notebook of any format into which pupils write and keep pieces of writing, anything from collections of words to unfinished themes. Not only should they be engaging in writing to help them remember what they are learning, but they should also be creating some of the activities. One technique is to provide an example or two and then encourage or tease them into developing additional sets or examples for themselves or others. After all, they are the ones who need the thinking and digging more than you do. And any time *they* build the exercise, they are much more personally involved than when the teacher does it. Nevertheless, don't forget to participate in completing some of the exercises with them!

Students may also be given sets of words to classify. For example, given the categories *noise, music, quiet,* they should be able to classify the following:

quiescence	dissonance	concord
harmony	cacophony	tranquility
serenity	attunement	disharmony

Semantic feature analysis can also be used, wherein students are to identify characteristics or features of a number of related items by indicating with a "plus" sign if the item has a given characteristic and a "minus" sign if it does not:

PETS	fur	feathers	tail	4 legs	can be held
cat	+	−	+	+	+
fish	−	−	+	−	−
dog	+	−	+	+	+
horse	−	−	+	+	−

Other methods of handling classification include giving students a category—anything from "jobs" to "vehicles" to "emotions"—and having them list the specific words and then identify the characteristics. Or you may prefer the reverse, giving them a mixed list of words that they are to classify under common properties.

Word Origins and Language History

Based on a summary of 197 studies, Hillerich (1980b) found that the best way to develop vocabulary is to provide experience with words in a variety of meaningful contexts, whether this is at kindergarten or at upper grades, whether oral or in print. This finding has been verified in many research studies, including a comparison of reading in context with use of the dictionary (Eeds and Cockrum, 1985) and from the fact that sixth graders demonstrated vocabulary development with *no* instruction merely from being exposed to new words in their reading (Nagy and others, 1985). Of course, this is not to suggest that teachers ignore vocabulary development since another reassuring conclusion from Hillerich's summary was that *anything* a teacher did to develop vocabulary was better than doing nothing!

From another standpoint, in developing norms for the 190 Starter Words with 344 first graders, Hillerich (1974b) found that the average child, in January, recognized 92 percent of the 50 most frequently used words but only 38 percent of the last 50 of the 190 words, a finding which also suggests that the more frequently children see a word, the more likely they are to remember it. Of course, to this major finding about the importance of exposure to words in meaningful context, we should also add a final point. Yes, vocabulary is best developed through exposure to words in a variety of meaningful contexts, but that learning is enhanced even more if we add "with an interest in language."

Hence, many of the following suggestions are designed to provide enjoyment with and in the language. While there is certainly no evidence to prove it, even experience—if pleasurable—in the history of language is one way to engage older students in manipulation of English, whether they take a historical view of influences or of the syntax or spellings of words.

Intermediate and middle grade students can enjoy books such as the following, dealing with the history of English:

Applegate, Mauree. *The First Book of Language and How to Use It.* Franklin Watts, 1962.

Cutler, Charles. *The English Language: Anglo-Saxon to American.* Xerox Education Publications, 1968.

Denison, Carol. *Passwords to People.* Dodd, Mead, 1950.

Hogben, Lancelot T. *Wonderful World of Communication.* Doubleday, 1959.

Laird, Charlton, and Helene Laird. *Tree of Language.* World Publishing, 1957.

Lambert, Eloise. *Our Language.* Lothrop, Lee and Shepard, 1955.

Pei, Mario. *All About Language.* J.B. Lippincott, 1954.

Sparke, William. *Story of the English Language.* Abelard-Schuman, 1965.

The English lexicon is a composite of words from all the languages of the world. Older students might enjoy classifying words according to the country of their origin, or they might like to see how many words they can collect from a given country, perhaps the country of their own ancestry. For example, they might compare the terms for meat that came from two sources—the Anglo-Saxon animal names as compared with the French table names:

Anglo-Saxon	cow	sheep	calf	pig	deer
French	beef	mutton	veal	pork	venison

To continue with foods, students will find that we "borrowed" *chop suey* from the Chinese, *chili* and *taco* from the Spanish, and *pizza* from the Italians (even though they wouldn't recognize what we call "pizza"). Or they might like to continue with parallels from Anglo-Saxon/French, such as bequeath/devise, give/grant, deed/act, and so on.

Have students investigate word origins, many of which can be fascinating. For example, left-handed individuals are "sinistrals," a term connoting evil. If it had not been for a confusion in direction on the part of the Romans as they copied a Greek religious custom, it would be right-handed people who were sinistrals! Incidentally, it can often be challenging to write imaginary origins for words or phrases we use—again, getting students to enjoy playing with language.

Taking a different tack, not only can students discover interesting word origins, they might trace the changes in meaning that many words have undergone. For example, some words have broadened in meaning: a bonfire was originally a fire of bones; to manufacture was to make by hand; and a maverick was merely an unbranded calf. Other words have narrowed in meaning: Browning referred to a mouse as a "wee deer" since the term referred to any four-legged animal. To be a miser meant to be miserable, and an acre was merely any field of any size.

Of course, other changes are just as interesting as words become up- or downgraded in connotation. Propaganda merely referred to anything disseminated (propagated); to be silly was merely to be happy; a vulgar dress was an everyday dress; and an outlandish one was merely from a different land. In contrast, some words have been upgraded: a mansion was once any farmhouse; to be innocent was to be ignorant; and paradise was any enclosed park.

Useful references dealing with word origins include the following:

Asimov, Isaac. *Words from the Myths*. Houghton Mifflin, 1961.

Epstein, Samuel, and Beryl Epstein. *The First Book of Words*. Franklin Watts, 1951.

Ernst, Margaret S. *Words: English Roots and How They Grow*. Alfred A. Knopf, 1954.

Funk, Charles E. *Heavens to Betsy*. Warner Paperback, 1955.

_____. *Thereby Hangs a Tale*. Warner Paperback, 1950.

_____. *A Hog on Ice*. Warner Paperback, 1948.

Funk, Charles E., and Charles E. Funk, Jr. *Horse Feathers*. Warner Paperback, 1958.

Mathews, Mitford M. *American Words*. World Publishing, 1959.

Morris, William, and Mary Morris. *Dictionary of Word and Phrase Origins* (two volumes). Harper and Row, 1968.

Partridge, Eric. *A Dictionary of Catch Phrases*. Stein and Day, 1977.

A major reference for teachers or superior high school students is Eric Partridge's *Origins* (Macmillan, 1963).

Furthermore, your students might like to collect examples of words that have become generic. Do they really care when they ask a friend for a "kleenex," whether they get a Kleenex, a Puff, or a Scottie? And do they still "dial" numbers on a push-button phone? How many remember grandparents who called that GE refrigerator a "Frigidaire"? Do their parents remember grandparents who called those first refrigerators "iceboxes"? Today, this tendency is a problem to major manufacturers in protecting trade names from becoming generic. How many people still "ditto" material on an A.B. Dick duplicator or "Xerox" on an IBM copier?

Other words originate as eponyms, names of people. Begin with some of the more common origins, such as *sandwich, ferris* wheel, or *maverick*. Have students discover the origins of words such as *leotard* (Jules Leotard, a French aerial performer) or *saxophone* (Antoine Sax, a Belgian instrument maker). Useful references here for older students are *People Words* by Bill Severn (Ives Washburn, 1966) and *Word People* by Nancy Sorel (McGraw-Hill, 1977).

You might also have your students maintain a section in their language logs to collect literary allusions as they find them—or to identify new possibilities from their reading. These may include allusions from the myths, such as "the crash of Thor's hammer" or a "Janus-like personality." Others may come from literature: How many of your students would like to have "a friend like Brutus" or how many know an adult who is a "regular Peter Pan."

Perhaps they might extend their vocabularies by collecting or even inventing portmanteaus. These are new words formed from the combination of two existing words: *brunch,* from breakfast and lunch; *motel,* from motor and hotel. There are many others, including *boatel, smog,* and *newscast.* Can your students create portmanteaus for such combinations as a happy holiday or a messy paper?

Variations in Language

Sometimes vocabulary is best developed by focusing this interest in language on variations in meaning and making distinctions among related words. Many are the possibilities, and they contribute to student understanding of the use of particular literary forms and devices, both as recipients of their use in reading and as wielders of these forms in writing.

Idioms. The world of language is flooded with idioms, many of which we look upon as literal statements. Yet how many people actually "put the lights out" when they leave a room? Most leave the lights in that room! Have students collect idioms in their language logs. You might use some of the Amelia Bedelia books by Peggy Parish (Harper and Row) to encourage an awareness of idioms. Amelia is a maid who receives written instructions and always takes them literally. When the sun comes up, she is to "draw the drapes," so when the sun rises she sits down and sketches the drapes. She also manages to "put the lights out" and to "dress the chicken for dinner." Incidentally, your youngsters might enjoy writing their own "Amelia Bedelia" stories to demonstrate literal interpretation of idioms.

Differentiation. One way in which individuals expand their vocabularies is through differentiating meaning. After understanding *walk* and *run,* users of the language become aware of the difference and then differentiate even further: *saunter, stroll, jog, meander, amble,* and so on. Have your students collect and examine "synonyms" to differentiate meaning.

Tom Swifty. A Tom Swifty is a means of making youngsters aware of the many substitutes for *said* and *asked.* It is a verb that describes or relates to a quotation: "You lazy hound," he *snarled;* "Don't be catty," she *purred.*

Connotations. More important are variations in word choice that have an emotional impact on the listener or reader. This point will be discussed at greater length in Chapter 8, dealing with critical reading. Suffice it to say here that youngsters need to become aware of differences in the emotional effect created by words that are essentially synonyms. For example, when you won't change your mind, are you merely firm or adamant, or are you inflexible—or worse, stubborn?

Euphemisms. No one can find a garbage collector anymore; they are all sanitary engineers. Janitors are no longer custodians, but maintenance engineers, and undertakers are funeral directors—or could they be terminal engineers? In fact, one can't even buy a used car anymore; there are only predriven cars. Have your students collect—or make up—euphemisms.

Dysphemisms. These are the opposite of euphemisms and seem to be coin of the realm with teenagers. Dad is the Old Man, the car is the heap, and butter is axle grease.

Hyperbole. For effect, authors will sometimes use hyperbole—exaggeration. If youngsters collect examples and write some of their own, they are more likely to appreciate the use of hyperbole on them. You have probably used hyperbole yourself when you said, "I've asked you a thousand times to sit still." Or was that a literal statement?

Litotes. The reverse of hyperbole can also be fun and therefore affect our attitude toward what we are reading. Have your students try their hands at creating some examples: "We were not exactly a raving success" or "The *Queen Mary* isn't exactly a rowboat."

Onomatopoeia. Sometimes called "echo" words, these are terms that sound like the sound they identify: *buzz, zoom.* By locating and using such words in their writing, students will also add to their vocabularies. Provide them with onomatopoeic words such as *thump, splash, swish, gurgle,* and have your students name objects that might make the sounds. Or provide names of objects—*shoes, storm, ocean*—and have students think of onomatopoeic words to describe their actions.

Alliteration. Using words that begin with the same sound is a literary device that can encourage students to search for new words. In writing, they might want another adjective for "slimy slug" or a "bushy beard." To begin, read something like Lear's "A Flea and a Fly in a Flue" or have them attempt a rigmarole. This is a medieval roundalay where one person begins with a patterned statement such as "One weary wanderer washing windows." The next person is to follow the pattern, but begin the sentence with "Two," such as "Two tiny turtles tasting turnips." The game can go on as long as interest lasts or words can be found.

Acronyms. We are drowned in a sea of alphabet soup these days. Have pupils collect acronyms, from ALA to ZIP, and identify their origins. Students might even coin their own acronyms or decide why some are not good. For example, why did the North Umbrian Travelers Society change its name?

Dialect and Slang. Regional and cultural differences offer great opportunities for developing an awareness of and interest in vocabulary. Do your children refer to the noon meal as lunch or dinner; to the park object as a seesaw, a tilting board, or a teeter-totter; to that paper container as a poke, a bag, or a sack? Do they catch a cold, get a cold, or take a cold? After some examination of levels of usage, as will be presented in Chapter 10, you might have your students collect examples of different levels, from extreme formal to slang. Or use some of the old proverbs and have students translate from what is usually formal to their own informal: "These are the times that try men's souls" becomes "Some days you just can't win." Perhaps your students might even like to compile a slang dictionary of their own. Helpful materials for your use are *Discovering American Dialects* by Roger Shuy (National Council of Teachers of English, 1974) and *People Say Things Different Ways* by J.N. Hook (Scott Foresman, 1974). Two useful recordings, dealing with examples of dialect are "Americans Speaking" (National Council of Teachers of English, 1967) and "The Dialect of the Black American" (Western Electric, 1970).

Just Fun with Language

Many activities provide opportunities for enjoyment with language. Of the many suggested in this section, only homophones can be clearly admitted as contributors to skill in the use of language, and that in writing, not reading. Nevertheless, anything that helps youngsters become more familiar with and interested in the language is certainly going to add to their skill in that language.

Some books for children from third grade on include:

Fadiman, Clifton. *Wally the Wordworm*. Macmillan, 1964.

Merriam, Eve. *A Gaggle of Geese*. Alfred A. Knopf, 1960.

Rossner, Judith. *What Kind of Feet Does a Bear Have?* Bobbs Merrill, 1963.

Waller, Leslie. *Our American Language: A Book to Begin On*. Holt, Rinehart and Winston, 1960.

Homophones. Younger children can make collections of homophones on "pear/pair" trees. Students at any age can enjoy Fred Gwynne's books: *The King Who Rained* (Young Readers, 1970) and *A Chocolate Moose for Dinner* (Windmill Books, 1973). Pupils might even like to keep a section in their language logs for a homophone list. A helpful teacher reference is Harold C. Whitford's *A Dictionary of American Homophones and Homographs* (Teachers College Press, 1966), which lists 1,800 homophones and about 160 homographs.

Homophone fun can be extended by using riddles to be answered with a pair of homophones. Once you start, your youngsters should be able to make up other riddles to challenge the group.

What do a rabbit and a writer have in common? (their tails/tales)
What do a fireman and a farmer have in common? (their hose/hoes)
What do a bruised ballplayer and a window have in common? (their pains/panes)

Hank-Pank. A riddle to which the answer is a pair of rhyming words is called a hank-pank, hanky-panky, hankity-pankity, and so on, depending upon the number of syllables in the answering word.

A hard-of-hearing cook	a deaf chef
A cold swimming tank	a cool pool
A barber who cuts children's hair	a nipper clipper
A gruesome tale	a gory story

Oxymoron. An oxymoron is an apparent contradiction in terms, most often considered a favorite device of Shakespeare, who referred to "sweet sorrow" and "tragic mirth." Nevertheless, we have oxymorons all around us, or else how can we have "jumbo shrimp" or "authentic replicas"? The latter sound like "real imitations." One comedian even mentioned "military intelligence"!

Spoonerism. Usually spoonerisms are not considered a means to develop vocabulary, since they most often represent nothing more than a slip of the tongue, transposing sounds, as in "It's kisstomary to cuss the bride." However, these can be turned to interesting vocabulary exercises if you recall some of the anecdotes that went around using spoonerisms. For example, there was the story of the admiral who was a fanatic about painting. He kept the entire fleet busy painting until there wasn't a stern untoned. Another, too long to tell in detail here, relates the sad tale of an African chief whose heavy throne was stowed in a back room, thereby weakening the stilts holding his house. He was killed when the throne fell through on top of him, thereby proving that people who live in grass houses shouldn't stow thrones.

GENERALIZABLE INSTRUCTION:
THE DICTIONARY AND THESAURUS

The dictionary is the most valuable tool students have access to, and yet it is one of the most neglected. School staffs spend a year or more in deciding on a basal reading program, a science series, and so on, but when they need dictionaries, usually someone just orders them. Or worse, in many schools there are insufficient dictionaries, and the existing ones are outdated. Yet dictionaries change: In two years, between 1981 and 1983, G. and C. Merriam claimed thousands of new entries in the collegiate.

Not only is it important to be current in dictionary selection, it is equally important to understand that dictionaries differ. They differ in terms of where guide words and pronunciation keys are located; they differ in their diacritical marking systems and in their sequencing of definitions. Hence, I believe students should be exposed to a variety of dictionaries in their elementary school career so they do not get the mistaken notion shared by many adults that dictionaries are all organized in the same manner, and so that they learn to use dictionaries, rather than a specific dictionary.

Efficient use of a dictionary is essential for anyone hoping to be effective either as a reader or as a writer. A great number of specific skills are subsumed under the ultimate goals of dictionary usage. Nevertheless, those ultimate goals are the ability to use a dictionary effectively for meaning, for pronunciation, and for spelling.

As pointed out in that discussion, phonic skills are helpful, along with context, only when individuals are reading material that is in their listening/speaking vocabularies, that is, material where the word meanings are familiar and only the printed forms are not. Once individuals are reading at about third grade level or above, they meet words that are strange in meaning as well. Then only context and, if necessary, the dictionary will enable determination of meanings. Hence, formal teaching, dictionary "readiness," the preliminary development of basic skills, begins at the preschool or kindergarten level.

Although there are many dictionaries on the market, the following seem most suitable for elementary school. They are listed with an approximate grade level indicated. For example, at grades 2–3, because the dictionary is used for meaning, but not for pronunciation, no pronunciation is provided in those dictionaries.

Grades K–1 (Picture Dictionaries):
> *My First Dictionary* (600-plus words), Oftedal and Jacob (Grosset and Dunlap).
>
> *Houghton Mifflin Picture Dictionary* (800 words), Hillerich (Houghton Mifflin).
>
> *Picturebook Dictionary* (1,000 words), Hillerich and others, (Rand McNally).

Primary:
> *Houghton Mifflin Primary Dictionary* (Houghton Mifflin—Grades 1–2).
>
> *The Ginn Beginning Dictionary*, Morris (Ginn—Grades 2–3).

Intermediate:

> *Scott Foresman Beginning Dictionary,* Thorndike and Barnhart (Scott Foresman—Grades 3–4).
> *Webster's Beginning Dictionary* (G. and C. Merriam—Grades 3–4).
> *Houghton Mifflin Intermediate Dictionary* (Houghton Mifflin—Grades 3–6).

Grade 5 and above:

> *Scott Foresman Intermediate Dictionary,* Thorndike and Barnhart (Scott Foresman).
> *Webster's Intermediate Dictionary* (G. and C. Merriam).
> *Houghton Mifflin Student Dictionary* (Houghton Mifflin).

Advanced, Grade 6 and above:

> *Webster's Third New International Dictionary* (G. and C. Merriam).
> *Webster's Ninth New Collegiate Dictionary* (G. and C. Merriam).
> *The American Heritage Dictionary of the English Language* (Houghton Mifflin).

While every student should have a desk copy of the appropriate dictionary listed for "Primary" through "Grade 5 and above," obviously pupils are not expected to have personal copies of the collegiate or unabridged dictionary. The last category is intended to indicate the need for access to a copy of the unabridged and inclusion in each classroom of several copies of an advanced level so that those students will have access to dictionaries that provide information on etymology.

Dictionary Readiness

Dictionary readiness should begin with picture dictionaries. At this level, children use a dictionary as a picture book. They obviously do not have words in mind that they do not "know" since no one can think of a word that he or she doesn't know. These youngsters are not reading, so the only way they learn words and get meanings for them is through the oral language as they pick up those words. Hence, at this level, children do not use a dictionary for pronunciation or for meaning.

Through the use of picture dictionaries, youngsters should get the understanding that there is an order to a dictionary and that the order is alphabetical. It is therefore important that entry words be arranged in alphabetical order rather than merely by category. In addition to their use as picture books, when pupils begin writing, they also use picture dictionaries as sources of ideas for writing and as spelling dictionaries. Hence, kindergarten and first grade pupils should get enjoyable experience in using picture dictionaries to go from picture name to first letter and from first letter and picture to printed word (Hillerich, 1987).

Teaching the Locational Skills

In order to locate words in a dictionary, pupils must know alphabetical order. This should not be a major task if those youngsters have had appropriate experiences in kindergarten and grade one since:

1. They have used picture dictionaries.
2. Their teacher has used the alphabet at the front of the room to have them make words from phonograms such as *-an* by testing additional letters in sequence: *a, b, c,* and so on.
3. They have made simple spelling dictionaries in their language logs for the words they frequently write.

With all this experience, students will need little additional practice. Whatever practice they get should initially be with chunks of the alphabet rather than through attempts to recite the entire sequence in singsong fashion. They can be given sets where they fill in the missing letters:

$$f - h\ i -, \quad l - - o\ p -, \quad s\ t - - w.$$

The next step usually involves alphabetizing lists of words. When providing this kind of practice, keep the sets to be alphabetized to five or six words so pupils don't get lost in the detail of too many words in a set. Also, there is evidence that it is helpful to use nonsense words (Styer, 1972) since alphabetizing is a mechanical process, and pupils should not be distracted by trying to read the words or being concerned with meaning. You might also help youngsters in the early stages by covering all letters in the list words except the first letter of each. They can also use markers to do the same on their practice papers.

As usual, initial instruction and practice must be followed by application. Provide one dictionary for each pair of students. One holds the dictionary, spine inward, and says a word. The partner must take a card and slip it into the dictionary at the point where that word is expected to be found. By trading off after so many turns, partners can make this into a game. Using page numbers to count the degree of error on each word, they can keep score, with the lowest score winning.

Guide words are taught as an efficient aid in locating entry words. After clarification of what and where they are, children can be given the usual kind of practice on guide words found in basal reading programs. Illustrated in Figure 6-4 is both a simple and a more advanced form.

Figure 6-4

The underlined words below are the guide words on a dictionary page. Put a check beside each word you would find on this page in a dictionary.	The underlined words below are the guide words you would find on a dictionary page. Put a check beside each word you would find on this page. Write B if the word comes before this page. Write A if the word comes after this page.
<u>bake</u> <u>come</u>	<u>school</u> <u>second</u>
_____ been	_____ scull
_____ cake	_____ same
_____ baby	_____ scissors
_____ clue	_____ sea
_____ center	_____ seed
_____ cone	_____ second

Of course, before students in grade two or three begin to use a dictionary, they should be provided with an overview of that book, just as you would do with any text. As a result, they will learn what is in the dictionary, how it is organized, and what it can be used for. To accomplish this overview, use the introduction. Any good dictionary has an introduction that explains how that dictionary is organized and how to use it. In fact, if you haven't read the introduction to a good dictionary such as *Webster's Collegiate,* you have missed a whole education in dictionary usage and in language itself.

By about third grade, students must also be taught about cross-references and the handling of inflected forms. Imagine the uninitiated in this respect who wants the meaning for *geese* and finds it listed as "See goose"! Using examples, you can demonstrate that "regular" plurals and past forms are not given in a dictionary as entry words, whereas "irregular" ones, such as *geese* or *ran* are so listed. However, unless the user is familiar with the introduction of the dictionary, the question of which are considered "regular" in that particular dictionary is left unanswered.

Using a Dictionary for Meaning

The first use of a dictionary that is taught is for meaning since this is the first concern of one who hears or sees a new word, and it is also the easiest skill to teach. Such usage requires locational skills and use of context: There are very few words that don't have more than one meaning, so context is essential, both on the part of the teacher in providing practice and on the part of any user of a dictionary.

Once pupils have examined the dictionary at hand to see how it organizes definitions, we usually introduce use for meaning by providing a familiar word used in an unfamiliar sense: "The hunter tried to *bag* a deer" or "Dad built a *run* for the dog."

At this level, children should also be given practice in looking up homophones and homographs. Since homographs are different words, youngsters must become aware that there will be two entries for a given spelling: lead/ lead or pool/pool. In contrast, homophones usually present problems in spelling, not in reading. Obviously *red* and *read* will be separate entries. In order to handle them effectively, the writer must be aware of the two or three different spellings and then must use the dictionary to check that the correct homophone is being used.

Since most English words have more than one meaning, it makes no sense at all to provide practice in using a dictionary for meaning by giving students a list of words. All practice activities must include the words in context. The most effective and interesting practice, I believe, is to give the words in question form so students must use the meaning they find to answer the question. Begin with examples like the following, and shortly you should be able to turn still another job over to your students as they attempt to stump their classmates:

> Could you swim in a lampoon or a lagoon? Why
>   and why not?
> Which do you prefer, inspired or insipid people?
>   Why?
> Is a braggart likely to talk about his expiration or
>   his expertise? Why?

Finally, by about fourth grade, students must be acquainted with run-on entries or there is again likelihood of confusion. A run-on is merely a space saver: At the end of all of the information about the entry word *genial*, students will find "genialness *n.*" Unless they are taught differently, they may conclude this is another strange definition for the entry word.

By intermediate levels, students should also be taught about the etymological information following pronunciations and, as stated previously, should have access to more advanced dictionaries for such work.

Using a Dictionary for Pronunciation

A survey of dictionary authorities (Mower and Barney, 1968) indicated that the four most important dictionary skills dealt with pronunciation. Yet

House reported in 1944 that these skills were poorly learned, even through eighth grade, and the picture has not improved to this day, despite the fact that we usually introduce such skills by third grade.

In order to use a dictionary for pronunciation, students must have control of the locational skills, but they must also understand:

1. how the sound notation is indicated after the entry word,
2. that the strange symbols are "defined" in the pronunciation key,
3. where that key is and how to use it,
4. how stress is indicated,
5. how syllabication is marked for pronunciation and how that differs from the syllabication for the entry word, and
6. how to *apply* these skills in pronouncing a strange word.

Most of the foregoing is really not difficult for youngsters to grasp. Teachers can easily show them the "funny" spelling that indicates pronunciation, as well as the location of the key, and the fact that after each of the strangely marked symbols there is a word those youngsters know that contains the sound represented by the symbol. Nor should they have difficulty understanding the way in which syllables are marked in the pronunciation or that the "accent mark" tells the user to put stress or emphasis on that syllable.

Why then do individuals—not only children—have difficulty in using a dictionary for pronunciation? The point of difficulty arises after locating the symbol in question in the key. Then the user must isolate that sound, carry it up—mentally or orally—to the indicated total pronunciation and say it in the context of the other letters. Obviously this is an oral/aural skill; all the pencil-and-paper practice in all the workbooks of all the basal series will not provide the needed experience. However, teachers aware of this fact can make some of those practice pages effective by using them orally.

Begin instruction on this aspect of the skill by putting a one-syllable nonsense word on the board, such as /mȯn/. After having students use their dictionary keys to decide how the /ȯ/ is to be pronounced, have several pronounce it and then attempt to insert it in the context of the /m/ and /n/. Continue with as many examples as necessary until students get the idea.

The next step is to deal with multisyllable words. Here again any difficulty will not be resolved with pencil-and-paper activities since it is easy for children to understand what the accent mark means; it is only difficult for them to use it. Until this time, no child has ever consciously had to place stress at a given point in a word. Any word that child learned was learned with its accent intuitively placed. Hence, the new—and very difficult—task is to gain conscious control over stress.

Begin by writing on the board several pairs of homographs that shift accent, such as *rec' ord/re cord'* or *pres' ent/pre sent'*. Have students practice putting the accent on the syllable you indicate, constantly shifting back and forth until they gain some conscious control. Then put pronunciations for some multisyllable words on the board for students to practice—again, orally—on. These should not only be strange words to your students, but the regular spelling and pronunciation spelling should differ: *bizarre, parget, fustian,* and so on.

Using a Dictionary for Spelling

While use of a dictionary for pronunciation is usually poorly taught, its use for spelling is most often not taught at all. In a typical class, even at eighth grade, when a student asks about the spelling of a word, the teacher is likely to say, "You know how to use a dictionary. Look it up." You know the typical response: "How'm I gonna find it if I don't know how to spell it?" We must begin teaching children how to find it when they "don't know how to spell it"!

Use of a dictionary for spelling is a matter of educated guessing. However, we must provide that "education," and then we must take students by the hand to show them how to use it. The first step of that "education" can begin in first grade after children have been taught the sounds consonants represent. Once they realize that *m* at the beginning of a word usually stands for the sound they hear at the beginning of *moon,* they should be made aware that when they want to spell a word that begins with that sound, it will usually begin with that letter.

Then, as soon as pupils are introduced to the alphabetical sequence in a dictionary, they can take the next step. Say a word that begins like "moon" or "monkey," and ask in what section of a dictionary they would expect to find that word. They should be able to say in the "m" section.

By grade two, it is time to explore the possible spellings of vowel sounds, as discussed in Chapter 5. Through this experience, youngsters become aware of the ways in which a given vowel sound might be spelled. Then teachers can provide students with a word and have those youngsters begin their educated guessing with their dictionaries as the check. For example, given the word /fān/, pupils should be able to suggest that it will begin with *f,* and therefore be found in that section of the dictionary. "Now, what vowel sound do you hear?" "The long a." "How could that be spelled?" Here some might guess *a* consonant *e,* as in *bake,* check, and be disappointed. Soon the suggestion of *ai* will enable them to find the word.

Not only do youngsters need to explore spellings of vowel sounds, they must also have that kind of experience with initial consonant spellings or they will never find the *pn* spelling of /n/ in *pneumonia* or the *mn* spelling in *mnemonic*. Of course, with these variant consonant spellings as well as with the vowels, students need practice in application. This is easily accomplished by putting the pronunciation spelling for a few words on the board each day, having students use their dictionary pronunciation key to identify the pronunciation, and then having them find the correct spelling. Soon, some of your students will be taking over this job to challenge their classmates. What better way to get them into the language?

Using a Thesaurus

Although more a tool for the writer than for the reader, the thesaurus is another vocabulary builder for the individual who becomes interested in improved word choice. This important tool should be introduced as a means for precision in word choice as low as grade three with a simple thesaurus and should be expanded to *Roget's Thesaurus* by grade six.

At the early level, *In Other Words: A Beginning Thesaurus* by Schiller and Jenkins (Scott Foresman) is the appropriate book, followed by *In Other Words: A Junior Thesaurus* at fourth or fifth grade. By sixth grade and above, students should have access to and be taught how to use *Roget's Thesaurus*.

Some people prefer an alphabetical thesaurus to Roget's; however, many more entries will be found in the latter because of its organization. And it is not so difficult to teach children to use. One begins in Roget's by using the index in the back of the book to find a word that is close to the one desired. For example, I want a more appropriate word than *proclivity* to express "an inclination toward." After locating *proclivity* in the back section, I find listed under it: *inclination 634.3, preference 637.5, tendency 174.1,* and *trait of character 525.3,* where the numerals are referring me to a section and paragraph. Since my intent has to do with a "trait of character," I go to section 525, paragraph 3, where I find forty-three words or phrases expressing that meaning, extending from *disposition* to *tendency, propensity,* and *warp.* In contrast, for *proclivity,* an adult alphabetical thesaurus lists only the definition "an inclination to something" and the synonym *bent.* To include all of the nearly synonymous words found in Roget's would require a tremendous amount of duplication and therefore make the size of an alphabetical thesaurus prohibitive.

Chapter 7

Using Reading and Writing to Develop Comprehension: Literal and Inferential Skills

In a sense, this book—like all others on the teaching of reading—is written backward: It began with decoding skills and only now gets to comprehension, even though in actuality comprehension begins long before one learns anything about reading. In fact, we might say that there is no such thing as a "reading comprehension skill." All that we call "reading comprehension skills" are actually thinking skills applied in a reading situation. In another sense, they can also just as well be classed as listening skills.

As thinking/listening skills, these "reading comprehension skills" begin long before a child enters school. Consider the four-year-old who touches the hot curling iron and gets burned. The next day, on seeing the iron plugged in, that child draws a conclusion—predicts an outcome: "If I touch it, I will get burned." This is not only comprehension, it is a higher order comprehension—inferential, as opposed to literal, thinking.

Such facts indicate that the comprehension skills to be presented in this chapter can be developed in nursery school or kindergarten as well as in middle school or high school. At the nonreading level, the skills will be developed through listening and reacting to selections read by an adult, whereas at higher levels, the student will do the reading as well.

It is here also that writing comes into its own. It is here that reading and writing are truly integrated through the use of both modes for meaningful communication. In fact, in a sense, both are composing processes. As Wittrock (1983) pointed out:

> When we read, we generate meaning by relating parts of the text to one another and to our memories and our knowledge. When we write with clarity we generate meaning by relating our knowledge and experience to the text. (Wittrock, 1983, pp. 600–601)

CATEGORIES OF COMPREHENSION

One way to examine comprehension skill is through the traditional three categories: literal, inferential, and critical reading. Literal comprehension is a matter of understanding what the author said; inferential, what the author meant by what was said; and critical reading is a matter of going beyond what an author said and meant to judge or evaluate that piece of writing. Dale (1965) put it cleverly when he referred to the three categories as "reading the lines...reading between the lines...and reading beyond the lines."

Notice that I refer to these three as "categories," not "levels" as most writers do. I also called them levels until a few years ago when a graduate student expressed great pleasure that there were "three levels of comprehension" since she had three reading groups: the low group worked on the literal level; the average, on inferential,... Shake and Allington (1985) observed the same misconception among classrooms in their study. These are not levels of difficulty by any stretch of the imagination. In fact, the only hierarchy that exists, supported by both research and common sense, is indicated as follows:

Inferential	Critical
Literal	

Research (more recently, Hillocks and Ludlow, 1984) and common sense indicate that one may be able to answer a literal question but not be able to answer in either of the other two categories. Conversely, if one can answer an inferential or critical reading question about a selection, that reader obviously must have understood literally what the author said on that point. For example, imagine that you have read about a character who had a blue wagon, and somewhere in that selection there were some clues revealing the importance of that color in the wagon. If asked what color the wagon was (literal), you might be able to answer that it was blue. Asked why the character had a blue wagon (inferential), you might shrug: "It didn't say." However, if you could answer initially why the wagon was a particular color, you must have known what color it was.

From another standpoint, inferential comprehension and critical reading are placed side by side to indicate that, even though both presume literal understanding, they operate independent of each other. Work with students on inferential comprehension will increase skill in that category but will have no effect on critical reading; work on critical reading will increase critical reading skill but will have no impact on inferential comprehension. Is it any surprise that children learn what we teach and do not learn what we do not teach?

This traditional hierarchy or taxonomy is most familiar to reading teachers, and I find it most helpful in classifying comprehension skills for reading. Nevertheless, there are other taxonomies, including Bloom (1956) and Barrett (1968). More recently, Pearson and Johnson (1978) suggested another tripartite taxonomy: textually explicit, textually implicit, and scriptally implicit.

"Textually explicit" is equivalent to literal: the answer is in the text. "Textually implicit" is equivalent to inferential in that one uses information from the text along with background knowledge (schemata) in order to answer a question about what an author intended. This category presumably includes, without separate distinction, critical reading. Finally, "scriptally implicit" questions require answers that come from background experience where the text itself merely provides the jumping-off point. Hence, such questions would more likely classify in the affective category as creative reading.

Since the newer classification seems to offer a confusion of cognitive and affective domains, we will stay, in this text, with the traditional three categories of comprehension and will treat "scriptally implicit" reactions as part of the affective domain, as creative reading or literary appreciation.

COMPREHENSION: A PROBLEM AREA

Most educators view reading as a meaning-getting or meaning-building act. Yet it is in this area that we seem to have failings in our teaching of reading. Four national assessments in reading, from 1971 to 1984, indicate that we continue to improve in the teaching of decoding skills and literal comprehension. However, when it comes to inferential comprehension, critical reading, and the study skills, we have failed to improve and, in some cases, have regressed (Educational Testing Service, 1985).

The reasons for our shortcomings in this area are multiple. First, it has been only in recent years that research attention has been focused on this complex act, so evidence is still in short supply. Second, the traditional emphasis on specific skills is coming into question, but as I see it, the case is not closed on this point. Third, emphasis in developing comprehension skill has been on questioning. Not only has that questioning been poor, but it may not be enough. It may reveal that we have actually not taught comprehension. Let's examine a few of these points.

"Teaching" Comprehension

Durkin (1978–79), reported that her observations revealed that teachers devoted less than 1 percent of time to teaching comprehension. She found that the majority of time was given over to "testing" comprehension. She considered questioning as "testing" rather than "teaching."

Perhaps Durkin was a little harsh in her categorizing. True, if a teacher asks a question, the child answers, and the teacher nods or in some manner reacts to the "correctness" of the answer, that teacher has NOT TAUGHT ANYTHING! The child merely used what he or she already knew, so nothing was taught. However, I'd consider that an intermediate step between teaching and testing. I'd consider it "practice." Nevertheless, we owe children more than practice; we owe them some teaching.

How does one "teach" comprehension? Comprehension probably cannot be taught directly any more than "understanding" can be taught directly. We must teach the methods of achieving that comprehension; that is, we must teach children what they must do in order to comprehend. That can be done in a number of ways—through modeling, through improved questioning techniques, and beyond—that will be expanded upon throughout this chapter.

Modeling is a matter of the teacher thinking out loud, demonstrating the process of comprehending for students. As Davey (1983) pointed out, poor comprehenders may not (1) form good hypotheses, (2) form mental images, (3) use prior knowledge about a topic, (4) monitor how well they are comprehending, or (5) know what to do if they don't comprehend.

These are the very things a teacher can do in front of the class, as that teacher reads a selection and thinks aloud:

1. Form hypotheses—"From what I've read so far, I think..."

2. Mental image—"I have a picture in my mind of this room. Over here I can see..."

3. Prior knowledge—"This reminds me of the time..."

4. Monitor comprehension—"This doesn't seem to make sense." (Leads to number 5)

5. Fix up—"I'd better check that last paragraph again."

Another step in "teaching" comprehension has to do with questioning. For example, suppose your fourth graders had read the following paragraph and you want to teach an inferential skill:

> The boy ambled down the street. He gazed in one
> store window after another. Tarrying by store
> after store, he shuffled home.

Too often the "teaching" is a matter of asking "Was the boy in a hurry?" If children answer "No," the teacher is ready to go to something else; if they answer "Yes," she will likely just ask another child in order to get the "right" answer. This kind of activity is practice, not teaching.

Teaching can take place if that teacher will follow up the initial answer with "How did you know?" or "What made you think that?" or merely "Why?" in the case of some answers. Then, if children cannot explain, it is up to the teacher to demonstrate how an answer can be arrived at. And it is "how" or "why" that is so much more important than "who," "what," "when," or "where."

Yet, in the 1979 assessment of reading (National Assessment of Educational Progress, 1981), seventeen-year-olds could answer literal comprehension questions but could not explain "why." Is there a reason for this phenomenon? I believe so. If we ask a kindergartener a question, get an answer, and follow up with "Why?" or "How did you know?" we are likely to get a reason. However, by about second grade and beyond, the "why" question is most likely to be answered with a shrug. Too early, children discover that teachers ask only questions to which they know the answer, and they want to find out if I do. Teachers don't care "why." We've got to let children know that we do care WHY, and that WHY is usually more important than the original answer.

Questioning Techniques

Traditionally, questions have been asked after students completed the reading. Nonetheless, a variety of other placements are possible and have been investigated. Summaries of this research (Tierney and Cunningham, 1984; Gall, 1984) reveal the confusion. Whether one uses prequestioning, interspersed, post-, reciprocal, self-, or student–student questioning, almost any kind, since it requires active participation on the part of students, seems beneficial. However, if the questions—especially pre-questions—are too specific, students may miss some of the broader ideas; they will be reading for detail only. It is also clear that youngsters learn what we question and fail to retain what we ignore.

Despite these findings and depending upon the study examined, from 70 to 97 percent of the questions teachers ask are still literal, factual questions. Is it any wonder that literal skills are improving at the expense of the other two categories? Considering the need for inferential and critical reading skill, as well as the fact that inferential and critical reading presume literal comprehension, the percentage of effort ought to be reversed, with the literal receiving minimal attention. Furthermore, if a basic goal of the discussion is to increase children's enjoyment of reading, we certainly do not accomplish that with the usual quiz or by emphasizing boring literal detail.

Let's take a closer look at three ways to improve your questioning technique.

Use the Basal Series

One way in which teachers could improve their questioning techniques is by following the guide in their basal series. In contrast to teacher performance, basal guides usually provide no more than 50 percent literal questions. While this is also too many, it is a step in the right direction.

Ask Inferential Questions

Teachers can also improve their questioning techniques by practicing the development of inferential questions. In fact, a good bootstrap in-service can be conducted at a faculty meeting. Using a story that everyone knows, to save time from reading at the meeting, have teachers make up a question for each of the inferential skills (presented later in this chapter). Then, as a group, evaluate the suggested questions to determine if they are truly inferential and if the specific skill intended was actually tapped. As a follow-up, teachers might tape record the discussion in their classes and evaluate the quality of the questions they asked.

Not only will this change in focus from literal to inferential increase interest in the discussion, it will improve language. Students who are asked inferential questions not only engage in more sophisticated thinking, but they also use more sophisticated language in their responses (Smith, 1978). Again, common sense verifies this evidence. If I ask, "What color was the wagon?" I usually get one word: "Blue." However, if I ask, "Why did the character have a blue wagon?" the answer is much more involved, usually beginning: "Well, because..."

Wait Between Questions

Another difficulty with questions has to do with wait time. Lucking (1975) reported that the average adult takes about fourteen seconds to begin responding to a question; children in the classes he observed were allowed 5.6 seconds, one-third the time. In one school, reader asked 5.1 questions per minute—machine-gun fire! Gambrell (1983) found that reader allowed one second of wait time and posed a question every forty-three seconds. In another situation, teachers waited three times as long for a bright child to respond as they did for a slow student.

This implementation of the self-fulfilling prophecy, this difference in the treatment of good and poor readers, has been demonstrated in another way. Good and Brophy (1969) reported that when a good reader was asked a question and failed to respond, the teacher rephrased the question or provided some support. When a poor student was asked a question and failed to respond, the teacher asked someone else.

Hassler (1979) verified the work of Rowe (1969) to report that increased wait time increased length of student responses, increased confidence, and decreased failure to respond. Furthermore, increased wait time usually means fewer and more sophisticated questions as well as higher-quality answers because both teacher and students have a little time to think. Check your own wait time with a tape recorder. There is something about silence that invites a response!

One good questioning technique is to prepare students for the discussion by having them get paper and pencils ready. The teacher asks an open-ended question, and all students are given time to write their thoughts on that question. Only then are they allowed to respond to the question. This technique avoids the usual concern for behavior during wait time, and it avoids the situation where one child is called upon and answers while everyone else breathes a sigh of relief at having avoided another question. Instead, it combines good wait-time, every-pupil response, and the integration of writing.

Even in the literal category, questions are often poor. Suppose one wanted to check comprehension of the sentence "The girl found a penny." The typical questions are: "Who found a penny?" and "What did the girl find?"

Such questions are pure recall and provide no indication of comprehension beyond structural meaning. For example, given the same pattern, "The stripling unearthed a krone," anyone who could say the words could respond in the same manner to "What did the stripling unearth?" and "Who unearthed a krone?" The reader need not have any notion of what a stripling or krone is. All the individual is demonstrating is knowledge of the structural patterns of English sentences. At the ridiculous extreme, one might ask the same pattern of questions of "The gip gapped a gop" and get accurate recall responses, even though the sentence is nonsense.

To check on comprehension at this literal level, one must require translation at the very least. Admittedly with such a basic sentence as "The girl found a penny," not much translation is possible, but at least the questioner can use, or expect in the response, words like "she" for *girl* or "money" for *penny*.

FOUNDATIONS FOR COMPREHENSION

In recent years, some researchers have focused on additional considerations related to reading comprehension. Not the least important is the attention given to vocabulary development.

Obviously if one is to comprehend a selection, that person must know the meanings of most of the words in that selection. However, as demonstrated by Fleisher and others (1979), a reader may know the meanings of all the words and still not comprehend. These researchers pretaught to mastery the meanings of all the words in a selection and still some of these middle grade students were unable to comprehend that material. Knowledge of vocabulary is a necessary but not sufficient element in reading comprehension.

Other recent concerns have to do with schema theory, story or text grammar, and metacognition.

Schema Theory

A schema is a mental structure from experience that enables one to interpret new experiences or observations: Schemata are the blueprints of experience—the background knowledge—that enable the individual to make sense out of the world.

Evidence is accumulating that background knowledge is essential to comprehension and, according to Pearson (1985), is more important than IQ in reading achievement. In fact, it controls comprehension to the extent that different individuals, depending upon their backgrounds or schemata, will get different interpretations of the same material, whether read or heard. For example, test your perception or mental set as you read the following:

> We'd had a full week of nothing but rain and
> humidity. Still the newspaper predicted the rains
> would continue.

Many of my graduate students are reminded of vacations. If that is a current description of weather, they just say it's a typical day. However, mental images are strengthened when the excerpt is continued:

> Even the sheets were damp.

What associations do *you* have now? Often my students recall a camping trip, a vacation cabin, and so on. Then another line reinforces this view for many and changes it for a few:

> Every line looked as if it were spotted with
> mildew.

To some, this is the blurred print of the newspaper in the second line of the exerpt. To others they recall a clothesline. Some fail to make any true connection. Finally, how much does this final sentence clarify for *you?*

> We knew we'd have to put the sails out to dry if
> ever the sun came out.

This last sentence separates the sailors from the landlubbers! Anyone who is familiar with sailing immediately puts it together: The "sheets" and "lines" are what a landlubber would call ropes. However, those not familiar with sailing fail to connect previous sentences to the last one.

The following practical implications of schema theory are basically what good teachers have long recognized:

1. An individual cannot be expected to comprehend material that is outside that person's experience. In order to meet such a problem, teachers must be certain children have the necessary prior experience or else provide it for them.

2. Youngsters will comprehend better if associations are made between prior experiences and the new material. One technique to activate prior knowledge is through writing. Have students write what they know on the topic and discuss their work before they read the selection.

Langer (1984) has suggested PReP (PreREading Plan) as an effective way to tap and activate schemata: (1) Make an initial association—"Tell me anything that comes to mind when..." (2) Reflect on this association—"What made you think of...?" (3) Reformulate ideas based on new experiences— "As a result of our discussion, do you have any new ideas about...?"

Less apparent is a danger identified by Alvermann and others (1985). They found that when the prior knowledge of sixth graders was activated and was incongruent with information in the text, prior knowledge overrode textual information. In other words, these children seemed to separate school information from their "real world" knowledge. It behooves teachers to model the necessary activity or thinking when text and experience are in conflict if students are to learn from that incongruous information.

Story Grammar

Another concern of researchers, related to schema theory, has to do with story grammar. Just as any language has a grammar—rules for use—so too stories have a "grammar." As a mature reader, you know that intuitively. If

Figure 7-1

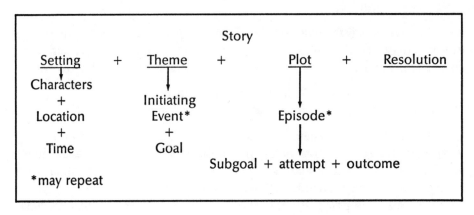

someone handed you a recipe and said, "Here is a good story," you would certainly consider that strange. You have a schema for story. You know what a story is: It is a narrative—written or oral—that has certain elements. In fact, a simplified form of Thorndyke's (1977) story grammar looks like Figure 7-1.

Very similar, although organized a little differently, is the Johnson and Mandler (1980) grammar shown in Figure 7-2.

If any one of these major elements is missing, one does not have a "story." In a sense, then, concern for story grammar represents a concern for providing children with another kind of context: With a knowledge of story grammar, the reader knows what to expect in the selection—knows there will be a character or characters engaged in a goal orientation, and so on.

Evidence is that children understand well-formed ("grammatical") stories better than poorly formed ones. With ninety-six first graders, Feldman (1985) compared understanding of stories from preprimers with understanding of those same stories when rewritten following the elements of story grammar. Children understood the rewritten stories significantly better.

What is the best way to provide this knowledge of story grammar? Children will gain some knowledge through experience in hearing and in reading stories. Conversely, let's hope that no one begins to "teach story grammar" the way we too often teach that other kind of grammar: by drill on labeling or by expecting students to list the elements.

Probably the best way to provide greater knowledge of story grammar is by having youngsters write stories. In so doing, both in prewriting discussions and in the actual writing, they will have to consider what the necessary elements in a story are—what is the grammar of a story.

Fowler (1982) suggested using story frames. For example, to summarize a story with one character, children might complete something like this:

This story is about _____. _____ is an important character in the story. _____ tried to _____. The story ends when _____.

Another way to summarize is to provide headings to be completed:

Character: "Who?"
Setting: "When?" "Where?"
Initiating event: "What happened?"
Goal orientation: "What does the character want to do?"
Resolution: "How did it end?"

In addition to listening to stories, reading stories, and writing stories, retelling them has been found to contribute to comprehension, whether in kindergarten (Morrow, 1985) or eighth grade (Gambrell and others, 1985). In a

Figure 7-2

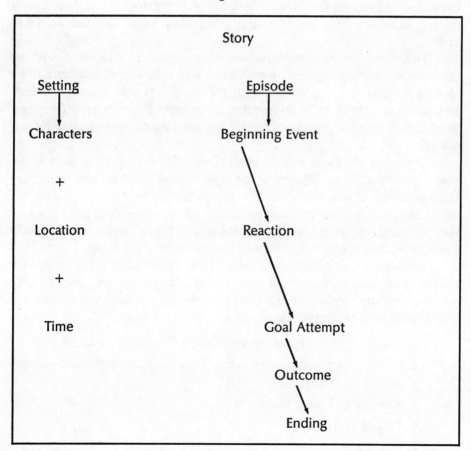

similar vein, Pellegrini and Galda (1982) found that thematic-fantasy play also contributes to improved comprehension.

Metacognition

While the term is relatively new, the idea of metacognition has always been a standby of good teachers. In fact, returning to the beginning of this chapter, any time you ask a student "How did you know?" you are dealing with metacognition.

Simply defined, "metacognition" is knowing about knowing. It has to do with knowing when one does or doesn't understand and what to do in order to gain the needed understanding. It includes monitoring one's own comprehension, and it is this "comprehension monitoring" that is referred to by reading people when they use the broader term "metacognition." For example, recall in Chapter 4, in introducing new words, when the teacher asked children how they knew the word was *water* and not *wagon* or *pond,* that teacher was dealing with metacognition—making pupils aware of how they knew what the word had to be.

This focus on metacognition was also implied in Chapter 5 with its emphasis on introducing new words in order to review how they were to be identified rather than merely to teach the words. At this point, of course, instead of using the term "metacognition," we could as well borrow the magic word from writing—"process." Yes, we are speaking of emphasis on process, not product.

Children's ability to recognize all the words in the present story is not nearly so important as developing the skill that will enable them to identify unknown words in new or unstudied printed material. As in writing, we need to shift from the traditional focus on product or outcomes—knowing the words or the "answers"—to an emphasis on process or "means," and we need to help students become consciously aware of the means they are using.

Furthermore, this shift must extend to a repertoire of skills so that the student is aware of alternatives in approaching an unknown word. Review with your students the "tools" they have for figuring out a strange word, tools that might be used in this approximate sequence:

1. Context. (This, at least, establishes parameters of meaning.)
2. Phonics: Consonants and vowels. (Try long, then short sound—Harris and Sipay, 1985, p. 397.)
3. Analogy to known words.
4. Prefixes/suffixes.
5. Dictionary.

The need for metacognitive—comprehension monitoring—training is apparent from a variety of studies. As compared to poor readers, good readers are aware of inconsistencies in text, and they do significantly more self-correcting of their own miscues. Furthermore, they understand what reading is all about. In a variety of studies at different levels, for example at fifth grade (La Fontaine, 1984) and at seventh grade (Garner and Kraus, 1982), students were asked "How do you know when you are doing a good job of reading?" Consistently, good readers replied with something like "When I understand what I am reading." Poor readers said, "When I know all the words."

Thus far, research has told us the obvious about comprehension monitoring: Good students do it better than poor students; older, better than younger. Research has not offered a solution as to how to increase this ability. However, until further evidence, let's abide by the practices of good teachers and probe with children "How do you know?" "How can we find out?" Furthermore, let's model comprehension monitoring with them, as discussed in a previous section.

THE SKILLS APPROACH TO COMPREHENSION

While current research interests offer some exciting and valuable new insights into reading comprehension, most of us are not ready to completely abandon work with specific comprehension skills. Admittedly, as Rosenshine (1980) pointed out in his excellent summary, research has been unable to isolate much more than "word knowledge" and "reasoning in reading" as discrete skills. Nevertheless, this inability to separate out additional skills is most likely a weakness of our tests and certainly should not imply that subskills do not exist nor deter our use of this variety of ways of looking at reading comprehension. If we improve our teaching in this area, we can certainly also contribute to increased comprehension on the part of our students.

In this chapter, we will discuss only the literal and inferential comprehension skills since critical reading is better associated with the reading of factual matter and hence, with the study skills, as presented in Chapter 8.

The literal and inferential skills to be discussed in this section are as follows:

I. Literal Comprehension
  A. Understanding Word Meaning
    1. Using phonic skills
    2. Using structural skills
    3. Using picture context
    4. Using printed context

5. Using a dictionary
6. Recognizing synonyms, antonyms, homophones, homographs
7. Identifying words with multiple meanings
8. Recognizing the effect of stress on meaning

B. Understanding Sentence Meaning
   1. Using typographical aids
   2. Identifying referents for pronouns and adverbs
C. Detail—Recognizing and Recalling
D. Main Idea—Recognizing and Recalling
   1. Topic of a paragraph
   2. Main idea of a selection
E. Sequence—Recognizing and Recalling
   1. Plot development
   2. Character development
   3. Argument
F. Comparisons—Recognizing and Recalling
G. Cause/Effect Relationships—Recognizing and Recalling

II. Inferential Comprehension
   A. Drawing General Conclusions
   B. Inferring Topic or Main Idea
   C. Inferring Sequence
   D. Inferring Comparisons
   E. Inferring Cause/Effect Relationships
   F. Making Judgments
   G. Identifying Character Traits
   H. Predicting Outcomes
   I. Interpreting Figurative Language
      1. Simile
      2. Metaphor
      3. Personification
      4. Idioms

Developing Literal Comprehension

Beside most of the literal skills is the expression "Recognizing and Recalling." Students "recognize" when they have read a selection, are asked a question, and have the material in front of them to find the answer. They "recall" when they have read the selection but do not have the material in front of them in order to find the answer to a question asked. There are some who would say that the latter is a memory skill and not a reading skill. However, good readers have to perform in both ways, and therefore I would provide students with experience in both.

Literal comprehension skills are most often developed through practice, that is, through questioning techniques and verification of answers. Nevertheless, some students may need modeling even here.

At any reading level, these skills are most often developed through the use of a basal reader, although this doesn't have to be the case. They can also be developed through the use of trade books. In any event, before children read the selection to be used, that selection should be introduced to them. The introduction should provide any necessary background children may need to understand the story or to tie in with their existing schemata. It is here again that preliminary writing on the topic can help to bring to the surface prior knowledge on the subject. In keeping with the goal of making youngsters independent of us, I believe that, when prior background information is necessary to the understanding of any selection to be read, teachers should provide printed material containing that background for children to read and discuss so that they can get their own background instead of having it handed to them.

In the case of most primary level basal stories, however, the content is within the experience of the children and the introduction usually is nothing more than a brief motivating statement just to get youngsters into the reading: "What do you think will happen? Let's read it and find out."

At middle grades, and especially in factual material, some clarification of purpose needs to be made. No one gets everything from reading a selection. We all read for particular purposes, whether consciously or not. Furthermore, if children have had the typical experience identified in studies of questioning techniques, they are most likely to read every selection for detail because that's the kind of question they are expecting to get. Finally, if the selection to be read is a factual one, the research evidence indicates that discussions are more fruitful and retention is enhanced if clear purposes are established prior to the reading.

Understanding Word Meaning

Understanding word meanings requires using the word recognition and identification skills previously discussed: recognition vocabulary, phonic skills, structural skills such as identifying past and plural markers, context, and—when necessary—the dictionary. Students will also need vocabulary experience in order to identify words with multiple meanings and will have to recognize the effect of stress on words such as CONtest and conTEST.

Reading programs usually provide for experiences in recognizing synonyms, antonyms, homophones, and homographs. Actually, these have little if anything to do with reading and relate more to writing. Obviously, the first two are important when the writer wants to think of another word that means approximately the same or the opposite of a given word. Homophones are words that have the same pronunciation but may differ in derivation, meaning.

and/or spelling: *pair, pare, pear.* Homophones present no problem in reading, since no one, upon reading about a *pair* of shoes, even thinks of the other two homophones. On the other hand, homophones are a serious problem to the writer who, in writing about that *pair* of shoes, becomes confused with the spelling of the other two homophones.

Homographs are words that are spelled the same but may differ in derivation, pronunciation, and/or meaning: *wind, wind.* The only way to interpret these is through use of context, and if the individual is using context, it is not difficult to interpret "The *wind* blew" or "Please *wind* the watch."

Understanding Sentence Meaning

Part of the skill in getting at the meaning of sentences, in addition to making use of word meaning, requires use of typographical aids such as punctuation or special type.

In the former case, children should be taught to interpret end punctuation, commas as short pauses in speech, and even ellipses when they come to them in their reading material. The interpretation of the latter can be taught only through use of context and, in general, as an indication of omission or interruption. Sometimes ellipses are used to indicate that a speaker was interrupted, sometimes instead of *etc.*, and sometimes to indicate a change of thought or direction.

Likewise, teaching students to interpret special type requires the use of context. Boldface is used to attract attention or to indicate emphasis. Italics may also be used for emphasis or to indicate that the writer is referring to a word rather than to what the word represents, as in "How do you spell *cat*?"

Comprehending sentences also requires interpretation of referents for pronouns and adverbs. Most of the research has not dealt with method here; it has dealt with the obvious, reporting that difficulty increases with increased distance between anaphoric form and referent or when the referent follows the anaphoric form.

Despite the fact that very young children seem to have no difficulty with anaphora at the oral level, third graders still seem to have considerable trouble with printed materials. Could their problem be merely with the mechanics of the practice material itself?

Most often that practice material is in the form of a half-page selection, with pronouns (or adverbs) underlined and numbered, followed by a list of the numbered anaphoric forms with blanks where students are to write in the referents, as in the following oversimplified sample:

> Sue saw a rock in the chair. (1) <u>She</u> picked (2) <u>it</u>
> up.
> (1). She _____
> (2). it _____

Merely reproducing the selection with blanks where the pronouns are, and providing a list of pronouns from which to choose, results in a much easier task for youngsters. But that is "writing," not "reading." However, taking a cue from that, I also found that they are more successful with these kinds of activities if they are told to ignore the bottom portion of the page and merely to draw an arrow from each underlined word to the person, place, or thing that it refers to. In other words, the problem seems to lie not in the skill but in the double-think mechanics of the activity.

Regardless of the cause of the difficulty, teachers are probably well advised to provide some instruction—through demonstration and practice—in the various types of anaphoric relationships. Following is an abbreviated listing of typical noun, verb, and clause substitutes, based on the work of Irwin (1986):

Type	Example	Usage
Pronouns	she, we, that, who	*Lena* is my friend. *She* . . .
Place/time	then, after	*Winter* is cold. *Then* we . . .
Alternate word	child: kid; cat: kitty	That *child* is some *kid*.
Arithmetic	some, two	We picked *apples*, but *some* . . .
Null		Dogs *bark*, but cats don't ( ).
Inclusive	do, so	*Is it raining?* I think *so*.

Recognizing and Recalling Detail

As stated previously, children already get too much practice in recognizing and recalling detail. However, there are times when this skill is important, so they should be provided with some experience here. First of all, if youngsters are to read for detail, that detail should be significant to the story and not merely a matter of trying to "catch" them on some fine point. For example, in the case of a story about an artist known for her unusual color combinations, it would be a good purpose to read for that kind of detail, to discover what were the unusual color combinations that made the artist famous. Also, in reading for detail—as well as for any other purpose—it is important to establish that purpose before youngsters begin reading.

Recognizing and Recalling Main Idea

Identifying the topic of a paragraph or the main idea of a selection of several paragraphs is a difficult skill for young children. They have a tendency to want to repeat the entire selection, whereas application of this skill requires abstracting from several ideas to find the summary statement. There is confusion in the literature, not only about the distinction of these two terms, but about "main idea" itself (Baumann, 1986). Clearly, a topic is a word or phrase that states the gist of a paragraph or selection. This is also one of the definitions in *A Dictionary of Reading and Related Terms* (Harris and Hodges, 1981). Some distinguish main idea from topic by specifying that the topic is a word or phrase whereas the main idea is a sentence telling what the entire selection is about. Without wanting to quibble, I would suggest that either a sentence or a word can designate the topic or main idea and that the distinction lies in the fact that any well-constructed paragraph has only a topic (one idea), and therefore one would not ask for the "main" idea; a selection has more than one topic, but it has an overriding or "main idea."

Regardless of definitions, whether one asks for topic or main idea, the technique to be taught to children is essentially the same. In fact, most often this is in inferential skill since the topic or main idea is usually not stated directly. However, when it *is* stated, one merely looks for the word, group of words, or sentence that best identifies the gist or thesis of the paragraph or selection. The following paragraph, whether read to kindergarteners or read by beginning readers, can be used as an example:

> We had fun at Mary's birthday party. We played
> all kinds of games. She got lots of presents.
> Mary's mother gave each of us a hat.

Ask pupils to find the one sentence that tells what the "story" was about. If you want, you could ask for the topic by telling them to find just a few words in the story that they would use if they were going to give that story a title (a "name," in the case of younger children.)

This same technique can be applied when children read a selection of several paragraphs to identify the main idea. Teaching can take place by having pupils analyze, sentence by sentence, or paragraph by paragraph, to decide what each is about. Then they are to find the group of words or sentence that best states that idea. Reinforcement of the skill can take place by the teacher asking children *how they knew* and having them go back to verify their decision. If necessary, the teacher may also model the process of identifying topic or main idea.

Recognizing and Recalling Sequence

This skill most often begins with a sequence of events since this seems to be the easiest kind of sequence to recognize. It can also be developed at higher levels with a sequence of character development, sequence of arguments, and so on.

Of all the comprehension skills, this seems to be the one that is given the most unrealistic practice on worksheets or workbook pages. To begin with, this skill is most often used when a person has read or heard something rather lengthy and wants to have "pegs" on which to hang that narrative so it can be retold or retraced. In other words, that person usually wants to have in mind three or four major events or items that will serve as a mental outline in the proper sequence for retelling the story. There is no excuse, first, for giving children a selection that has no real sequence and, second, for giving them a dozen to fifteen petty details to rearrange in the proper sequence.

Appropriate practice can be provided with a selection that does have a significant sequence, having the children read the selection, and then having them either recall "What happened first, what happened next, . . . " or having them recognize from a collection of three to five jumbled major events which is the proper sequence. Any teacher taking such a realistic approach will find that most children do not have difficulty in recognizing or recalling a sequence of events. For those who do, it behooves that teacher to drop back to the oral level and deal with the skill, as discussed in Chapter 3.

Still another avenue lies in writing. Youngsters who are involved in constructing their own stories must consider sequence; they must decide the order in which events should be told. This can be brought out even more clearly in factual writing, where students record, in diary fashion, experiences of any kind, from field trips to science experiments.

Recognizing and Recalling Comparisons

Comparisons are easy in the literal category since they are stated in so many words: "Sean was taller than Kari." Even here, it is important to use or to ask for translation: "Who was shorter?" Youngsters can enjoy making comparisons and writing about them, whether characters or their actions.

Recognizing and Recalling Cause/Effect Relationships

Again, in the literal category, this is not a difficult skill, since the relationships are stated. However, even here youngsters can be aided if you call their attention to those special words used to indicate cause/effect relationships: *because, as a result, when, after,* and so on. Get your pupils started when they meet one or two of these signal words. Then have them search their reading material for other words that signal cause/effect relationships, and let them keep a record in their language logs for sharing at a later date.

Developing Inferential Comprehension

This is the category to which most of the discussion and teaching time should be devoted. In this category, the reader is not provided with "the answer" in so many words. Answers are only implied; that is, they are textually implicit. Hence, inferential comprehension requires making use of what is stated literally, plus intuition and experience. It is somewhat like working a math problem: The reader is given this fact and that fact and must put them together to arrive at a conclusion not stated.

It is especially important here, if you follow the advice of spending most time in the inferential category, that you establish purposes for reading. If your students have been exposed to the traditional literal kind of questioning, that is what they will be reading for. Imagine their consternation if, without warning, you suddenly become creative and begin asking inferential questions.

Since the terms *inference* and *conclusion* are synonymous, you might question using the latter as a subskill under inferential comprehension. It is only used to identify a particular kind of inference, that is, a general conclusion. Also, since all the other "inferential skills" are also conclusions, why are they listed as if they were unique skills? The only reason for this listing it to assure that students get some instruction and practice in each of these different types of inferences or conclusions. Otherwise, we might merely list the major category "Making Inferences" and dispense with the balance of the variations.

If you follow the suggestion of a bootstrap in-service by employing a faculty meeting for everyone to develop inferential questions for each of these skills, you might save time by using a story that everyone is already familiar with. In my graduate classes I use "Goldilocks and the Three Bears," so example questions for that story are offered with each of the following skills.

Drawing General Conclusions

Work on this skill can begin at a very simple level with a riddle-type paragraph such as the following:

> I ride on a big red truck. I usually wear a coat
> and boots. My truck has ladders and hoses on it.
> We hurry to fires. Who am I?

If anything more than practice is to take place, it is necessary to take the students back to the selection to point out the clues they used to decide that this was a firefighter.

Also at a simple level, because of the number of clues, would be a paragraph such as the following:

> John was bigger than anyone else in his class. He
> was also the fastest runner in the school. You
> should see him throw a football! He was just
> made captain of the football team.

A very simple and obvious question to ask is, "Do you think John is a good football player?" followed by "What makes you think that?"

At a more sophisticated level, use any library selection that students enjoy. It is a good idea to have them prepared with pencil and paper so that they can jot down notes or reasons for their answers since not all conclusions are clear-cut, and students should not get the impression that there is only one right answer. Perhaps a story is about a character on the way to a party. He may get hurt on the way, so walking is difficult. Even though the party will include running games, the character wants to see friends and has a very positive attitude about the party. Will this character have a good time at the party? The positive attitude suggests "yes," but the injury implies "no." The important part of conclusion-drawing experience is to have students verify the conclusions they draw; it is not to arrive always at a preconceived answer.

With Goldilocks, one might ask, "What time of day do you think it was when Goldilocks went into the bears' house?" At times people have suggested, "Why do you think Goldilocks went into the house?" This question is certainly not literal or text explicit, but, depending upon the version, it could require drawing a general conclusion or it could be a cause/effect question since the implication in the story might be that she was hungry or tired. While the most important point in this questioning practice is to encourage inferential as opposed to literal questions, it is also helpful if we can tap the skill we are attempting to tap.

Inferring Topic or Main Idea

The same procedures employed in the literal category can be used for the inferential. The only difference is that the inferred topic or main idea is not stated in the selection read. It must be deduced by the reader based on clues given in the selection. For example, even the simple paragraph about Mary's birthday party could be read to children with the word *birthday* omitted; the children should be able to infer that the topic is "Mary's birthday party."

One technique for determining topic or main idea is the mechanical one of analyzing what each sentence or each paragraph is about in order to determine what all the sentences or all the paragraphs are about. Another technique, especially for younger pupils, is to ask them for a title—or new name—for the story. A little more creative for older students is to ask them to pretend they are newspaper reporters reporting on the selection as if it happened in their own town today. What headline would they use?

The writing of headlines can go beyond the discussion of a single story. Sometimes it is fun to have older students take stories they know and write headlines (as will be suggested in Chapter 9) for others to guess what book is referred to. Doing this with "Mary Had a Little Lamb," one group arrived at the headline "School Board Says Baaaa to Ewe."

With Goldilocks, some teachers take the easy way out by saying they would simply ask, "What is the main idea?" This is satisfactory with older students who understand the question, but a follow-up is still necessary in order to reinforce the skill.

Inferring Sequence

This is a skill completely ignored in most basal reading programs. It is required in order to decide what must have happened between two immediately adjacent stated events. For example, imagine reading about two characters who are playing ball in a vacant lot when the neighborhood bully comes down the street. The paragraph ends, and the very next paragraph begins with these two characters running through the alley to their house, equipment in hand. To get at inferred sequence, the question would be, "What must have happened between their sighting of the bully and their running down the alley?"

In the case of Goldilocks, again depending upon how much is stated in the particular version in mind, there are lots of opportunities for inferring sequence: "What must Goldilocks have done between the time she finished eating and when she sat in the first chair?" In fact, any question beginning with "What must have happened between..." or "What must _____ have done between..."—so long as the answer is not stated in the text—will be a question asking for an inferred sequence.

Inferring Comparisons

This skill is developed in the same manner as was done in the literal category except that the comparisons to be made are not specifically stated in the story: The reader is not told that Sean was taller than Kari. The reader is merely told that Sean and Kari were going to explore a cave. When they arrived at the entrance, Sean had to bend over to enter, but Kari could walk through without bending. Who was taller?

Incidentally, there is no reason to limit discussions to a specific selection; it is better to get students thinking across stories or books. Have them compare different dogs, mice, or children they have read about. They might even like to make their own books of "Mighty Mice," "Fantastic Females," or "Bombastic Boys." With whatever characters your students know, from Frederick and Anatole to Homer Price and Henry Huggins, comparisons can be made.

In the case of Goldilocks, opportunities for this skill abound. Goldilocks can be compared with Baby Bear, Baby Bear with Mother or Father, or any of the characters with people or other characters your youngsters know.

Inferring Cause/Effect Relationships

Here, students are asked to identify cause/effect relationships when they aren't given the clue words supplied in literally stated relationships. For example, the selection read may indicate that "The weather was too dry for crops. The shortage of corn led to..." Here a question could be asked about why there was a shortage of corn, since the selection did not state in so many words that there was a shortage *because* of poor weather conditions. This kind of situation is also a good example of the fact that schemata—past experiences—are necessary, along with understanding of the printed material, in order to answer such a question. Obviously anyone with such limited life experience as not to know about a relationship between moisture and successful crops could not arrive at a satisfactory reply to the question.

In the case of Goldilocks, one might ask—assuming the answer was not stated literally—"Why did Goldilocks run when she saw the bears?" or "Why did Baby Bear's chair break when Goldilocks sat in it?"

Making Judgments

A judgment requires that individuals bring their own values to bear on a situation. It is here that teachers, while avoiding imposing their own personal values on students, can help youngsters to develop values. The progression in value development goes something like this: The toddler is not even aware of behavioral choices to be made; through experience, an awareness of choice—but without preference—is developed; next grows a preference for this choice of behavior over that one; eventually, the individual truly values this choice above all others and will make judgments accordingly.

Hence, teachers can contribute by helping students become aware of choices and reasons for choice. Questions to be asked would be questions such as "Do you think _____ should...?" or "Would you have...?" Of course, any such questions need to be followed with "Why?" or "What makes you think that?" In the case of Goldilocks, the obvious questions are "Do you think Goldilocks should have gone into the house when no one was there? Why? (or Why not?)" or "Would you have gone into the house? Why? (or Why not?)"

Identifying Character Traits

Often character traits are brought out in the process of other questions since this category relates closely to making judgments. Children may be asked what kind of person they think the character was and why they have this view, or "How would you like to have Goldilocks living next door to you? What makes you say that?"

Charts can also be made with each character name as a column heading. Characteristics of each can then be listed in each column for comparison. Conversely, students may begin by writing down characteristics of people they know. Greater depth of analysis can be achieved through comparisons of characters and through writing about familiar characters in new, hypothetical situations where students must infer behavior and justify their inferences.

Predicting Outcomes

Practice in predicting outcomes should not be expected until a selection has been read in its entirety. Too often, if we interrupt a story in order to ask youngsters what they think is going to happen, we imply that the author's conclusion is *the answer.* If we do this, we are encouraging convergent thinking, giving students the impression that there is only one correct answer.

Have students complete a selection and provide practice in predicting outcomes by having them respond to a changed situation. In fact, if you want extended writing, let them write a whole new ending for the story. Regardless, the prediction can be elicited after reading is completed by asking, "What do you think would have happened if...?" By changing an event or situation, you open up a whole new set of circumstances or possible behaviors, thereby encouraging divergent thinking.

If you are working on this skill as opposed to creative thinking, you should expect answers to reflect understanding of the characters and setting. In other words, students should be brought back to clues and understandings from the selection in order to justify their predictions. While you would obviously grant more freedom of response to younger children, even kindergarteners should be helped to use their understanding of the text. For example, we might ask a kindergartener, "What do you think would have happened to Goldilocks if the bears had been home when she got there?" If the kindergartener replied "The bears would have eaten her," I would be compelled to follow with, "Is that the kind of bear who lived in this house?"

Interpreting Figurative Language

At the primary level, about the only figurative language children will meet are similes, metaphors, personifications, and idioms. By intermediate and middle school, many others are possible, but only the few common ones will be mentioned here. It is most important to recognize the purpose for dealing with elements of figurative language. It is not to provide instruction in the proper labeling of these elements. It is to enable students to understand the meaning intended and to appreciate the manner or style through which that meaning is conveyed.

A *simile* is really literal, not inferential, and usually presents no problem to youngsters. They are told in so many words how one thing is being compared with another: to borrow from Tresselt, "The cars looked like raisins in the snowdrifts."

Metaphors present a different problem. Because of their tendency to interpret literally, even middle grade students have difficulty here. Stated as a metaphor, the preceding simile becomes, "The cars were raisins in the snowdrifts." In this case, children are likely to envision raisins in the snow, cars shaped like raisins, or who knows what.

One way to teach understanding of metaphors is through a mechanical, step-by-step process: "What two things are being compared? How could cars and raisins look alike? From the balance of the context, how did the author intend for us to compare them?"

A much more interesting method—and I believe, more effective—is through writing. After a few examples of similes from their reading, have students write some similes. Then show them how to convert the similes to metaphors and let them write additional metaphors. Having engaged in the process themselves, they will find it easier to interpret what other authors are doing.

Personification is usually not a difficult figure for children to interpret. For example, they readily understand the sentence "The trees reached out their arms" since they know trees don't really have arms. Most often the emphasis on personification should be in helping youngsters appreciate why an author said something that way, asking if trees really could reach out, and what the author was comparing the trees to. Once more, writing can be a great help in the interpretation of personification. If children use the figure themselves, they are more likely to understand it when someone else uses it. Ortony and others (1985) also found that playing creative verbal games related to figurative language improved understanding.

Idiomatic expressions must be interpreted on the basis of a knowledge of those expressions. Anyone from a different language background, or even from a different geographic area, is likely to have difficulty interpreting certain idioms. While context can sometimes help, experience is the only sure way to cope with them. In one classroom, I was momentarily taken aback by an idiom new to me when the teacher asked her pupils to "pick up the floor."

As suggested in Chapter 6, an enjoyable method of familiarizing youngsters of any age with idioms is through the Amelia Bedelia books by Peggy Parish. Even though these are primary books, they can be used effectively through high school or college. Students can then be encouraged to write their own "Amelia Bedelia" selections or draw pictures depicting literal interpretations of idioms.

THE AFFECTIVE DOMAIN

Although there is a need to develop comprehension skills through teaching and practice in the discussion of a selection, the most important purpose for that discussion should be to increase students' enjoyment of their reading. This is accomplished not through a quiz but through delving into the meaning, reacting to what was said and implied, sharing and enjoying the way in which an author expressed ideas, and engaging in the kinds of activities suggested in Chapter 9. At times, this may be nothing more than an opportunity to give an emotional response to the material: "Did you like it? Why (or why not)?" This is the affective domain where, in most cases, there are not specific patterns to be adopted, but rather it is the lead—the interests— of the readers themselves that should be followed.

Creative Reading

As opposed to the more convergent analysis that will be discussed in the next chapter as critical reading, creative reading is a matter of using statements in the text to jump off on one's own ideas, experiences, or fantasies. It is here that youngsters need to be encouraged with questions such as "What does that remind you of? What else could the character have done? Have you ever had an experience like that? What happened to you?"

In order to extend ideas with a little more depth, it is here that youngsters can be encouraged to write their own experiences based on reading they have done. Or they might want to expand the possibilities of whatever was suggested in the text they have read.

Literary Appreciation

Many of the inferential questions should help to increase children's appreciation for selections read. For example, appreciation deals with the amount of empathy the reader develops for characters in a story. This identification is enhanced through questions dealing with the character: "Why do you think the character did that? What would you have done? Why?"

Visualizing is an aid to identification and interpretation of ideas presented in fiction. Teachers can improve children's ability to image by modeling, where the teacher verbalizes the mental picture created by the text. Another aid is to have youngsters draw or write descriptions based on something they have read. Then have them go back to the selection to compare what they recalled with the description given there. More interesting practice results if you invite youngsters to select a character or scene from any of a number of selections they have all read and have them write their own description. Then share descriptions to see if they are clear enough for others in the group to decide who or what they refer to.

Awareness of and appreciation for the language used by an author should be developed early at the primary level. This awareness of language includes recognition and interpretation of the figurative language, as discussed in the previous section. It should also include an awareness of rhythm in certain selections, whether poetry or prose, such as that used by McCloskey: "The giggling gull teetered on the tip of the tiller and laughed fit to split." Youngsters can more readily appreciate such language when it is read orally.

It should go without saying that labeling is worthless; there is no need for children to know or to identify the terms given to these devices. However, they do need to become aware of the ways authors use words to appeal to our ears as well as to our minds. Again, using some of these techniques in their own writing will contribute to the youngsters' understanding and appreciation.

Alliteration, as also demonstrated by the McCloskey sentence, is another device of which youngsters should become aware. They can be helped in this awareness by developing their own alliterative sentences, possibly starting with an alphabetical list of animals to which they add first names: Andy Ardvaark, Becky Beaver, and so on. They may then pick an animal about which to develop an alliterative sentence: "Slurp, the slimy slug, slid slowly down the slide."

Onomatopoeia is best developed through children's own writing. They may collect and enter into their language logs words that sound like the action or situation expressed: *crunch, munch, splash, tinkle,* and so on.

Another device particularly enjoyed by younger children is the *repetitive building* found in all kinds of cumulative tales, from "The House That Jack Built" to *A Fly Went By.* Becoming aware of this technique helps children understand why they like or don't like a particular kind of story and enables them either to seek or to avoid more of the same kind.

Humor comes in all forms. Even first graders can recognize the humor in some kinds of puns, such as that in *The Biggest Bear,* when Johnny Orchard tells Grandfather that there is a bear in the orchard. Grandfather replies: "Better a bear in the orchard than an Orchard in the bear." The nonsense poetry of Silverstein's *Where the Sidewalk Ends* or Prelutsky's *The New Kid on the Block* is surefire for reading to all ages or for middle grade youngsters to read for themselves. Furthermore, those middle grade reluctant readers can be teased into reading some of the stale jokes—from "knock-knock" to "elephant jokes"—in any of Schwartz's four collections of nonsense published by Lippincott.

Elementary students should also become aware of the genres of literature, beginning with distinguishing *reality* from *fantasy.* Later, they can be led to recognize *poetry* as opposed to *prose,* the general class of *folk/fairy tale* as distinguished from more *realistic fiction, biography, autobiography,* and so on.

Appreciation is largely developed through mutual enjoyment and having fun with selections read, whether they are in basal readers or in library books. True appreciation is not likely to be developed by pressuring children to read a variety of types if they don't want to. There are devices and gadgets to lead children to a "balanced" fare in reading. However, it seems to me that the major task is to keep them reading, whatever it is that they are interested in: From Nancy Drew to Judy Blume, all the series will eventually run out.

Furthermore, even at the stage when the development of literary taste becomes a goal, that taste is not developed by "requiring" certain reading material. It is developed by exposing youngsters to a variety, including some trading off with them: "OK, before you pick up another _____, why don't you try this book for a change?" After all, how does one develop understanding or appreciation of "good" literature if the reader has had no experience with "poor" literature?

Chapter 8

Using Reading and Writing to Develop Comprehension: Critical Reading and Study Skills

Critical reading and study skills are needed when reading persuasive or factual materials, whether newspapers or content areas in school. These study skills consist of the ability to locate, organize, evaluate, and retain information, and to read for various purposes. Critical reading, often presented in connection with the other two categories of comprehension, is the evaluative aspect of the study skills and hence seems more appropriately discussed here. However, because of its importance and sad neglect, it deserves a separate section.

THE STUDY SKILLS IN CONTENT AREAS

The study skills have generally not been well taught, partly because of the continued emphasis on literal comprehension but also for a number of other reasons. Let's examine those first since recognition of the problem is a first step toward its solution.

Problems in the Content Areas

One overriding problem is the fact that reading skills are most often taught through basal reading series, and the content of the pupil books has traditionally been fiction. Whoever would want to outline "Cinderella" or read it critically? In other words, these skills are usually not applicable to fiction; they are learned, practiced, and applied in factual/persuasive materials. However, additional problems are apparent.

Vocabulary

Content reading presents vocabulary problems beyond the usual. For instance, students meet familiar words with unfamiliar meanings: A "table" in science doesn't look like any table they have eaten from, nor do the "legs" of a triangle look like any other kinds of legs. And what is so odd about an "odd" number? Learning new meanings for a familiar word is often more difficult than learning a new word with its associated meaning. For example, one serious student, after learning that a factor was a number that divided *evenly* into another, had difficulty in accepting four as a factor of twelve because the quotient was an "odd" number.

Another vocabulary problem is presented by the many technical terms, from *adrenergic* to *zoomorphic*, and including *hemiptera* and *hemisphere*. Many of these can be understood through instruction in the Greek and Latin combining forms presented in Chapter 6.

There are also abstract terms to be dealt with, such as *freedom* or *democracy*. What understanding of these is held by a fourth grader or a tenth grader—or even an adult? Furthermore, there are other words that I call "loaded." For example, *photosynthesis* is hardly a word—it is a whole book! Yet it is dismissed in many science texts with little more than a parenthetical definition.

The solution to these problems lies in teaching such vocabulary items. Unlike basic fiction, where meanings of many new words are learned through context, and others through use of context and dictionary, understanding of much content material is dependent upon a prior knowledge of key terms. Tap existing schema and build through some of the vocabulary activities suggested in Chapter 6.

Reading Level

Awareness of the importance of proper placement in reading materials is apparent in most reading classes. However, that awareness often is not apparent in content reading, even in the *same classrooms*! Since science, social studies, and other content texts are to be used to gain information, we might expect such books to be written somewhat below pupils' reading levels so that they would not be using every bit of energy merely to read that material—so they would have some energy remaining to manipulate it mentally. In contrast, most content texts are written *above* the grade level for which they are intended. (To make matters worse, consider the fact that in any "average" classroom—by definition—only *half* the children could read the book even if it were written at grade level! See Chapter 10.)

There is no need for educators to waste time evaluating the readability of texts under consideration. Publishers have done this and will supply such information. However, unless educators specify that the readability is to include technical terms, publishers will likely provide reading level with those not included, rationalizing that such terms are familiar because they are defined in the text. Those terms are still new words and should be considered, so insist on readability that does include them.

What is the solution to this problem of reading difficulty? If the purpose is to transfer information from a single text to the heads of pupils, the only way this can be done when they can't read the material is to have someone read or explain it to them, put it on tape for them to listen to, or in some way translate the print for them. If the purpose is to provide greater understanding of a subject, a better method is to collect materials on that subject in a variety of sources at a variety of reading levels so that pupils can do their own reading at their own reading levels.

Lack of Clarifying Detail

Social studies texts in particular are highly abstract, presenting a skeletal outline with no meat on the bones; they present too many concepts too fast, with little or no detail to make them meaningful. Examine a paragraph at random from any middle grade social studies text to see what it would take for a student to understand what is stated instead of merely verbalizing back on a test the same words that were presented on the page.

You might even do a simple factual count, over just one page, of the number of vague quantitative terms—empty words—that appear to give information but do not, such as "*large* deposits," "*heavy* taxes," "the population increased *enormously*," or "France is *less* industrialized than West Germany." In terms of the latter, you can read, so how industrialized is France? Of course, it is "less industrialized than West Germany" and you can bet that is going to be a question at the end of the chapter.

There are many paragraphs where, if a teacher were serious about having students understand the information, one paragraph would represent half a year's work. Hence, the choice is whether you want to "cover the book" or uncover some of the information. What you will do and how you will go about it should be determined by your position on the next point.

Objectives of the Teacher

Undoubtedly the most serious problem, and one that must be answered prior to any satisfactory solution to method, has to do with course objectives. What are your objectives in teaching science, social studies, or any other content area?

Most teachers deny that their purpose is merely to teach the facts. However, examination of a social studies or science test gives lie to such denials. Yet, with the rapid accumulation of "facts," what is one to do, teach twice as fast each year or delete some of last year's important "facts" to make room for the new? And what are "facts" anyhow—usually substantiated theories in science and agreed-upon biases in social studies. Are you one who, as I did, learned "facts" about atoms and molecules, not to mention some from economics or even geography, that are all wrong today?

Probably the best statement about "scientific fact" was made by Neurath:

> Scientists are like sailors who have to rebuild their ships at high sea, without being able to seek port. Each plank in the hull may be jettisoned in the process, but it is not feasible to jettison all of the planks at the same time. (As quoted in Harste and others, 1984, p. 50)

In contrast, most teachers claim to teach "concepts," broad understandings or generalizations that usually fall into the category of "motherhood and flag." There seems to be little agreement on what concepts are the essence of social studies in particular or on what information is necessary to develop these concepts.

I would like to suggest that the purpose for social studies, science, or any of the content areas in the elementary schools should be to serve as vehicles for development of the study skills. Such skills cannot be developed in a vacuum, and they cannot be developed without the manipulation of "facts." However, the ultimate objective will determine how a teacher goes about working in the area. In social studies, for example, most schools provide a survey of United States history in grade 5, again in junior high school, and again in high school, with most students leaving high school knowing less about United States history than they did in the middle of fifth grade.

I certainly am not suggesting playing the game of shifting content around. Leave United States history placed as it is, if you like. However, instead of a superficial treatment for three years, let's take time to do what Norman Cousins, in a *Saturday Review* editorial, many years ago suggested as a "posthole" approach. Let's take time out from the surface treatment to dig a few postholes. Instead of verbalizing from the skeletal text, youngsters should be getting information, depending upon the particular subject under study, from a variety of sources—newspapers, historical fiction, biographies of the time, other factual books—so that they can contribute from different reading levels and from different sources.

The "process" approach to science came closer to doing this kind of thing in the 1960s. At that time, youngsters engaged in science instead of merely reading about it. For decades, good English teachers have been using a "process" approach to the teaching of writing. At this point, I am suggesting a process approach to social studies, where students will still need to locate information—indeed, gather facts—as well as organize, evaluate, and draw conclusions from that information to decide what is worth retaining. However, they will do this, for example, in the case of the Civil War, not to remember the "causes of the Civil War" but to gain the study skills so they will be able to avoid the threat of another war when they are young adults. Although no one can predict what facts they will need, we can be reasonably certain they will continue to need these thinking skills we call "study skills."

Locating Information

The locational skills include familiarity with and ability to use special aids, such as the card catalog (or computerized catalog), biographical dictionaries, almanacs and books of facts, encyclopedias, timetables, atlases, and so on. In addition to this ability to locate information from a variety of sources, students must also be able to locate information within a single source; they must be familiar with the parts of a book from title page to index.

Most such skills require little more than explanation or demonstration and practice through use. However, use of a table of contents and an index deserve further comment.

When dealing with the table of contents, youngsters need to understand how to use it, but more difficult is the understanding of *when* to use the table of contents as opposed to the index. They need to be aware that the table of contents is used when a great amount of information is expected to be found in the book; the index is used when only a brief mention of the topic is anticipated. Demonstration and practice with a variety of topics are then necessary.

Youngsters are usually taught the use of a table of contents and index in about third grade. By this time they have learned to use a dictionary and are therefore familiar with alphabetical order. The major task—and a difficult one it is—in using an index is the decision about what key word to use. Instruction usually begins with a key word stated in the question: With a book on agriculture, "Where are oranges grown?" Youngsters can usually decide that *oranges* is the operant word here. Next, they are given questions where there are two possibilities: "Where, in Florida, are oranges grown?" Now they might use *Florida* or *oranges*, either with the other as a subtopic.

A final challenge is to be given the question "Where are oranges grown?" when *oranges* is not found in the index of the book on agriculture. Then youngsters must search their own vocabularies for alternative words, and they might find the entry under *fruit* or *citrus*. It is important, when working on this skill, to help youngsters realize that there is no "right" or "wrong" answer; there are only answers that work and those that don't since different authors organize their indexes differently.

Organizing Information

The major techniques used to organize—and thereby retain—information are notetaking, outlining, and summarizing.

Notetaking

Research has focused almost exclusively on taking notes from lectures, usually at the college level. At that level the evidence suggests that it is not the taking of notes but the review of those notes that is most important. Using three groups of students, Annis and Davis (1975) had one group listen to a taped lecture and take notes that were reviewed after the lecture. A second group was not allowed to take notes but was given the lecturer's outline to review. A third group was only allowed equal time after the lecture to "think about" what they heard. There was no difference in achievement of the first two groups, both of whom scored significantly higher than the third group. Students also tended to remember what they included in their notes and did not remember what they did not include (Kiewra, 1984).

In contrast, at the elementary level, notetaking is usually a matter of getting information from printed sources. It may help to have youngsters put each note on a separate card so they can physically manipulate their notes when organizing their reports. It is also a good idea to get them in the habit of identifying the source of each note.

From the opposite view, I believe we get youngsters into encyclopedias too early and hence almost force them to plagiarize. When they write a report, children should go to more detailed sources and summarize them instead of going to the concise, tightly written encyclopedia article and attempting to put that information in their "own words." It is very difficult to summarize a summary! If they are going to use an encyclopedia, I would at least have a rule that they do not take pencil and paper with them when they use it.

Summarizing

Summarizing is a very difficult skill for young children. Most often they want to tell the entire tale, possibly even expanding on it in the process. Hahn and Garner (1985) summarized research on this topic and found six basic rules for summarization:

1. Delete trivial material.
2. Delete repetitious material.
3. Substitute a superordinate term for lists of times.

4. Substitute a superordinate term for lists of actions.

5. Select a topic sentence.

6. Create a topic sentence.

Obviously, such a list can be collapsed into three directions:

1. Delete all unnecessary detail.

2. Use a superordinate term for lists.

3. Find or create a topic sentence.

By beginning with instruction on topic sentence and providing practice in deleting the unnecessary and identifying the important information, students can become more skilled in summarizing and, as a result, will better comprehend material (Taylor, 1982). In fact, brief daily summaries in a language log represent one of the best ways of clarifying for themselves what students understand or fail to understand on a subject. In making these entries, students are forced to think about the topic and are therefore more actively engaged in the ideas. It is in writing that we identify what we know and *don't know* about the topic.

A variation of outlining and summarizing is mapping or semantic webbing. Just as vocabulary can be webbed, as suggested in Chapter 6, so too ideas can be mapped to show their interrelationships. If this is done before reading, it can serve as a pretest to determine prior knowledge and thereby activate schemata on the subject (Hillerich, 1985). For example, a study of animals may lead to the web shown in Figure 8-1 as a prewriting activity.

Figure 8-1

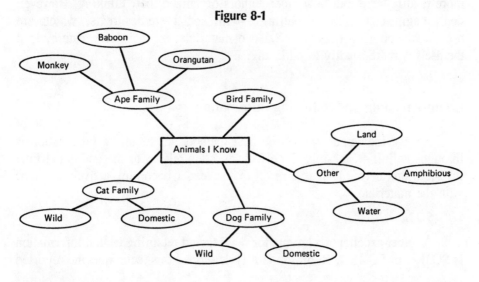

Source: Robert L. Hillerich, *Teaching Children to Write, K-8* (Englewood Cliffs, NJ; Prentice-Hall, Inc., 1985) p. 49.

Outlining

Outlining is probably one of the most important of the study skills, contributing more to comprehension and retention than mere reading, rereading, summarizing, or making a timeline (Miller and others, 1982). However, outlining is also one of the most difficult skills for students to master.

It is here that writing can again be most helpful, probably because when students begin by outlining their own thinking they better understand the function of outlining: It is merely a blueprint of an author's thinking. Hence, begin by giving students a topic with which they are very familiar, such as "What I Like to Do in My Free Time." Then ask them how they would like to subdivide this so their ideas will be organized: "at home" and "at school," or "indoors" and "outdoors," and so on.

You might put their suggestion on the board, as follows, and then ask for some of the specific activities that would be discussed under each of the two headings:

<u>What I like to Do in My Free Time</u>

Indoors

Outdoors

Your students have now made an outline, without concern for Roman numerals and capital letters. Those can come later, and I would make a chart with an example of outline form to be posted in the classroom for students' reference. Furthermore, after they have made a few outlines of their own, learned what outlining is and how to organize their own thinking, they can more readily ferret out how other authors organized their thinking. However, don't begin that kind of outlining with social studies texts, which are notoriously poorly organized. Science materials, by their very nature, lend themselves more readily to outlining.

Comprehending and Retaining Information

As just indicated, one of the best methods for retaining information is through outlining. Possibly the effectiveness is related to the additional time invested, and certainly it is a result of the reader becoming actively engaged with the material.

SQ3R

Another excellent technique for reading and retaining factual information is SQ3R—or SQRRR. Robinson (1961) developed this technique and reported on its effectiveness. Probably more impressive than the research is the fact that this had undoubtedly been the most imitated technique yet, as other researchers present minor variations to claim as their own: SQ4R, PQRST, OK4R, SQRQCQ, and so on. In simplified form, SQ3R consists of these five steps:

S urvey: Look over the material; read the title, picture captions, and so on, to discover what it is about.

Q uestion: Raise questions in your own mind about what you hope to find from the reading.

R ead: Read the material with your questions in mind.

R ecite: Think back over what you read in terms of the questions you wanted answered.

R eview: Reread to check your answers and to see if there was anything else you should have gotten from the material.

Robinson saw the value of SQ3R as being in the immediate recall of information, thereby leveling off the forgetting curve that would normally occur. While this may be, current evidence and concern for setting purposes suggests that the personal purpose established by the first two steps might also be a major factor in the effectiveness of SQ3R. Of course, there is no denying that any active involvement in print is also going to make a contribution to understanding and retention of information.

SQ3R is usually introduced to students late in third grade or early in fourth. There is no reason that the entire technique needs to be used at once. Why not introduce them to the SQ early in third grade so they get practice in establishing their own purposes for reading? Then, when this becomes habitual, they can take the next steps in the technique. Furthermore, unless they are reviewed and reminded frequently, students will not use and may forget this valuable study skill.

Typographical Aids

The "aids" to comprehension, such as the side headings and paragraph topics found in social studies texts, can become a handicap instead of a help if children are not taught how to use them (Christensen and Stordahl, 1955). They do become helpful if their function is taught to children.

Wide Reading

Equally important with outlining, as a technique for comprehending and retaining information, is wide reading on the subject. It is here that active participation comes into its own as the reader meets different views, and even conflicting views, on the same topic. Furthermore, as will be indicated in the discussion of critical reading, reading in other sources is the only way in which students can get another view against which to compare a first author when the students themselves have not had firsthand experience with the subject.

Advance Organizers

Other techniques for comprehending and retaining information from factual material are advance organizers and structured overviews. The former is an abstract framework that might help tie the new into existing schemata; the latter is an advance summary of the new material that may offer something as a result of the added repetition. Space will not be taken here to present either, since they are more appropriate to high school or college, are complex and time-consuming to use, and are of questionable value if one looks at summaries of the research (Barnes and Clawson, 1975).

Reading for Various Purposes

In order to read successfully for a variety of different purposes, students need instruction for flexibility of rate of reading, skimming and scanning, reading directions, reading in math and the content areas, and reading graphs and tables.

At the elementary and middle school levels, we have no business working on speed reading or reading rate per se. Of course, the evidence is clear that rate can be increased up to a point, with no decrease in comprehension. However, it is also clear that, once individuals complete the rate training, unless they are under pressure to maintain the increased speed, they will return to their original comfortable rate. Furthermore, while increased speed in college students did not reduce the information that they specifically read for, it did reduce the amount of incidental information recalled and also was a handicap to higher order recall (McConkie and others, 1973).

Additionally, evidence is clear that those who do want to increase rate can do so as effectively with a book, repeated practice, and a record of progress as they can with any of the hardware on the market. Braam and Berger (1968) found that college freshmen gained more through paperback scanning than they did through training with tachistoscope, controlled reader, or pacer. They also felt that the paperback experience was closer to reality and therefore would more likely lead to maintenance of the skill through continued application.

We do, however, have an obligation to teach children to vary rate with the type of reading they do, that is, to employ flexibility of rate. This can begin by third or fourth grade, and is "taught" through explanation and practice.

Students need to realize that they should not read a science text at the same rate they would read a fictional story.

Skimming and Scanning

Related to flexibility of rate, and possibly a means of developing it, are the techniques of skimming and scanning. Readers skim for an idea; they scan for something specific. In scanning, for example, for a date or name, they read nothing but merely have a mental image of four numbers or two adjacent words beginning with capital letters and try to find a visual match for that image. In fact, scanning is somewhat like looking for a four-leaf clover: One does not look at each blade of grass but has a mental picture of the clover and seeks a visual match.

Skimming is a matter of attempting to get the gist of a selection without reading the entire thing. It is very difficult for mature readers to describe exactly what they do when they skim, yet youngsters need specific directions in their initial experiences. I believe the best way to initiate this skill is to provide youngsters with a selection and to tell them that they will not have nearly enough time to read it; that you just want them to get the general idea of what it is about. Hence, they are to quickly read the first sentence in each paragraph. While this is not to imply that the first sentence is always—or even often—the topic sentence, it does give a specific direction and will usually enable pupils to get a good idea of what the selection is about without reading the entire thing. After students appear to have this technique fairly well in hand, you might then explain that we don't always read the first sentence, that we may skip around, may even skip a paragraph or two entirely as we "skim" for the general idea.

Reading Directions

Reading to follow directions is a skill that may be taught but is certainly poorly learned. In fact, even as adults, many of us are guilty of ignoring the directions until it is too late.

How does one read to follow directions? The technique is easy enough, but we must teach it to children and give them much practice in using it. The technique to be demonstrated and practiced is a relatively simple two-step process: (1) Skim over the material to see what it is about, what you need, or will culminate with, and (2) go back and reread carefully as you complete each step. Isn't this exactly what you do when you follow a new recipe? Or do you get to the middle and find you should have mixed the dry ingredients separately, or find that you don't have a single one of the required three eggs in the house?

One way to demonstrate to older students the proper way to read and follow directions is to use a variation of the old party game, announcing that you are giving a timed test, then distribute, face down, a paper such as the following:

<u>Can You Follow Directions?</u>

(Time limit: Three minutes)

1. Read over the entire paper quickly before you do anything.
2. Print your first name in the upper right corner of this paper.
3. Circle the word *paper* in the second sentence.
4. Draw three small circles in the upper left corner.
5. Make an "X" in each circle.
6. Draw a square around each circle.
7. Sign your name under the title of this page.
8. After the title, write "yes, yes, yes."
9. Jump up, then sit down and continue.
10. Make an "X" in the lower left corner of this paper.
11. Draw a circle around the "X" you just made.
12. On the BACK of this paper, multiply 703 by 28.
13. Draw a rectangle around the word *three* in sentence four.
14. Loudly call out your first name when you get this far.
15. If you think you have followed directions carefully to this point, call out, "I have it!"
16. On the reverse side of this paper, add 8950 and 9850.
17. Draw a circle around your answer.
18. In your normal speaking voice, count from ten to one backward.
19. Punch two small holes in the top of this paper with your pencil.
20. If you are the first person to reach this point, loudly call out: "I am the leader in following directions!"
21. Underline all the even numbers on the left side of this page.
22. Loudly call out: "I am nearly finished! I have followed directions!"
23. Now that you have quickly read everything, do only sentences one and two.

As you might guess, when given the signal to begin, even a group of eighth graders—or adults, for that matter—will "perform" while one or two sit quietly and smile. Is it that they have any difficulty in understanding the vocabulary or the sentences? Of course not. The problem is that they do not read the directions as they should, by skimming over the entire list first.

All students can benefit from being allowed to read their own directions on worksheets and workbook pages—providing those directions are written clearly enough to be understood! Younger ones might enjoy simple activities, ranging from the usual directions at first grade to "Make a blue circle," "Make a red triangle," and so on, to an activity such as shown in Figure 8-2.

Figure 8-2

> To see what is in the picture you will need four colors: red, yellow, green, and black.
>
> If a word in the picture names an animal, make it red.
>
> If the word names something we do, make it yellow.
>
> If the word names a place, make it green.
>
> If the word names a person, make it black.

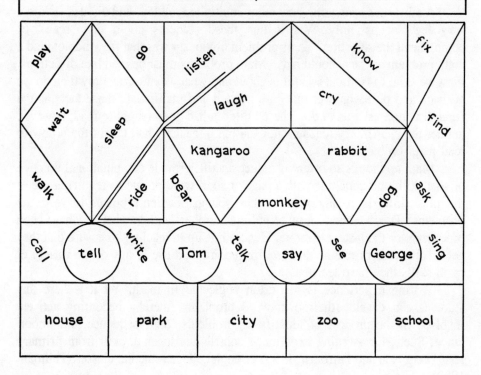

Attention to directions can also be attained by having students write their own directions for something they know, for example, how to use a jacket. I have had graduate students do such writing and followed their directions literally, to the amusement of the entire class. Students will discover the importance of clarity, detail, and sequence in directions, an awareness that may also contribute to their ability to read directions more effectively.

Reading Math

Closely related to the above skill is the ability to read math problems. After hearing math teachers at upper levels complain that children couldn't answer the word problems in math because "they don't know how to read," I made it a practice to visit middle school classes and to present students with a problem. After telling them to sit quietly if they finished before others, I put a problem such as the following on the overhead projector:

> Mary went to the grocery store. She bought 2 loaves of bread at 89¢ each, 3 pounds of pork chops at $2.79 a pound, a quart of milk at 99¢, and ½ dozen eggs at $1.29 a dozen. How much was the milk?

Again, it was amazing how many multiplied, added, and divided, while a very few sat patiently. Was it that these students could not "read" or comprehend the selection? Their problem obviously was that they did not read a math problem as they should have. Math problems must be read like directions: First we skim to find out what it is about and what we must do; only then do we go back and pull whatever facts are needed and manipulate those facts as the final direction asks us to do. These children had been taught to read; however, neither the elementary teachers nor the math teachers had taught them how to read math problems.

Math textbooks so often introduce a skill, provide computational practice on that skill, and conclude with a page or so of word problems requiring use of the new skill. Is it any wonder that youngsters don't bother to read the problems? They've been set up to pull the numbers and do what they have been practicing for the last week or so. Hence, it is up to teachers to ensure that they get mixed word problems that require reading and use of any of the variety of math skills they have learned.

Writing experience is too often neglected in math. Yet it is here that students can develop their own word problems, thereby becoming actively involved in the process of identifying problems, their sequence and importance. Such story-writing experience contributes to math skill from primary level (Ferguson and Fairburn, 1985) through college remedial classes (Pallman 1983).

Reading in Content Areas

In the content areas, teachers should be responsible for teaching their students how to read in that particular subject area. While there are some skills peculiar to each area, there are many that transcend a given subject to encompass all content areas. For example, recalling the discussion of text grammar in the previous chapter, factual materials also have a grammar whose understanding can assist students in comprehension. Both science and social studies texts share the following kinds of development:

1. By enumeration—students must identify the topic, then follow its development through subtopics and details.

2. By generalization—students must identify the generalization, then locate its support.

3. By sequence—students must identify and follow the sequence, whether chronological (as usually found in social studies) or procedural (as is usually the case in science).

4. By comparison/contrast—students must identify key words as well as the likenesses or differences discussed.

5. By cause/effect—students must identify the cause or effect, and relate the one to the other.

The importance of signal words was pointed out in the previous chapter. These are the "meaningless" structure words that youngsters too often merely gloss over, yet about 150 make up one-third of the words used in English. Robinson (1978) suggests having students collect and classify these words. For example, there are "go" signals that coordinate or continue ideas (*next, likewise, also, moreover*), "turn" signals that indicate a change of direction (*nevertheless, conversely, yet, on the contrary*), and "caution" or "stop" signals that say, in effect, that this is important so pay attention (*thus, hence, as a result, without doubt*). Don't give your students even this much of a list. When they meet a few of these signal words, call their attention to them, discuss what they mean, have pupils create headings or labels, and let them search the content texts for additional words to add to each of their categories.

Graphs and Tables

By upper primary levels, students should be introduced to the reading of graphs and tables since much of the information in factual articles is carried by these visuals. Teaching here consists primarily of going through examples, step by step, to learn how tables or graphs are organized and how to interpret them. For instance, present students with an example such as shown in Figure 8-3. You might begin by asking what the table is about; children should know by the title. Then questions of detail follow: "What is listed on the left side? What do the numbers stand for? What is the area of Lake Huron? Which is the smallest lake?" Such questions will lead children to understand and interpret the table. Facts that can be used to develop tables or graphs can be gleaned from any edition of *The World Almanac and Book of Facts* or *Information Please Almanac*.

Bar graphs, line graphs, pictographs, and pie graphs should also be introduced and their use taught. In addition, comparisons should be made as to their relative value. You might take the information from Figure 8-3 and present it in the form of a bar graph, as shown in Figure 8-4. Youngsters can be brought to see that a table provides more precision in comparisons, whereas a bar graph facilitates broad estimates or rankings. Pictographs are merely variations of bar graphs, whereas pie graphs provide the same kind of information but usually imply parts of a whole.

In contrast to these, line graphs usually report a relationship or trend, such as indicated in Figure 8-5. This kind of graph would not be appropriate for showing surface area of the Great Lakes.

Figure 8-3

Water Surface Area of the Great Lakes Within the United States	
Lake Michigan	22,400 square miles
Lake Superior	20,700 square miles
Lake Huron	9,100 square miles
Lake Erie	4,980 square miles
Lake Ontario	3,600 square miles

Figure 8-4
Bar graph showing water surface area of the Great Lakes within the United States.

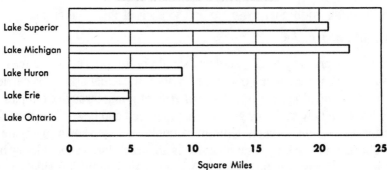

Figure 8-5
Line graph showing time of sunset in Illinois on the first
of each month.

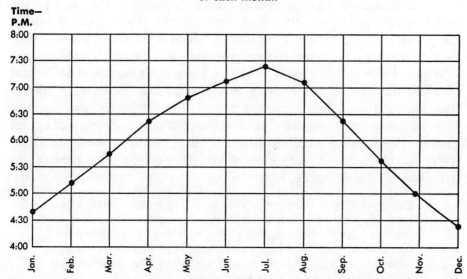

In addition to presenting examples of graphs and tables, and making comparisons of the different kinds, students can further understand and interpret them if they engage in making the tables and graphs. Again, factual books such as the various almanacs or books of records can be used as sources for data. Youngsters can also get practice in using graphs by graphing their spelling scores from week to week, percentages correct on math computation papers, library books read over a period of time, and so on.

EVALUATING INFORMATION: CRITICAL READING

Regardless of the purpose for reading, all factual or persuasive material should be evaluated as it is read. This very important aspect of the study skills is "critical reading," sometimes discussed with the other two categories of comprehension. And it is here, also, that writing comes into its own as an important means for introducing, practicing, and mastering these skills. In fact, due to the near void in instructional materials, writing is probably the best means any teacher can use.

Whether placed with the other comprehension skills or with the study skills, critical reading represents the most neglected, if not completely ignored, group of reading skills. This is true for a number of reasons.

Problems in Teaching Critical Reading

Examination of over one hundred research studies and a dozen professional textbooks on the teaching of reading (Hillerich, 1983b) revealed some of the problems in this area, not the least of which is the confusion over what "critical reading" is. Some leading professionals confound it with creative reading and with appreciation of literature. Many don't attempt to define it at all. Yet those who do usually bring in key words like "evaluate," "judge," "validity," and so on. Furthermore, a number of studies have shown that there is no unique variance between critical thinking, critical listening, and critical reading. Hence, while a definition is difficult, I will rely heavily on David Russell's (1956) classic definition of critical thinking in suggesting my definition of critical reading, which follows:

> Critical reading is a thought process applied to printed material that results in justified actions or conclusions on the part of a reader. It involves determination and evaluation of an author's stated or implied conclusions, based on objective evaluation of that author's supporting statements as well as on analysis of the means—the language and logic—used to arrive at those conclusions.

There are other reasons for the lack of improvement in the teaching of critical reading. Examination of a dozen professional texts revealed that they offer little space, much less help, on critical reading. Also, since basal readers traditionally contain fiction, they fail to provide the appropriate vehicle for developing critical reading since the latter is usually applied to factual/persuasive materials rather than to fiction.

Limiting students to a single text has kept them from evaluating viewpoints with which they are not familiar, but probably an even greater reason for failure to develop these skills is the desire to avoid controversy—the fear of "rocking the boat."

Of course, we might also blame the many misconceptions that exist about critical reading. Some believe it requires sophisticated skills of analysis and therefore cannot be taught until high school; Wolf and others (1967) demonstrated that these skills can be taught at primary level, and children so taught will read more critically. Some believe it is simply a higher level of general comprehension; as discussed in the previous chapter, critical reading and inferential comprehension develop independently of each other. Some believe it is taught through questioning; as will be demonstrated, many of these skills require initial instruction and practice aside from the reading before the skill can be learned and applied in actual reading.

To save space, references to research findings in the remainder of this chapter, unless otherwise noted, are based on a summary of over one hundred studies (Hillerich, 1983b). That research was clear that pupils taught critical reading skills will read more critically than those not so taught (1) regardless of grade level, (2) regardless of sex, and (3) regardless of IQ. Furthermore, students who cannot read the material, whether prereaders or remedial, can learn these skills by being taught through listening (Boodt, 1984).

Teaching Critical Reading

Obviously, anyone who is going to read critically must have material to read and must use the basic decoding and literal/inferential comprehension skills. Beyond that, the reader must have and use a variety of skills in order to evaluate or make judgments about a piece of material. Figure 8-6 is an outline of the critical reading skills.

The outline of skills follows the definition of critical reading given previously in that skills are clustered: support, language style, and logic used by an author. This organization is not to imply that one uses the skills in this fashion, but it does provide for an organized presentation. In actual practice, one might pick up a newspaper, be struck by the bias (listed under "language style") in the first paragraph, wonder about the author's purpose or background, and so on, jumping around among the various skills. (For another view of these skills, see Kneedler, 1985.)

Reserve Judgment

Reserving judgment is an important skill, especially if one is to read the newspaper critically. Evidence indicates that a preconceived negative attitude toward a subject handicaps the reader who is then unable to use even the critical reading skills already possessed. Yet what is the first thing one notices when picking up a newspaper to read it? The headlines. Have your students compare headlines from different sources on the same subject to make them aware of the way in which headlines can predispose them to the subject before they get the facts. Also have them write their own headlines, attempting both unbiased and biased headlines. Let them also know that headlines are usually written by a headline editor and not by the reporter who wrote the article, hence some misinterpretation can arise from this process.

Among the favorites in my collection are headlines from three sources dealing with one of the national assessments in reading and running the gamut, from positive to negative:

> NAEP Survey Shows Reading Skills Improving
> How Well Do Kids Read?
> U.S. Reading Exam Student Scores Low

Figure 8-6

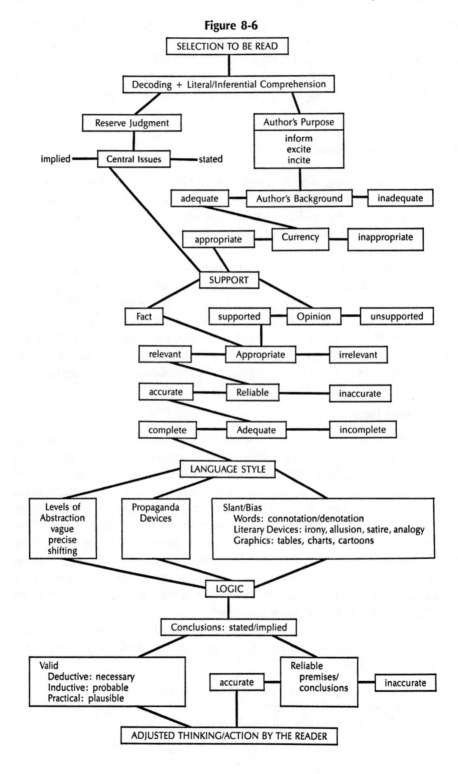

Would you care to guess which was from the local paper and which from the National School Public Relations Association?

Central Issues

If one is even to understand—much less evaluate—printed information, that reader must determine the central issues presented by the author. This identification requires no unique skills beyond literal or inferential comprehension. If the major points are stated, the former skills are required; if implied, the latter. Neither is meant to be a judgmental matter since it is perfectly acceptable to imply rather than literally to state all main issues.

Author's Purpose

Any careful reader will attempt to arrive at some judgment of an author's purpose, often related to that author's background. Is the author writing this merely to provide information—to educate the reader on the subject? Or is this a matter of attempting to change the reader's view in support of some new cause? Or even to oppose some existing establishment?

Earlier, I stated that critical reading skills are used with factual/persuasive materials. This is not always the case since humor and satire can sometimes be more effective than straightforward logic. I recall a column by one of my favorite humorists, Art Buchwald. He was quoting business firms and then adding his tongue-in-cheek translation. For instance, after an involved quote from an auto manufacturer disclaiming government charges about lack of safety in automobiles by blaming consumer misuse of the product, Buchwald's translation was, "Oh boy, it looks like we're in for another recall." Very funny, but the critical reader might question why several of these barbs related to the automobile industry. If one is to be a critical reader, the guard must be up at all times.

Of course, if you are using newspapers, evaluation of editorial pages should make students aware that articles there, whether editorials or by-line columns, are intended to present the writer's viewpoint. Have students write, on the same subject, a news article and an editorial or by-line column in order to emphasize differences.

Author's Background

First of all, the dichotomy "adequate" and "inadequate" on the outline is intended only as shorthand—as are all subsequent extremes—to indicate a continuum. It is not intended to imply that an author's background is either entirely adequate or entirely inadequate but only to suggest that the background be evaluated in terms of adequacy.

This is a skill that certainly needs work. Where else but in this country can an outstanding linguist or a noted nuclear scientist be looked upon by the public as experts in the teaching of reading? Or where else can a movie actress be looked upon as an expert in foreign affairs or in nutrition?

This skill can begin in kindergarten at the listening level. Tell children about the author of a factual book you have read to them, perhaps one about the life and habits of the white-tailed deer. That author was a ranger who spent fifteen years observing, photographing, and making notes about the white-tailed deer. Then tell them about the author of another book on the subject who is a television commentator living in a penthouse in New York City. Which author is likely to provide more reliable information?

Currency

Notice that the continuum suggested in Figure 8-6 for this point is "appropriate" versus "inappropriate" and not the usual "recent" versus "dated." I believe we do a disservice to youngsters when we stress copyright date alone. Only after considering whether the date is relevant should we consider currency. Assume that I want a book about space exploration and find one so titled. Upon checking the copyright date, I find that it was published in 1946. I will certainly search for another book! However, if I want a biography of Marie Antoinette and find the one by Belloc, I don't care that it was first published in 1909 since my concern is more for author's competence, style, and so on. In other words, students should be taught to look at the copyright date in terms of the subject matter.

Fact/Opinion

Of all the critical reading skills, if a basal reading series does anything, this is one skill area that is usually included—not always well done, but included nonetheless. For example, one published set of materials defines a fact as a statement that "is true." And what does that make all your opinions!

The first step in teaching this skill may be taken by third or fourth grade and is a matter of clarifying the distinction between fact and opinion. This can be done through definition and example statements. I have found that fourth graders have no difficulty in classifying two kinds of opinion statements as such, but one of the two kinds of factual statements they find very difficult—as do many adults. For example, of the following four statements, children and adults have no difficulty in classifying the first three as fact or opinion:

It is too hot in the room where I am working.   (opinion)

It is too cold in the room where I am working.   (opinion)

The temperature is 70 degrees where I am working.   (fact)

The temperature is 180 degrees where I am working.   (?)

The latter statement is often classified as opinion by both children and adults. However, it is a statement of fact (which I assure you is false). The distinction between statements of fact and those of opinion is that the former can be verified; the latter cannot. Given a statement of fact, we can observe, measure, feel, or in some manner objectively verify whether the statement is true or false; given a statement of opinion, we can only agree or disagree. Admittedly, in the latter case one can marshal facts to support a position, but the opinion itself cannot be verified.

Students need to be provided with the definitions and given practice in classifying statements. They can also write their own for classmates to classify. This is all a waste of time, however, if they don't ultimately apply this in a real reading situation. They need to read a piece of "factual" or persuasive material to check whether the author is arguing from fact or opinion, and if the latter, if that opinion is supported with facts. There is nothing wrong with presenting opinions, but if an author does only that, without supporting those opinions with fact, we might part company, and students should learn to do likewise.

The identified facts, whether basic or supporting, then need to be evaluated through the following three standards.

Appropriate

Some authors argue through a technique that I call the "sales syndrome." That encyclopedia salesperson who comes to your door never begins by asking, "Will you buy an encyclopedia?" Instead, the person may begin by asking if you are interested in education, believe in having books in the home, facts at your fingertips, and so on. After many a "yes, yes, yes," you are asked to sign in the hope that your "yeses" will continue.

Students need to be taught to examine the material to see that the great, true statements with which they agree have something to do with the conclusions. Have them delete the irrelevant and reexamine the selection and its conclusions. Have them attempt writing persuasive pieces of their own to see if they can slip in some irrelevant true statements that classmates will miss. Once more, by doing it themselves, they are more likely to recognize a technique someone is using on them.

Reliable

It is at this point, in evaluating the accuracy of material, that students must go beyond the single text. They usually have not had the life experience to judge the accuracy of most statements they encounter in a science or social studies text. However, by seeking out other authors judged competent, they can make comparisons and evaluate the accuracy of what they are reading.

Adequate

Adequacy has to do with relative completeness since no one can ever say *everything* there is to say on a point. It is here that authors can seriously mislead a reader by providing factual statements that are accurate and related to the conclusions but that reveal only half the story. Such partial facts can sometimes be more misleading than none. Yet it is here also that students must go beyond a single source if they are to know what the more complete picture is like since their experience will not be adequate for most of the information they get from social studies or science texts.

Levels of Abstraction

In dealing with language style, this first item may be the least serious, yet students ought to develop some awareness of the problem of shifts in levels of abstraction. For instance, if you had never seen or heard of a frog, I might bring a one-eyed, three-legged green frog to show you what a frog is. While neither you nor I could deny that what you see is a frog and what it looks like, for me to jump from this concrete specific to the broad generalization that all frogs are green and have one eye and three legs would certainly be a disservice to you in your understanding of frogs. And it is such shifts in levels of abstraction that can be dangerous to the reader.

You might begin with your students by using a pyramid of abstraction such as is shown in Figure 8-7, adapted from Hayakawa's (1949) "ladder of abstraction."

Figure 8-7

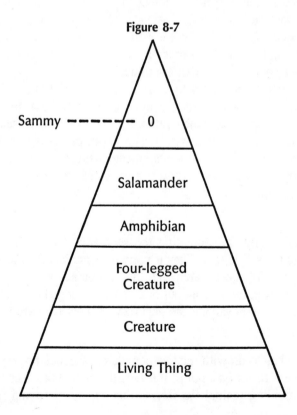

Sammy — — — — 0

Salamander

Amphibian

Four-legged
Creature

Creature

Living Thing

Clarify that as one goes up the pyramid, moving from the broad, abstract to the specific and concrete, the number of cases in the category diminishes until there is only the one unique individual example. Then have students complete other pyramids, even jumping in at the middle if you'd like, to complete one using "fruit," "transportation," and so on.

After they understand about levels of abstraction, have them write two versions of a story, one as specific and one as abstract as possible and compare the two versions. For instance, compare the following first sentences in my two stories:

1. The thing walked among other things in a place.

2. Rama, the battle-scarred tiger, crept among the other animals in the bush.

Which would you be more likely to toss? Of course, the first one is vague, dull, and actually meaningless; the specific one is clear and more interesting. Students should discover this in their own comparisons, that the concrete tends to be more clear and more interesting; the abstract, just the reverse. This is not to say that all writing must be specific; if one wants to cloud the issue, abstract is better.

All this practice is just a waste of time unless the understanding is now carried over to application. Have students examine a piece of persuasive or factual writing, marking the abstract statements. They can even attempt a rewrite at a more specific level to see if they still have the same reaction to the conclusions.

Propaganda Devices

This is a second area that is usually included in those basal reading series that do anything about critical reading. Yet if this is done to protect us as consumers, it is probably ineffectual since ad makers are so far beyond the classic devices. Vance Packard, in *The New Hidden Persuaders*, mentions a study where women volunteered to compare two skin creams. In order to differentiate the two, which were in identical plain jars, one jar had a circle and one a triangle on top. A large majority preferred one jar and offered a number of sound reasons for their preference. But the same cream was in both. The ad company was merely testing the packaging to see if women were more influenced by a circle or a triangle. How does one defend against this? Or against subliminal suggestions, which are still legal in many kinds of establishments?

Nevertheless, some experience with propaganda devices may be beneficial. Usually that begins by presenting the propaganda devices, giving some examples, and then having students locate magazine ads or TV commercials to classify according to the device used. In making such classifications, you need not be overly concerned about the labels since the point is to use them merely as "handles" in order to gain better understanding of the devices. Following are the most common devices considered:

> Bandwagon: Everybody is doing it, so you'd better too!
>
> Transfer: If you use this, you will be like...
>
> Testimonial: (A famous person sells the product.)
>
> Glittering generalities: (Statements that sound good but give no information.)
>
> Common folk: We're not fancy; we're just like you.
>
> Snob appeal: For the exclusive few: "Expensive, but you're worth it."
>
> Veiled threat: This could happen to you.
>
> Appeal to research: "Ninety-five percent of the ———'s surveyed..."
>
> Name calling: (Trying to ridicule the competition.)
>
> Card stacking: (Presenting only one side.)

Students may enjoy classifying different types of ads. They will find that certain types of businesses seem to favor particular devices: insurance companies, veiled threat; fast foods, bandwagon; pharmaceuticals, appeal to research. Also they may classify in more than one category. For instance, cereals using sports figures can be considered an example of transfer or of testimonial. Furthermore, they will find that many TV commercials don't use the classic devices so much as they use the old political device: "I don't care what you say about me, just mention my name." They use humor just to get attention so consumers remember the name.

While not often included in the classic devices, the "hidden source" is a favorite of news reports: either the passive voice, "It has been reported that..." or, even more impressive, "According to a reliable source..." In either case, the receiver has no means of checking the original source.

After they understand the devices, your students might enjoy making up a test of the most familiar slogans to see how many people in other classes can recognize the product being advertised. Some of us may do poorly on such a test and feel proud that we have resisted the ad makers. However, don't congratulate yourself unless you are certain that the craving you get for a particular cereal isn't a result of some ad, the name of which you cannot recall.

Students will enjoy writing their own commercials for an imaginary product. Of course, no matter what else you do, it has all been a waste of time unless ultimately youngsters apply their newfound knowledge to reading and analyzing a piece of text. Yes, propaganda devices can as well be used in editorials, by-line columns, or even "news" articles as in TV commercials.

Slant/Bias

Of all the critical reading skills, the most important, especially if one is to read the newspaper critically, is the ability to detect slant or bias (Kimmel, 1973). Most writers don't attempt to persuade through half-truths or lies; they merely insert emotionally loaded words to gently bring the reader around to their way of thinking.

Begin instruction in this skill at third or fourth grade by making children aware of the fact that many "synonyms" have different emotional effects on the reader. For example, ask for all the words they can think of that mean the same as *house*, a place where people live. They can probably arrive at the following or more:

		abode		
	shack		home	
palace		house		hovel
	mansion		residence	
		pad		

Now ask them to sort these terms by positive and negative connotations—or "good sounding" and "not-so-good sounding" for younger pupils. They will certainly recognize that *home* and *hovel* have a different effect on the reader, even though both denote a place where people live.

After experience with different examples, possibly including "automobiles" or "dogs," give students a paragraph without adjectives to add all the positive adjectives they can, then—reversing the slant—to add the negative. You might even want to use Aesop's Fables since these are bare-bones stories. For instance, have half the class slant the story of "The Fox and the Stork" by making the fox the good character and the stork the "bad guy." Let the other half of the class do the reverse, with no one being allowed to make any changes other than to insert adjectives or adverbs. Students might also like to reverse the slant on TV commercials or magazine ads.

Application of the skill comes when youngsters use this in reading factual or persuasive materials. Have them strike out the emotional adjectives and adverbs to see if they still agree with the author's conclusions. They might even like to reverse the slant to judge the effect. Excellent reading material for this practice—if students are reading at a high enough level—is the sports page of any newspaper. Kimmel (1973) found that sports writing was the most biased of any kind of writing. Sports writers don't seem to be able to merely give the facts: One team either "clobbered" or "squeaked by" the other. Students might even like to write some parodies or exaggerated sports articles.

Figure 8-8
IMPROVEMENT IN READING
IMA TRYIN SCHOOL DISTRICT

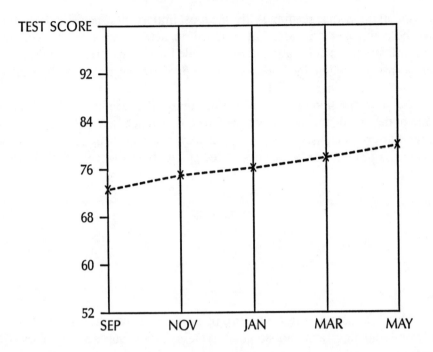

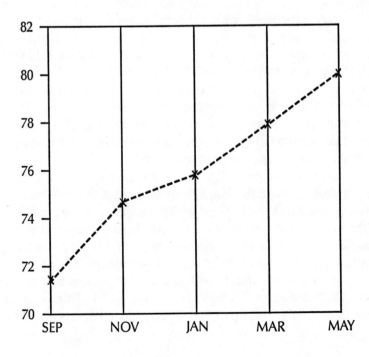

Don't forget how graphs can be used in a biased manner. The same facts can be shown quite differently by enlarging or truncating a graph, as shown in Figure 8-8.

Which graph do you think was done by the local paper and which by the school? Helpful for this kind of information, if you teach middle grades or above, is a little book called *How to Lie with Statistics* (Huff, 1954). Also, don't throw away that "junk" mail. It can be a marvelous source of material for analysis of slant/bias or propaganda techniques. The emotional language in one included statements about living a "righteous enough life," "make you shape up," "terrifying," "scares you, too." Another used the (not so) "veiled threat" in addressing the recipient as "Dear Potential Handgun Victim" and raised questions about "being pushed around," "deception," and "weapons of murder."

Students can also benefit from comparing newspaper headlines. How do headlines of small-town newspapers compare with city papers? Many times they tend to be more sensational. Compare "White Supremacist Explodes in Anger at His Sentencing" with "Racist Given 2 Life Terms in Shootings of 2 Joggers" or "Two Friends of Reagan Given Posts" with "Reagan Adds Two Wealthy Friends to High Level Jobs."

You can also use those political surveys that presumably want to know what constituents wish, but are really loaded to get the answers the legislator needs for ammunition. How can anyone answer questions such as "Do you see a need to alleviate the unsafe working conditions the police and fire departments have been working under?" (Of course not; we like to have them work under unsafe conditions?!) Youngsters get very good at these kinds of biased questions. They never ask, "Do we have to go out for recess?" It's "Do we *have to* do math?" and "Do we *get to* go out for recess?" Have them collect the biased statements they hear and record them in their language logs for sharing at a future date.

Logic

Even here, we are not talking about high school skills. In fact, I will not go much further than what can be done at primary level, but which should be developed—if it hasn't already been—in twelfth grade.

First graders can learn about deductive logic, evaluating the validity of categorical statements, when intentions are both stated and implied. For example, in the literal category, they can identify that *some* is intended by the statement: "Out of six cats, only one scratched." Likewise, they can determine the implied intention of *all* in the statement: "Cats are good pets."

First graders can also learn to draw conclusions from premises in the use of simple syllogisms. Few such children would have a problem arriving at the logical conclusion for the following:

If I touch a hot stove, I will get burned.
I touched a hot stove.

Where even older students face a problem is when they are asked to evaluate the pure logic of a syllogism when the conclusion goes against common sense and experience, as in the following:

All bananas fly.
This is a banana.

You might like to use simple Venn diagrams, such as shown in Figure 8-9, to work with the "all, some, none" categories, raising questions such as "Are all salamanders animals?" "Are all animals salamanders?" "Are some animals salamanders?"

Youngsters should also get experience in evaluating practical arguments. For example, inductive arguments are evaluated on the strength of the premises and the logic of the conclusion.

Ivan is sneaky.
Ivan is Russian.
Therefore, all Russians are sneaky.

In this case, knowing that the premises are true, is this the logical conclusion? One technique in evaluating is to draw Venn diagrams based on the

Figure 8-9

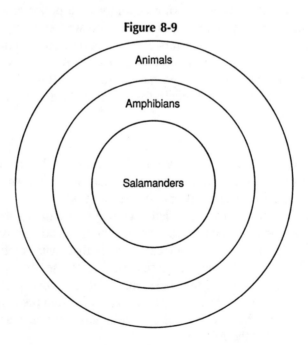

two premises to discover the many other conclusions possible, always including the fact that Ivan is only one of many sneaky people and many Russians.

Arguments by enumeration are evaluated by the size of the sample:

Three apples had worms.

Therefore, apples are wormy this year.

Arguments by analogy are evaluated on the strength of the analogy:

Motorcycles and bicycles are similar.

Therefore, riding a motorcycle is like riding a bicycle.

Some Final Comments

Not only do we find it important for youngsters to write in the "reading" class, but they should also read in the "writing" class. What better opportunity to apply critical reading skills than in reading their own or classmates' writing?

It is important not only to step aside for teaching and initial practice of the preceding critical reading skills, but it is necessary to apply them holistically to a piece of printed material. The dearth of materials for this purpose—possibly because publishers also don't want to "rock the boat"—means that teachers are left to their own devices. In addition to the writing suggested throughout this chapter, use two or more different newspapers in order to get articles on the same subject to compare. Brief biographical sketches, historical fiction, and so on—when you can find two versions—can be ideal for this kind of comparison, where students find they must check the author's background to infer purpose, determine fact/opinion, validity, use of emotional or biased expressions, and so on.

Chapter 9

Using Reading Skills: The Independent Reading Program

A total reading program has two major emphases: the sequential development of essential skills, and the enjoyable application and practice of those skills. A good basal reader, *used with discrimination*, is still undoubtedly the best vehicle a teacher can have for basic skill development. However, it must be remembered that this is only half the job of teaching reading; the other half—literally 50 percent of the time called "reading" in any classroom—should involve the enjoyable application and practice of these skills in the independent reading program. In fact, the proper purpose of a basal reading program is to get children *out of* basal reading programs; the purpose is to provide the consistent, sequential skill development so they can and do read.

The independent reading program refers to those activities conducted with library books or trade books, as opposed to textbooks. Use of these trade books includes much more than the allowance of time for the reading of those books in school. Of course, time for the reading is important, too, but unless youngsters have an opportunity to do something with that reading—that is, to *use* the reading they do—half their pleasure and development is unattained. After all, the best teacher of reading is wasting time teaching children *how* to read if that teacher does not, in the process, develop in them *the desire* to read.

This insistence on library reading as 50 percent of the total program is not based on hopeful hunches. Anyone who would question the contribution of the independent reading program to total reading development need only look at the research evidence on Individualized Reading that was developed during the late 1950s and early 1960s. At that time, a number of educators (Lazar, 1957;

Veatch, 1959; Barbe, 1961) insisted that children not be kept locked in basal readers for their total reading program: Children are interested in different subjects, therefore they need self-selection; children learn at different rates, therefore they need self-pacing; children read at different levels, therefore they need a variety of types of materials; children need different skills, therefore they should be taught individually in teacher-pupil conferences.

In the process of their enthusiasm, many proponents of this library approach to individualized reading conducted exciting and active reading programs in library books, but they often forgot, neglected, or just didn't have time to teach the basic skills. In spite of this fact, any examination of the research evidence from the late 1950s indicates that children in these kinds of programs did at least as well in skill development as those in basal readers (Sartain, 1960)—and they certainly had a lot more fun! Actually, we need the best of both worlds: the basal reading program for the consistent, sequential skill development and the trade books for the application and extension of those skills, as well as for the stimulation of enthusiasm and interest in reading. Success in reading on the part of any individual is a direct result of two major factors: skill and interest.

Of course, a frequent complaint of teachers is, "I just don't have time for library books!" Such a statement implies that the reading of library books is a frill, a reward for getting work done. This it is not! The library reading must be an integral part of the total program *for all children.* In fact, it is usually the good reader who knows that reading can be fun, while the poor reader still tries to finish the workbook pages. All children need to discover that, no matter how minimal their skills, they can still enjoy really reading.

No time for library reading? We might point to Yap's (1977) evidence: He found a higher relationship between the amount of reading done and achievement than he found between IQ and achievement. While teachers might not be able to do much about IQ, they can do something about the amount of reading their youngsters do. It cannot be emphasized enough that children also learn to read by reading.

THE WORLD OF CHILDREN'S BOOKS

The world of children's books is relatively new. In fact, historically speaking, children's literature is an infant. Of course, we can go back to Bunyan's *Pilgrim's Progress* of 1676 and say that was a book children read. However, that book—and many of the subseqent books that children read, from *Gulliver's Travels* to *Black Beauty*—was not intended for children.

Except for Mother Goose, first published in 1697, and a few fairy tales, it was not until the mid-nineteenth century that children's literature even began, and it began with the fairy tales of the Grimm brothers and Anderson and the nonsense of Lear. In fact, children's books of the seventeenth century bear little resemblance to what we call children's literature today. Sloane (1955) listed 261 books written in the seventeenth century for children to read. Here, for example, in what appear today to be uninteresting summaries of some religious catechisms, are two *titles* from this collection.

> The apprentices warning piece. Being a confession of Peter Moore, formerly servant to Mr. Bidgood, apothecary in Exeter, executed there the last assises, for poysoning his said master. Wherein is observed such lamentable expressions proceeding from him, as may produce a trembling to all who reade or heare thereof, and be a warning to such leud servants who walk the same steps, lest they receive the same punishment. (Edited by Joseph Foster, 1641; see Sloane, 1955, p. 146.)

> The vanity of childhood and youth; wherein the depraved nature of young people is represented, and means for their reformation proposed: being some sermons preached in Hand-Alley, at the request of several young men. To which is added, a catechism for youth. (Daniel Williams, 1691; see Sloane, 1955, pp. 206-207.)

Such were all that children had as books to call their own. The general pattern during the seventeenth and eighteenth centuries was a pedantic, moralistic approach, reaching a height in France in the grandiloquence, didacticism, moralism, and floods of tears presented by Berquin (1749–1791), of whom Paul Hazard (1947) commented: [He was] a man so dreadfully serious, says one of his critics, that no one ever saw him smile during his life— with the result that, after his death, no one ever spoke of him without smiling." (p. 36)

The middle nineteenth century began to offer a few books, still not written for, but more appropriate for children: Cooper's *Deerslayer* and *Last of the Mohicans,* Ewing's *Lob-Lie-by-the-Fire* and *Jackanapes,* and finally Dodges' *Hans Brinker,* as well as Kingsley's *The Water Babies* and Hawthorne's *Wonderbook* and *Tanglewood Tales.*

The first American literary work for young children was Wanda Gag's *Millions of Cats,* published in 1928. And, for the very young child just starting to read, the beginning-to-read books did not begin for practical purposes until the publication of *The Cat in the Hat* and its four companion books in 1957.

The teacher interested in greater depth about the history and development of children's literature is referred to the intriguing and often humorous work of Paul Hazard (1947) or to complete works such as those by Huck (1986), Glazer and Williams (1979), or Norton (1983).

In contrast to the dearth of children's books before this century, today we are swamped, as over 3,000 titles a year are recommended for children. The problem today is not to search out or locate books for children but to sort out and evaluate the best from the thousands that are available.

THE SELECTION OF LIBRARY BOOKS

The selection of trade books is not the exclusive responsibility of the children's librarian in the school or public library. It is also the classroom teacher's responsibility if that teacher is going to recognize the role of library reading in the total reading program. And that responsibility includes not only providing a good selection of outstanding books for children to choose from, but it also includes *knowing* those books.

Good literature for children has many of the same qualities as good literature for adults. As stated by Arbuthnot (1966), children's books, like adult books, show "compassionate love and the kind of courage that is another phase of achievement" (p. 16). As children mature, they shift from admiring the characters to identifying with them.

Criteria for Selection

Good literature is well written in terms of style, with content that meets persisting needs for self-understanding or for understanding of the world, or it offers some worthwhile escape in humor or in fantasy. Put another way, some refer to good literature as dealing with elements that are universal and permanent: universal in that it treats the problems of mankind everywhere; permanent in that it deals with those problems that persist throughout time.

Such criteria may sound somewhat pretentious when talking about primary children's books; however, reduced to application at that level, there certainly are such books: Hoban's *Bedtime for Frances, Baby Sister for Frances,* and so on, deal with problems faced by young children. *Tom and the Two Handles,* also by Hoban, is a beginning-to-read book dealing with a persistent problem of young boys and treating it in an enjoyable manner.

Good books for children have a sound plot. In fact, plot is one of the most appealing elements for youngsters. A good plot is one that unfolds as a natural outgrowth of personalities, decisions, and situations of the characters; it is not contrived, accidental, or coincidental.

Characterization must ring true. The personalities and/or the "animalities," as Huck calls them, must be real and lifelike. There is no place in children's literature—any more than in adult literature—for the stereotypes and cardboard characters of the soap opera or Western, where every character is either all good or all bad. Good characterization will be realistic in that the reader will get to know the character as a person; it will have consistency in that, knowing the character, one can predict in an unmentioned situation how that character might react; and, in the process of interacting with the plot, the character will show growth just as a real person grows through experience.

Again, these are not exotic criteria to be applied only to adult books. Who could confuse some of the mice children should meet? *Anatole* (by Eve Titus), the self-possessed chief cheese taster in a French cheese factory, could not be confused with *Frederick* (by Leo Lionni), the dreamer and poet, or with Amos, the subtle braggart in *Ben and Me,* by Robert Lawson.

The content and theme of children's books must be appropriate for them. Usually, the manner in which an author handles the content is more a determinant of appropriateness than is the content itself. An author's theme should be developed through characterization and plot. If authors are so poor that they have to tell their readers what the point is, youngsters will not accept them any more than adults would. For example, when Bunyan found that his *Pilgrim's Progress* was being read by children—because they could read it as an adventure story at the literal level—he wrote a book specifically for children in the vein of books of the time. This book, called *Divine Emblems,* was rejected by children because of its typically didactic approach.

While we certainly don't want to expose children to books that are objectionable or that are pure trash, there are some worthy books that may not meet all the criteria of great literature but that could be called "stepping-stones" to good literature: A youngster must begin somewhere, and the early beginning-to-read books can be classed in that area since they are interesting, appealing, often humorous, and written at a level that the beginner can read.

Tools for Selecting Children's Books

Although there is no substitute for personally reading the good books available for your children, it is impossible to rely on personal review for the selection of books. One would have to read about eight books every day just to review all the books recommended. Of course, it also should go without saying that we cannot rely on publishers' catalogs to make our book selection. Has any publisher ever listed a book that was not "stupendous, fantastic, and the greatest book ever published"? Hence, as an aid to book selection, it is important that the classroom teacher become familiar with the tools used by the children's librarian for the selection of books.

Children's Catalog (H. W. Wilson Co., 950 University Avenue, Bronx, NY 10452) is the "bible" of children's books, a comprehensive listing with annotations that is revised every five years with paperback supplements provided during the intervening years. Every book listed in this catalog is recommended by the American Library Association. In addition to the annotations in the body of the catalog, it contains indexes of authors, titles, and subject heading. For example, the teacher who wants to find more titles about rockets at the primary level can use the subject listing. Some entries are also starred (*) or double starred (**) to indicate that they are considered most important for first purchase by schools or libraries.

Every elementary school should have a copy of this catalog, and it should be kept in the teachers' lounge or at other locations readily accessible to all the staff at any time. In addition, each school should have at least one periodical subscription to help teachers keep informed about children's books, authors, illustrators, and so on. The major periodicals are:

> *School Library Journal* (R. R. Bowker Co., 245 West Seventeenth Street, New York, NY 10011)
> *The Horn Book* (585 Boylston Street, Boston, MA 02116)
> *Booklist and Subscription Books Bulletin* (50 East Huron Street, Chicago, IL 60611)
> *Wilson Library Bulletin* (H. W. Wilson Co., 950 University Avenue, Bronx, NY 10452)

School Library Journal includes the greatest number of book reviews per issue, and they are usually a paragraph or two in length. It is the precursor of *Children's Catalog* and includes the starred and double starred notations.

Horn Book doesn't review as many books per issue, but it reviews the books in greater depth. Also, it reviews some books in galley proof, so the reader will see the reviews before these books are actually available.

A handy catalog for the teacher's personal use is the inexpensive paperback *Best Books for Children* (R. R. Bowker Co., 245 West Seventeenth Street, New York, NY 10011). This is compiled by the American Library Association also, and it includes about four thousand book entries, with notes indicating various recommendations. It is revised annually, and changes about 10 percent with each revision. It also includes only recommended books, with one-sentence annotations and indications of approximate grade level for use.

Scope of Materials

Students at any level should be exposed to a variety of all kinds of books. This variety should include fantasy, realistic fiction, fact, and poetry.

Mother Goose and nursery rhymes should not be neglected. Following is a list of Mother Goose books:

> *Brian Wildsmith's Mother Goose,* illustrated by Brian Wildsmith. New York: Franklin Watts, 1964.
> *Marguerite De Angeli's Book of Nursery and Mother Goose Rhymes,* illustrated by Marguerite De Angeli. New York: Doubleday, 1954.

Mother Goose, illustrated by Tasha Tudor. New York: Henry Z. Walck, 1944.

Real Mother Goose, illustrated by Blanche Wright. Chicago: Rand McNally, 1965.

Through the use of Mother Goose rhymes, the teacher can expose children to various literary devices. Rhythm can be demonstrated through many selections, such as "To market, to market, to buy a fat pig" or "Tom, Tom, the piper's son."

Rhyme can be enjoyed through almost any of the Mother Goose selections. Alliteration is shown in some selections, such as "Little boy blue come blow your horn." Onomatopoeia is demonstrated through "Hark, hark, the dogs do bark."

Imagination is tickled with items such as "If all the world was apple pie, and all the sea was ink." Humor runs through many of the rhymes, including "Jack and Jill" or "Georgey Porgey."

In addition to Mother Goose, every teacher should have a book of poetry from which to pick selections to read to children. Arbuthnot's *Time for Poetry* (Scott Foresman) is probably still the best collection for the primary level. Another very attractive one is *The Golden Treasury of Poetry,* illustrated by Joan Walsh Anglund (Golden Press, 1959). At middle grades, a popular anthology is *Favorite Poems, Old and New* by Helen Ferris (Doubleday, 1957), and an excellent newer one is *A New Treasury of Children's Poetry* by Joanna Cole (Doubleday, 1984).

Folk tales are important for reading to young children, and these may be selected in individual books or in anthologies such as those by Huck (1986), Norton (1983), or Glazer and Williams (1979). From the folk tales, children should be exposed to the cumulative tales, such as "Henney Penney," the talking beast tales ("The Three Little Pigs"), the magic that is in most fairy tales, and some of the simple myths, such as *Arrow to the Sun* by McDermott (Viking, 1974). The fables of Aesop can be enjoyed at any level.

Factual books are also important to youngsters and appeal at all ages. Even though publishers' catalogs are usually not reliable sources for judging books, a few can be trusted for some series of factual books that include consistently well done titles. Among these are the following:

TRUE BOOKS— (Childrens Press) Science and other factual topics for grades 2–4.

FIRST BOOKS— (Franklin Watts) Science topics for grades 4+.

ALL ABOUT BOOKS— (Random House) Science topics for middle school and above.

LANDMARK BOOKS— (Random House) Social Studies, including historical fiction for middle school and above.

ENCHANTMENT OF AMERICA— (Childrens Press) One book on each state, for grade 5 and above.

ENCHANTMENT OF THE WORLD— (Childrens Press) One book on each country, grades 7–9+.

William R. Morrow also has some exceptional natural science books by authors such as Selsam, Zim, and McClung. The latter's series about various members of endangered species can be read from about grade 5 and includes such sure-fire titles as *Sampson, Last of the California Grizzlies,* and *Rajpur, Last of the Bengal Tigers.*

Good book lists are available from a variety of sources. Annually, in the December issue, *School Library Journal* publishes a list of the "Best Books of the Year." Reviews are also available in most elementary professional journals and in many newspapers. Whitehead's guide (1984) is an example of the many good reference books available.

While numerous awards are given for outstanding children's books, the two major honors each year are the Caldecott and Newbery awards. The former is presented to the children's book that is considered the best illustrated for the year; the latter is awarded to the best book in terms of literary quality. Hence, while there are exceptions, the tendency is for the Caldecott books to be largely primary picture books and for the Newbery books to be directed more to the upper elementary and middle school levels.

Unfortunately, these award-winning books, especially the Newbery winners and runners-up, are not always the most popular with students. Because many do not have a fast-moving plot that reaches out and grabs the reader in the first sentence, many youngsters feel they are dull. One good method for getting these books read is to begin them by reading to the class.

Caldecott books are primary picture books, but the text is not of the high-interest, low-vocabulary type, so they are not easy reading. Usually these are read to kindergarteners or first graders who then "read" the pictures.

This brief discussion of award-winning books is not intended to suggest that children be presented with a required reading list. There is no book so important that everyone must read it. On the other hand, there are many books so important that everyone ought at least to know about them. Among these are the Newbery and Caldecott books, lists of which can be found in any anthology of children's literature.

ENSURING ACCESSIBILITY OF GOOD BOOKS

If students at any level are to make use of library books, those books must be accessible. By this we mean, at the elementary level, they must be in the classroom. In fact, research evidence still supports classroom libraries as opposed to central libraries at the elementary level. Powell (1966) reported that children who had classroom libraries checked out twice as many books as did those who had to go to the central library. Hillerich (1966) reported three times as many books checked out from classroom libraries. In contrast, the only evidence found to support the opposite view is a study by Gaver (1963), who compared six schools and found that students checked out more books in the schools with central libraries. The difficulty with that study was that the schools without central libraries also had less than half as many books and spent less than half as much per child on library books. It is difficult for children to check out books, no matter what the housing, if there aren't many available.

Role of the Library

While we could recite other advantages besides accessibility for the classroom library, the central library—when properly run—need not be a handicap, other than the tendency for teachers to rely on the librarian as the one responsible for this portion of the curriculum. Teachers need to realize that their knowledge and children's use of library books are equally important with knowing and using a basal reading program.

Most school libraries these days are well handled. The librarian doesn't see the job as one of keeping the books neatly shelved and keeping those dirty little hands off the books; librarians see their job as one of storytelling, "selling" the books, and getting them worn out through use.

The good school library is an "open" library. Why should I go to the library at "9:30 on Tuesday" when I'm not finished with the book I got last Tuesday, or—just as likely—I was ready to go back at 10:00 last Tuesday because I didn't like the book I got. Of course, this is not to suggest that classes need not go to the library on a schedule; it is only to insist that youngsters also be allowed to go at any time they and their teacher agree they may go.

Some schools have only volunteers instead of a qualified librarian. This should not mean that the library can be open only when a volunteer is present. Teachers can still take a class to that library, and I would contend that children can be taught how to check out their own books when no one is there—or do we really believe children will come into the library in order to *steal* a book. (Would that it were so!)

The elementary library also is not the place for youngsters softly to tiptoe in, quietly select a book, and sit down to read it. One librarian realized this. In her library she had added, above the "Quiet Please" sign, another sign of her own: "NO." The library is a place for youngsters to call to each other about books, to recommend books to friends, and to get excited. The quiet reading can be done in the classroom, the hallway, or even outdoors if the weather permits.

In defense of the librarian, let it also be said that the library is not the place to "dump" a class while the teacher goes for a cup of coffee. Who knows the interests of those children better than the classroom teacher? That teacher should be there, guiding, encouraging, and helping, whether or not there is a librarian present.

Finally, most school librarians these days encourage teachers to take twenty-five or thirty books to the classroom and keep them until the group is ready for another collection. Most public libraries also allow teachers to check out classroom collections on their library cards. Hence, there is really no excuse for not having the books readily accessible for youngsters, and—if teachers will only make their wishes known to administrators and other faculty—more can be done. In one school, teachers were using extra work-books in self-defense to keep youngsters occupied while they worked with a reading group. When they agreed on the greater value of library reading—if only they had the books!—an administrator present saw to it that available funds went to classroom library books instead of to more consumable materials.

Censorship

Schools have no right to spend tax money on books that can be considered little more than trash. Library books should be selected carefully, based on local evaluation or authoritative opinion. However, these days various social, ethnic, religious, or political groups often bring pressure to bear on the school to eliminate certain books. In some communities, a single book has been the spark setting off several years of turmoil and upheaval. Many of these attacks are not made by an individual but by organized groups, some nationwide and with considerable money behind them. Does your school district have procedures and an official position when a complaint is made about a book in your school? For example, many schools have adopted the position—or a similar one—stated in the American Library Association's "Library Bill of Rights":

> The American Library Association affirms that all libraries are forums for information and ideas, and that the following basic policies should guide their services.
> 1. Books and other library resources should be provided for the interest, information, and enlightenment of all people of the

community the library serves. Materials should not be excluded
because of origin, background, or views of those contributing to
their creation.

2. Libraries should provide materials and information presenting all
   points of view on current and historical issues. Materials should
   not be proscribed or removed because of partisan or doctrinal
   disapproval.

3. Libraries should challenge censorship in fulfillment of their
   responsibility to provide information and enlightenment.

4. Libraries should cooperate with all persons and groups concerned
   with resisting abridgment of free expression and free access to
   ideas.

(Reprinted by permission of the American Library Association from
the Library Bill of Rights, adopted June 18, 1948; amended February
2, 1961, June 27, 1967, and January 23, 1980, by the ALA Council.)

As you see, this statement affirms the rights of all to information, rights
that may not be abridged by any group or individual. However, even if your
school district officially adopts such a position, it must go further. It must have
a materials evaluation committee and procedures, in writing and approved by
the board of education, that enable maintenance of this position. Such
procedures should spell out who is responsible for the selection of materials,
criteria and methods used in selection, and action to be taken with anyone who
objects to any of the materials selected. Of course, such procedures for
handling objections must be made known to all staff.

Following is a brief outline of the procedures used in some school
districts:

Initial Complaint

Various schools handle the details differently, but most have information
for teachers about dealing with objections. That information may include
directions such as the following:

1. Be courteous and demonstrate shared concern for the welfare of the
   child.

2. Do not immediately become defensive about the book. Inform the
   person complaining that it was selected carefully and that it will be
   reexamined.

3. Notify your principal.

4. Set a date or have the principal set a date for a conference with the
   person lodging the complaint.

Follow-up

The teacher and principal should reexamine the book as well as check on
reviews or other professional opinions about the material in question. At the

subsequent parent conference, the findings will be shared. If the complainant will not accept the findings, that person should be invited to submit a formal request for reconsideration of the material so procedures for the formal complaint can be initiated.

Formal Complaint

For this phase, additional steps must be clearly established, such as:

1. The complainant will be provided with a form for written complaints (Figure 9-1 is an example) and invited to submit it for consideration.

2. The superintendent will be informed.

3. Materials objected to should be temporarily withdrawn, pending a decision of the School Materials Evaluation Committee.

4. The School Materials Evaluation Committee must conduct a thorough and objective evaluation of the objectionable material, including its possible merits, faults, other reviews, and so on, concluding with a written report of its findings and recommendations to the superintendent.

5. The complainant will be notified of the decision and that decision will be implemented.

In any school, ultimate responsibility for a decision may be retained by the board of education or it may be delegated by them to the committee. Of course, this too should be carefully defined in writing, but regardless of the statement, authority and final responsibility rests with the legally elected members of the board of education.

Figure 9-1 represents a sample of a formal request for reconsideration of material, adapted from forms recommended by the American Library Association and the National Council of Teachers of English (National Council of Teachers of English, 1978). The procedure is not designed to intimidate anyone or to hinder any legitimate complaint but is offered as a protection against the selfish interests of an individual or group who would attack material used in the school. Usually schools that have such written procedures and adhere to them find little difficulty with the self-appointed censors.

IDEAS FOR USING LIBRARY READING

While selection and accessibility, as well as time to read books, are essential to the conduct of a good library reading program, they are not enough. Just as you or I can enjoy reading a book, we appreciate it that much more if we

Figure 9-1

Author: _____Book: _____Periodical: _____Other: _____

Title: _____Publisher: _____

Request initiated by: _____

Address: _____City: _____State: _____Zip: _____Telephone: _____

Do you represent yourself: _____An organization/group(name): _____

1. What do you object to in the work? (Please be specific. Cite pages.)

_____

2. What do you feel might be the result of exposure to this work? __

_____

3. Is there anything good about the work? _____

4. For what age group would you recommend it? _____

5. What do you think is the theme of this work? _____

_____

6. Did you read (view or hear) the entire work?_____ What parts?_____

_____

7. Are you aware of judgments of this work by literary or other critics?
(Specify):_____

8. What would you like the school to do about this work?

_____ Do not assign/lend it to my child.

_____ Return it to the Selection Committee for reevaluation.

_____ Other: Explain:_____

9. In its place, what work of equal literary quality and subject treatment
would you recommend? _____

Signature of complainant:_____ Date:_____

Source: Robert L. Hillerich, *The Principal's Guide to Improving Reading Instruction.* Copyright © 1983 by Allyn and Bacon, Inc. Reprinted with permission.

can share it with someone. So, too, children need opportunities to do something with the reading they engage in:

1. Books must be promoted so that youngsters become more aware of the exciting world of children's books.
2. Students must see that they are making progress in reading.
3. They must be able to share with each other about that reading through creative activities.
4. They must have ample opportunity to share through discussing and through writing.

The following sections deal separately with each of these elements of the independent reading program. This is not to imply, however, that the elements are completely discrete; they are all interrelated and contribute to each other. Activities are not organized by age or grade because most of them can be adapted to almost any level.

Developing Awareness of Books

The first step in helping make youngsters more aware of good books is to be certain that those books are around all the time. A second step, reading to children, is an essential part of every day's activity. A third effort in many classrooms is the use of Sustained Silent Reading (SSR).

Following are some additional ideas that can be used or adapted to help stimulate youngsters to become more aware of the fun of children's books. Of course, the many additional suggestions for sharing about the books in the remaining sections of this chapter are also contributors to this awareness of books.

1. You can "sell" good books to your youngsters. Every time you bring a new collection of books into the classroom from the central library, you have a perfect opportunity to say a few words about each book as you hold it up. You'll find some takers in the process.

2. Specific selling can be done by calling individual children's attention to a book on their favorite subject.

3. Youngsters can become reviewers for the class. When a new collection of books is brought into class, ask each child to take one book home for a quick review the next day. Based on these cursory examinations, the class can decide which books to keep in the class collection and which to exchange immediately for more appropriate titles. In the process, of course, some are going to get hooked on their book.

4. Newspaper or magazine articles about children's books, authors, or illustrators should be called to your pupils' attention.

5. You can promote movies or television shows based on or about children's books.

6. A different book button, made from a miniature book jacket, can be worn each day by the principal or teacher. Any child who can demonstrate having read that book gets the button.

7. Poor readers in intermediate and junior high will read primary books if you can find ways to remove the stigma. Ask how they would like to look at some first grade books to see what those books look like to them now that they are grown up. You might also have them read or retell stories to kindergarten or first grade youngsters.

8. Book fairs and exhibits of books within the school are good ways to promote library reading. Classes are usually scheduled to visit and browse. Such affairs also present excellent opportunities for older pupils to become reviewers for lower grades. Perhaps fourth grade can be reviewers each year, with the better readers reviewing upper grade books for those classes and the less able readers reviewing for lower grades.

9. You can present a book "joke wall." Construct a wall-like board with doors. Children behind the wall will open a door and say a riddle relating to a book. Others must guess what book is being referred to.

10. A paperback flea market can be held where students bring their old paperbacks for sale or barter. Some schools require a 3" X 5" card containing evaluative comments on the book as a "ticket of admission."

11. Having authors talk about writing or about their books is a certain means of motivating interest in the books.

12. Storytelling or reading-to sessions by teachers or the school librarian are excellent ways of motivating and encouraging reading of the books discussed, whether an entire book or only a part is read.

13. Chalk talks by authors or librarians are always fun.

14. Younger children might enjoy having a grab bag filled with all kinds of little toys, trinkets, and gadgets. One child will pull out an object and others will tell what story it reminds them of and why. This technique can also be used by the teacher, with selected objects, to decide what story should be read to the group.

15. Listening to radio or TV reviews or commentaries about children's books can help youngsters become more aware of such books and of their importance.

16. A library corner—complete with displays, a rug or other inviting seating, and lots of books—is essential in any classroom.

17. You can have students play "What's My Name?" The name of a book character is pinned to the back of each player. Players must discover their identities by asking "yes" or "no" questions.

18. Matching characters and books can make students more aware of the world of books. Write names of characters on numbered slips, the names of books on unnumbered slips. Give each pupil several of each. The child with character number 1 calls out the name, and the first child who holds up the appropriate book title for that character gets the character slip. The player with the most character slips wins the game.

19. Taped reactions to a book might be kept in the library corner along with that book. Anyone interested in knowing something about the book may turn on the tape recorder.

20. Book "Rummy" or "Fish" might be played by any number of students. Make, or have pupils make, playing cards, each with one of three major elements from a book they have read (title or plot, character, author or setting). A "spread" consists of one card from each of the categories of a given book. A variation might use two cards to a set, with the game consisting of a match between a character and that character's description. Another simple variation is merely to "spread" a set of cards with each of the elements, regardless of the books they were from. Then youngsters might try to identify which books each element was found in.

21. Book bingo may be played with characters, authors, and/or titles. "Call" one of the three elements not on the bingo cards, and players must mark—by association—the appropriate item on their cards. For example, you may have character names on the bingo cards and call book titles. When you pick *Call It Courage,* pupils who have Mafatu on their cards should cover that name.

22. Favorite poems brought to class and read by pupils (after appropriate preparation) stimulate further reading of poetry.

23. A Book-of-the-Week or Book-of-the-Month contest also promotes discussion. Children may compete to "sell" the group their book as the best. They may also become involved in nominating new books for their own "Newbery" or "Caldecott" award.

24. Contests are sometimes held where pupils collect the names of all their classmates who have read their book and agree it should be the Book-of-the-Month.

25. Dust jackets from the library might be posted on the bulletin board to advertise some of the new books in school.

26. Newspaper or magazine articles about children's authors or books should be brought to class, posted on the bulletin board, and discussed. Encourage youngsters to be alert for such materials.

27. You can visit the library—school and public—with the class regularly, allowing adequate time for browsing and for you and youngsters to assist classmates in identifying and selecting good books.

28. You can invite the librarian to visit the class to talk about some of the new books that they might be interested in. In many communities, the public librarian would be pleased to be invited to visit a class.

29. A pantomime of a major segment of a book might lead others to want to read that book.

30. Pictures may be collected that have nothing to do with children's books but could have. You can begin the collection, and soon students of all ages will join in to challenge their classmates. Others are to guess what book the picture "could have been from." For example, on the front page of a newspaper, there was a picture of bull sitting under a tree—obviously a possible illustration from *The Story of Ferdinand*.

31. Headlines also make good attention getters. You can begin this activity by putting on the bulletin board or chalkboard a headline that could refer to a book. For example, "Trio Takes Trip through Time" or "Chief Cheese Taster in Danger" might refer to an intermediate and a primary book respectively that youngsters ought to know and be able to guess the titles.

32. "Who Am I?" envelopes can be placed on the bulletin board. Inside each envelope are slips of paper, each with a sentence or two giving clues to a book or character. Youngsters are to guess who is referred to, for example, "I'm an elephant who's faithful one hundred percent." (Naturally, it's Horton, from *Horton Hatches a Who*.)

33. "What Am I?" envelopes can be produced and used in the same manner.

34. Information about favorite authors may be presented to the class, either by the teacher or by other students. Good sources of such information include book jacket blurbs as well as *The Junior Book of Authors*, edited by Kunitz and Haycraft, and *More Junior Authors*, edited by Fuller.

35. You can decorate the bulletin board with appropriate pictures for book incidents: pictures of people laughing for funny incidents; people crying for sad incidents; horses for horse stories, and so on.

36. Sound filmstrips and films of award-winning books are available for purchase or rental from Weston Woods (Weston, CT 06880) and serve as good motivation for reading those books.

37. Rebus titles can be put on the bulletin board for children to guess the books they represent. Eventually pupils will begin making their own rebus titles for others to guess. Figure 9-2 gives three examples.

38. Acting out the behavior of familiar characters is another method of keeping youngsters aware of books. One student will perform while others try to guess the character being depicted.

39. The game of charades is an additional means for children to act out book titles or characters and to have others guess what they are referring to.

40. "Name That Character" may be played, where a leader begins by naming a character from a book. The next person must name a second book character whose name begins with the last letter of the name of the first mentioned character, and so on.

41. Oral reading of a portion of a book can increase motivation. A student (or the teacher) might read the funniest part, the most exciting part, the first chapter, and so on.

42. "Who would you most like to be?" Another way to acquaint children with books and characters is to have a youngster tell what character he or she would most like to be and why.

43. A class chart of favorite books should be posted in the room and constantly added to as children decide on another book they like as a favorite. Incidentally, research evidence suggests that the most important recommendation to young children is a recommendation from peers or the teacher.

44. You can have a book parade, where each student dresses up as a book or book character to represent a favorite book. "Books" may even be organized into sections according to subject matter, as in the library.

45. You can involve students in making suggestions for book purchases in the library.

46. Books that *you* read during SSR or that you merely have lying on your desk will arouse curiosity. This is one of your best advertising devices.

Figure 9-2

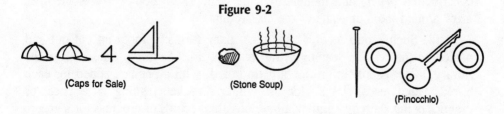

(Caps for Sale)   (Stone Soup)   (Pinocchio)

47. You can poll the class or have students poll other classes to determine favorite books and authors. Keep the results posted for all to use.

48. A "Books I'd Like to Read" section of the bulletin board also aids book promotion. Students can add their choices for all to see. You might even want them to justify any addition they make to the list.

49. Miniature book clubs can be formed in the class. Each "club" may consist of six to eight students who elect a chairperson. That chairperson selects a collection of books, makes a routing sheet, and has each member take a book for quick evaluation. Any member who doesn't like a book simply passes it on to another and waits for the next book to be passed.

50. Once each year, invite the public librarian to come to school for a day. Any students who do not have library cards can be excused to go see the librarian in order to make out an application for their own card.

51. Magazines are important too. Have students do a survey of the school and public library to see how many different magazines are available to them. Each student might select a different magazine to review for the class. They might be amazed at the number of good magazines they are missing.

Recording Progress

Since it is important for children to see that they are making progress when they start to read, there is certainly justification, especially at the early levels, for extrinsic kinds of records and motivation. The point is, however, these records should be noncompetitive. There is no excuse for making charts where children get stars for books read. Under such conditions, the child who is a good reader gets many stars easily, while the poor reader, who needs encouragement, gives up and withdraws from the competition entirely. All records should be noncompetitive unless only equals are competing.

Following are some examples of motivating activities that can result in a sense of accomplishment:

1. Bookworms are often used as group records of accomplishment. In this case, a circular "head" is made for a bookworm, and every time anyone reads a book, the name of that book is put on another segment (circular piece of construction paper) and mounted on the wall. These bookworms sometimes grow around the four walls of the classroom.

2. Such group records may take many forms: a footprint cut out and pasted on the ceiling, leaving a trail of book titles from the classroom to the library; a large sailboat on the bulletin board, with a pennant added for each book anyone reads; "nuts" for the winter; "rockets" going into space; or dragons being slain by knights; all are possible records of progress for a group.

3. A "Bookthing" is the most unusual record I've seen. Some second graders, completely on their own, decided they did not want a bookworm or any of the conventional records for books read. Instead, they decided on a bookthing. This was nothing more than a shapeless mass of all kinds of paper, hanging on the wall. Every time one of them read a book, another hunk of paper was added to the bookthing.

4. Personal card files or charts might be kept by each child.

5. Keeping a personal scrapbook might appeal to some. With one page for each book read, the pupil might write a few words or draw to illustrate important points about the book.

6. A simple listing of "Books I've Read," in the form of a little booklet, can serve as an individual's proof of progress throughout the year.

7. A permanent bingo card might be kept, where each column is a category: horses, biography, science fiction, sports, and so on. The pupil will color in a square when a book of that type is read. (Note: I don't believe it is a good idea to force a "balanced diet" of reading on children. The major concern is to keep them reading. However, if they choose their own four or five categories, most likely the choices will be favorites of theirs.)

8. A collection of "books" can serve as a more elaborate record of progress for individuals. Prepare empty matchbook covers by pasting a plain white paper over the outside of the cover. Every time a child reads a book, the title of that book is printed on the spine of a matchbook, and the child adds this "book" to his or her collection. Even some sixth graders get excited about seeing such a "bookshelf" grow.

9. Teachers who work on a one-to-one or small group basis can more easily tailor records to the desires or interests of those with whom they work. I recall a third grader in the reading clinic who was wildly enthusiastic about Snoopy in the "Peanuts" cartoons. His record of progress was his own drawing of Snoopy sitting on the doghouse, complete with goggles, scarf, and machine gun. Every time this youngster read a book, he added one of the Red Baron's planes going down in flames around Snoopy.

Sharing Through Creative Activities

While language activities, talking and writing, are much more valuable, construction and graphic art projects are certainly legitimate methods of sharing books children have read and enjoyed.

1. Youngsters may prepare displays of characters or important objects from their books. These may be made from clay, sawdust and paste, Styrofoam, soap, balsa wood, wire, papier mâché, or merely from paper.

2. Collections or scrapbooks may be developed, relating to books or subjects that each pupil is interested in.

3. A cutout of favorite characters can form a bulletin board display entitled "Friends from Books."

4. Book jackets may be designed to illustrate a favorite book.

5. Even first graders can make "Wanted Posters" for characters, indicating what the character is wanted for.

6. Original illustrations might be created for a book read.

7. Life-size characters can be drawn on mural paper and used to decorate the walls or halls in a school.

8. Book posters, illustrating books read, make interesting bulletin board or hall displays.

9. A map of a favorite character's travels might be of interest to some youngsters. Others might like to make a travel poster based on sites in the book.

10. Bookmarks can be made to illustrate a favorite part of a story or a favorite character.

11. Dioramas may be made depicting favorite scenes from books.

12. Shadow boxes or "peep shows" may be made from shoe boxes as another means of sharing about books.

13. A shoe box may be painted or decorated to look like a book, with scenes from the story inside.

14. Students can do a comic strip summary of a book read.

15. Some youngsters might like to do a cartoon of the funniest part from a humorous book.

16. A TV show or movie can also be made from a large box. Cut out one side to form the "screen." The movie or strip can be wound around broom handles and run through the screen.

17. You can make a scribble mural. On a large sheet of paper, make a scribble outline with heavy black crayon or paint. Each child may choose a space and illustrate some incident from a book read.

18. A quite different kind of mural can be created on the bulletin board. Have pupils add their own individual cutout characters as they finish a book. As each character is added, the pupil explains how that character fits into the mural.

19. Children may make elaborate drawings or paintings of "the best part" of a favorite book.

20. Pupils may dress dolls or clay figures as characters from books.

21. The youngsters themselves may dress up as favorite characters to put on a pageant or tell about a book they have read. A large frame might be made to set up a tableau.

22. Paper bag masks might be made of favorite characters and worn by pupils.

23. Mobiles can be made of characters or objects from books.

24. "A Line of Good Books" can be made by stringing a cord and using clothespins to hang paper "cloths" about books or characters.

25. Youngsters can find magazine pictures to illustrate the story they have read. They may even like to keep a scrapbook of such pictures from a variety of books they might read.

26. Some students might enjoy making a photo album that could have belonged to one of the characters in the book they read.

27. Felt-board demonstrations may be used by some children to tell others about a book they have read.

28. Collections made from "How-to" books may be brought to class and displayed. These may include rocks, leaves, stamps, insects, and so on. Similarly, collections assembled or objects constructed from such books may be displayed.

29. Sectioned bulletin boards may be established for children to complete: "favorite make-believe people," "favorite heroes," "favorite cats," and so on.

30. Pupils might enjoy making a storyboard of a favorite book. To do so, they would need to visualize key passages from the book. (Information on storyboards is available from the Eastman Kodak Audiovisual Department.)

31. Large silhouettes may be made of characters, each with a few descriptive sentences about that character.

Sharing Through Talking

Youngsters should be encouraged to talk about books, authors, and characters. In so doing, they not only increase their own enjoyment of books, but they also motivate others to read the books and, in the process, increase their own language development.

1. In talking (or writing) about their books, youngsters may give a straightforward summary or reaction, or they may tell about a humorous (exciting, sad, serious) part. They may also select a particularly appealing paragraph for oral reading to the group.

2. Conferences with the teacher about books read are an essential element in the library reading program. Their value was clearly demonstrated

through studies of Individualized Reading. This conference should not be a quiz session; it is not an effort by the teacher to find out if the child read all the words or even all the sentences or chapters. Rather, it is an opportunity for mutual sharing about the book and for the teacher to show a personal interest in what the student likes.

3. Holding a trial for a character or characters in a book is another way to get the group to react and to talk about the characters. The trial may be held to hear arguments: Is the character innocent or guilty of the charges placed? Of course, the trial may also be held for the book: Should it have been published or not?

4. You can let youngsters use the school public address system to present a radio broadcast. This may be a discussion between a "character" and the "author," two "characters," or an interview with an "author" or "character." Even more fun is to have conversations between "characters" from different books.

5. Regular book reviews can be presented over the public address system to promote new books or old favorites.

6. Whether over the public address system or through personal appearances, a particular grade might be chosen that will do an annual review of Newbery and Caldecott winners, with better readers reviewing the Newbery books for upper grades while less capable readers review the Caldecott books for lower grades.

7. Reviews by older students may be presented to younger ones. Such activities are especially helpful for the slower reader, who can then read beginning-to-read books without stigma. Children will also find, even through middle school or high school, that those simple books can be fun to read.

8. The class may be broken into groups of five or six to form book clubs. Such clubs may prepare skits about books, tell about them, do oral reading, or—in any other manner they choose—promote book reading among other classes in the school. This is often an effective method for getting reluctant readers involved.

9. Radio shows can be presented within the classroom, using a tin can "microphone" or the tape recorder.

10. Panel discussions about books can be held. As early as fourth grade, students can hold panel discussions even though no two members of the group have read the same book. They can still discuss and compare their readings in terms of the problems faced by major characters and how these problems were resolved: through magic, intrinsic character qualities, accident, and so on.

11. Similar discussions may be held dealing with books on a common theme: horses, science fiction, space, famous people, or even famous mice.

12. Instead of having one child tell about a book, break the class into small discussion groups so that more may be talking at once. You might even have each group select one person whose story is so important the whole class should hear about it.

13. As worthwhile "homework," have older students read a book to a younger child and report to the class on that child's reaction to the story.

14. As a means of motivating more reading as well as sharing, play "Stump the Experts" or "Trivial Pursuit." Individual students may raise questions about books, characters, or authors for others to answer. (In order to keep this reasonable, questions should be limited to books that have been in the classroom collection.)

15. Students may tell why they believe a particular person in the class would enjoy reading their book.

16. You can hold debates, where class members discuss why certain books should or should not be read by everyone. As a variation, you might like to hold a Book-of-the-Week (Month) contest, where individuals try to persuade their classmates that the book they have read should be selected.

17. You can play a musical selection and have students describe a scene from a book for which the music would be an appropriate sound track. Of course, musical accompaniment may also add something to storytelling.

18. Younger children might like to dress as book characters and tell what that character did in the story. Several members of the class may participate to form a scene or chapter from the book.

19. Older students may have an "author's party," where they dress in the costumes of their author's day. Each of these author's may react with the others in terms of their books, times, and so on.

20. Youngsters may also pretend to be the book. Dressed in a box with appropriate illustrations, they may speak for the book, not hesitating to brag a little as they tell of the joy and sorrow, adventure and humor that lie within, or what struggles and efforts the author experienced in order to create them.

21. Pantomimes are also appealing. The rest of the group may try to guess the book or character being pantomimed.

22. Puppet shows may be used to dramatize. Puppets can be made from a piece of clay on the end of a pencil, a handkerchief over the hand, or a paper sack.

23. If several students in the class have read the same book, they may want to get together and dramatize it for the class.

24. You can have youngsters show a book jacket or important illustrations on the opaque projector while telling about the book.

25. The overhead projector is ideal for dramatizations. In this case, provide students with clear transparency plastic on which they may draw and color the characters and backdrops. Then the characters may be cut out and taped on a cotton swab stick. When the story is dramatized with the projector, children see full-size characters in action on the screen.

26. You can present a "Man on the Street" TV show. Use a box or wooden frame large enough for two heads. An "interviewer" can ask different children questions about characters, authors, or books. Of course, the story itself can be dramatized over the "TV."

27. Greater depth of character interpretation can be accomplished by older students. A student may play the part of a character who feels maligned or unfairly represented in the story. Similarly, youngsters may take the role of a minor character and describe the main character as seen through another's eyes. Also, students may pretend to be a character and tell what they would do in a given situation.

28. "Meet the Critics." One student, as author, must defend the book—characters, plot, theme—against class members who serve as critics. (This is especially interesting when some class members truly love, and others hate, a book.)

29. Pupils who read biographies might like to hold "Recognition Day" ceremonies for the biographee, complete with speeches and presentations.

30. Comparisons of characters can be enjoyable. Youngsters might like to compare boys they have read about, such as Homer Price and Henry Huggins, girls they have read about, or even mice they know.

31. In this same vein, books may be compared that deal with similar themes or topics, for example, books about courage, such as *Call It Courage, Li Lun, Lad of Courage,* or *The Matchlock Gun.*

32. You can play "Twenty Questions." Form two teams for competition. Team members take turns trying to guess a book or character by asking questions that are to be answered only "yes" or "no." The team getting the answer in the fewest questions wins the contest.

33. Books can be promoted as a TV program in the format of "I've Got a Secret." The panel of experts must ask questions to discover what book is being reviewed.

34. Simple interviews may be held, similar to "Twenty Questions," where participants attempt to guess who the "character" is by asking questions that may be answered only with a "yes" or "no."

35. After reading a book up to a crucial point, have students suggest endings for the story.

36. Authors are also important. Especially by middle grades and above, youngsters should have information about authors and should engage in discussion and comparisons of authors and their works. If possible, invite an author who relates well to children to come visit your class.

37. A first grade buddy system is another way to encourage those first steps in reading. Pair children and let each pair find a nook where they can take turns reading to each other from books at their independent reading level.

38. School magazines afford a wealth of material that can serve as springboards for lively class discussions. You might have students bring in their favorite magazines for discussion and sharing.

39. Tape recordings may be made by pupils of their reactions to the book. Some teachers have found it motivating to keep the tape recorder and the taped reaction on a table with the book so that others can look at the book and hear what a classmate said about it.

40. Chalk talks or flannel board presentations may be made to the class or to other classes.

41. Some youngsters might like to prepare a monologue from their book.

42. Reports may be made where the reporter tells the plot up to the point of climax. Then pupils who have not read the book decide on a good ending for the book. The reporter may then complete the report or may leave it to classmates to discover how the book was concluded.

43. The overhead projector may be used to show a map of the character's travels, which may be traced while the book is being presented to the class.

44. Pupils may present a slide show by making "slides" of transparencies that can then be shown in series on the overhead.

45. "How-to" books can be shared with a demonstration of one of the activities explained in the book. If appropriate, a sample trick, experiment, or construction may be taught to the class.

46. Pretending to be a character, youngsters may tell what they would do in a given situation if they were the character under discussion.

47. Crystal-ball gazing can be fun. In this case, the reporter will sit before the crystal ball and begin giving clues about a book such as "I see a mouse half asleep in the sun...His brothers and sisters are busy gathering food for the winter...Another day, and he still seems to be daydreaming while they work." Others in the class should be able to guess the ball-gazer is seeing Frederick.

48. "The character I liked/disliked most" is always a good topic for youngsters to share with the group.

49. "The same thing happened to me!" In this case, youngsters may tell of something that happened to them that reminds them of a character or situation in the book they've read.

50. If a travel book has been read, pupils may give an illustrated lecture, using postcards, photos, or still pictures from magazines.

Sharing Through Writing

Thus far, no mention has been made of the official "book report," and no mention should be made except to say that formal book reports are probably the best method ever invented by teachers to discourage children from reading library books. Yet children can—and should—have an enjoyable time writing about books they have read. In some cases, they will approximate the kind of experience they would be getting in the distasteful required book report.

1. A file may be kept on favorite books. Youngsters may report on index cards the author and title of a book they have read, as well as whether or not they recommend the book and why. This file can then be used by others in the class who might want to check on a particular book or discover what one they might like to read next.

2. A cumulative folder may be kept on favorite books, wherein each child may add his or her personal comment about that book for others in the group to read.

3. A class booklet of favorite books may be compiled. In this case, each child is allowed to write a brief summary and reaction to a favorite book. These are compiled into a class folder, with one page for each child. At anytime during the year, a child may change the original page for a more preferred book, but no one will be required to write more than one during the year or allowed to have more than one page in the book at a given time.

4. New endings for favorite books or new adventures for favorite characters may be written. Conversely, youngsters might also create a new character for some favorite action.

5. Headlines and "Who Am I?" riddles, as suggested in the previous section, might be used as teasers and motivators of interest.

6. On-the-spot reporting is an interesting way to write about books read. Students will write a news item about a book as if they were reporters who were there at the time the events actually occurred in their hometown. Entire class newspapers have been made up of such "news items."

7. Pupils might write a publisher's description of the book, or merely an advertising blurb.

8. Pupils may write a lost-and-found ad for a character or object.

9. You can have youngsters make comparisons, for example, two books on a similar theme, different versions of the same story or fairy tale, or two characters from different stories.

10. Comparisons of factual books, such as biographies, may also be made to identify author bias or differences in the information presented.

11. Comparisons can be made of the artwork in different books, pointing out how the illustrations fit the type of story, the artist's use of color, and so on.

12. Pupils might like to tell how events in a book are similar to or different from what they experience in their own lives.

13. Vocabulary development is enhanced by encouraging youngsters to keep a log of new, interesting, or unusual words and expressions they discover in the process of their reading. These may be shared periodically or may be placed in a section reserved on the bulletin board.

14. Some students might even like to compile a dictionary of interesting words from library books.

15. Time lines may be kept, by the group or by individuals, to record events from factual books or to record publication dates, authors' lives, and so on, as a means of interrelating events or people.

16. Letters may be written to the librarian in appreciation for certain books or as requests for the purchase of other titles.

17. A lettter might also be written to a friend or classmate recommending a favorite book.

18. Some might enjoy writing to a character in the book, making a complaint, a suggestion, or asking a question.

19. Students may also write letters between characters. What might Paul Bunyan say to Pecos Bill, or Frederick to Anatole? Some may prefer to write their own letter to a book character, discussing some action or event in the story.

20. You can have pupils write a letter to an author telling why they liked that author's book. If letters are mailed in care of the publisher, pupils can usually expect a response of some sort.

21. You can have youngsters use a familiar song to write a parody of a book read. They may also write parodies of poems or fairy tales: "Goldie Bear and the Three Locks."

22. Analogous stories may be written in the manner of types of stories read, whether tall tales, limericks, or "Just-So" stories.

23. Let pupils tell about a book through poetry, or write poems in response to those listened to or read. For example, *Hailstones and Halibut Bones* by Mary O'Neill may lead to writing poems about color.

24. After reading a biography, the student may write about an imaginary visit with the biographee when they were both the same age.

25. You can have youngsters advertise a book by writing a magazine ad or a radio or TV commercial to "sell" a favorite book.

26. You can have students write a poem about the book they have read.

27. After deciding who the narrator is, students may rewrite one scene in the book from the point of view of another character.

28. Ten or fifteen interesting words may be listed from the book and the pupil may tell why they were chosen.

29. An original reference booklet may be developed by a youngster who reads a nonfiction book.

30. Scrapbooks may be constructed by some pupils, perhaps of favorite poems, jokes, riddles, or even interesting paragraphs of a certain type. Of course, there should be opportunity to share these.

31. Children who have read the same book may collaborate on a set of questions (inferential, not literal) that they believe anyone who has read the book should be able to answer. The questions may be used to interview others who have read the book.

32. Those interested in dramatics might like to write and produce an original play about a book or about the joy of books.

33. You or your students may develop annotated booklists for the benefit of others in the class.

34. Brief biographies may be prepared about favorite authors. In fact, the class might like to prepare a booklet, complete with illustrations, about favorite writers, including information on their works.

35. Character booklets may be compiled to include favorite types such as "Gallant Girls," "Clever Cats," "Dynamic Dogs," or even "Mighty Mice."

36. A category game may be played by the group. Provide each child with a paper divided into columns, as indicated below. Whoever can write in the most items wins. The game can be modified and become a little more difficult by using a word or the alphabet vertically as indicated at the left. Then every entry in the row must begin with the letter indicated at the left of that row. (See Figure 9-3.)

37. Based on their reading about authors or characters, youngsters might like to develop a factual (or fictional) "Who's Who."

38. Students may write articles for the local newspaper or the school newspaper about the library program or its services.

Figure 9-3

	Animal	Person	Poetry	Fairy Tale
L				
A				
K				
E				

39. A large piece of chart paper, cut in the shape of a thumbnail, may be posted on the bulletin board as the basis for pupils' "thumbnail sketches" of characters, authors, or books.

40. This same type of bulletin board activity can produce sections devoted to "suspense," "action," "laughter," and so on.

41. You can have pupils invite a character to dinner and explain the invitation to their mothers.

42. Students may develop five interview questions to ask the main character in their book.

43. Students can pretend they are casting a film for their book. What actress would they choose for the leading female character? What actor should play the male character?

44. Students may pretend to be the author and explain why they chose the particular title for the book, what part was most interesting to write, and so on.

45. Students can collect outstanding paragraphs of a particular type. During one period they may be looking for outstanding examples of character description, at another time, mood, action, scene, and so on. These paragraphs can be shared and can serve as an excellent basis for discussion of the ways in which an author can handle writing problems, as well as a source for teaching pupils about their own writing.

46. Youngsters who read books about codes might like to write about that book in the secret code of the book.

47. Pupils may write a joke or riddle about the book to share with the class.

48. Older students might like it interpret the setting and plot of their book in terms of life today in their own town. You might assist here by discussing how this was done with "West Side Story."

49. Have older students suggest how a story or character made an impression on them or gave them greater understanding of their world.

50. What would be the reaction of a space traveler in the year 3001 who finds your book in a time capsule?

51. Pupils may write a rebus of an incident from their book

52. Students can use magazines or catalogs to collect pictures of people, animals, locations, or objects that relate to those read about. They might develop a booklet of these items along with brief captions or descriptions telling how they relate to the book.

53. A regular column should be reserved in the school newspaper or magazine for articles about library books.

54. To develop or illustrate their understanding of major characters, pupils might write what that character would like for a birthday present, where he or she would most like to vacation, like for dinner, and so on. They might even find newspaper or magazine articles that the character would enjoy reading and tell why they believe this is so.

55. Youngsters might like to explain why they believe the reward or punishment of the major character was justified.

56. Students may write an explanation of what the main character would be least likely to do and why they believe this.

57. In considering the characters in their book, students may write how and why a particular character might have changed in the course of the book.

58. Pupils can write about why they would or would not like a particular character to live next door to them, or why they would or would not like this character as a friend. In this same vein, they may write what character they would like to take a vacation with, what they would do, and why they would choose that particular character.

59. You can place a collection of twenty or so library books on a table. After a pupil has read a book, that youngster is to make up five questions (inferential, not literal), put them on a 3" × 5" card, and put it in a file. After several youngsters have read the same book, they can form a panel and use the questions as the basis for a discussion.

60. Students may pretend to visit the character when that person was their age and then explain what happened.

61. Youngsters may write one-line captions under favorite books at the library.

62. Writing a movie script for an action story is a good way to give youngsters practice in arranging events in sequence.

63. "Telegram" (condensed) book reports may be a helpful method for getting pupils to make brief summaries.

64. In the pattern of some biographies they have read, pupils might like to make a biographical dictionary of characters they know from books.

65. Older students might like to rewrite their story, or an event from it, as a picture book, using a simple vocabulary, so younger children can enjoy it.

66. Anyone who reads a factual book about space might like to write a science fiction story using the information gleaned from the factual material.

67. Using vocabulary from the book, some students might like to make a crossword puzzle for others to attempt.

68. Students who have seen a movie based on a book might like to read the book and make a comparison. Such activities can range in difficulty from *Charlotte's Web* to *Gone With the Wind*.

Chapter 10

Recognizing and Adjusting to Individual Differences

This chapter will review some of the major points about individual differences and how we can recognize and accommodate them. The most important point is that while we give lip service to the existence of individual differences, in practice we sometimes act as if they don't exist. For example, to say of a child, "She is a second grader" is no more descriptive than to say, "She is a female." The latter says nothing about the individual except her physiological makeup; it doesn't even indicate the length of her hair. Likewise, saying, "She is a second grader" indicates nothing more than that the child is roughly seven to eight years old.

THE RANGE OF DIFFERENCES

Children vary in their reading levels just as all individuals vary in their achievements in any activity. The differences are more than merely differences in measured IQ. They have to do with some of the points mentioned in connection with language development in Chapter 3, as well as with differences in aptitude and interest, instructional methods and materials, time on task, and with many factors we have not yet identified or understood. We do, however, know that these differences exist, and we should expect and respect them.

When educators talk about "reading levels," do they know whereof they speak? About ten years ago, the Silberbergs (1977) found they did not. In fact, on a multiple choice question, only 22 percent understood "grade level"—and, with only five choices, 20 percent should have known the correct answer by chance. Of course, I knew that lay people did not understand "grade level," but I had assumed educators did. That assumption was shaken when I saw a newspaper report that two reading teachers attempted to justify additional assistance in reading because, according to their recent standardized testing, 42 percent of students in the district were reading below grade level. Isn't that terrible? Of course not!

In the past year, I have asked this question of 2,210 educators, ranging from experienced teachers in graduate classes and reading councils to principals and administrators: "In a typical classroom—at any grade level— which of the following percentages comes closest to identifying the percent of children you would expect to be reading below grade level on a standardized test: 10, 30, 50, 70, or 90 percent?"

What is your response? While a little better than Silberbergs', my groups' average to only 36.7 percent with the correct answer. However, an additional group of principals who had been working on test score interpretation in their school district did better—66.7 percent of them knew the answer.

Obviously—but not so to too many educators—the answer is, by definition, *50 percent!* Grade level is an average, following the normal curve in a typical class; therefore approximately half the class is above and half below average. Grade level is not a floor, below which no one is supposed to sink.

Figure 10-1 shows a normal "bell" curve, with distributions in percentages by standard deviation, where—for all practical purposes—three standard

Figure 10-1

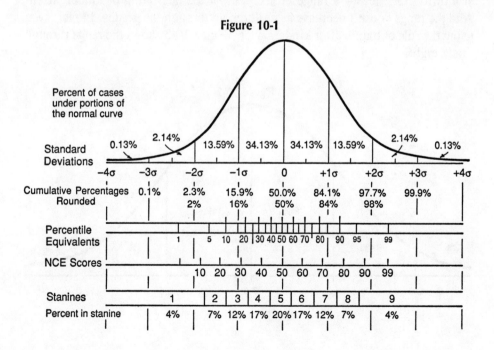

deviations above and three below the mean encompass a total population. Also shown on the figure are distributions for percentiles, NCE scores, and stanines.

The test manual for any standardized test will provide you with the standard deviation of that test. Use it to determine the range and percentages of youngsters you would find at different levels on the test. For example, a typical standard deviation on a reading test is a grade equivalent of 2.5. If you used such a test at the beginning of grade seven (7.0) and had a perfectly average class, you would find the distribution shown in Figure 10-2.

As shown in Figure 10-2, in a typical class at grade seven, 50 percent are above and 50 percent below grade level. If, by some magic, we could accomplish the public's desire and move the lower half of the curve into the top half, you know what would happen. Test publishers would re-norm the tests and we would be back to square one.

As also shown in the figure, 2 percent of the students tested are reading below grade two and 2 percent above grade twelve, a range of ten years. There has been a rule of thumb in the teaching of reading that the range of reading levels in any classroom is equal to at least the grade level plus one year: at grade 5 we would expect a range of (5+1) six years; at grade 3, (3+1) four years, and so on. I believe this range is an artifact of the tests themselves and grossly *underestimates* the range in any classroom.

Given the above rule of thumb, what is the range in a kindergarten: zero plus one? With 916 beginning kindergarten children, Hillerich (1978b) found a range from a few operating in oral language like two-year-olds to those reading at a third grade level—a range of six years at the beginning of kindergarten! And the range doesn't decrease as children go through the grades. In fact, even using the rule of thumb after kindergarten, Figure 10-3 shows the range through grade eight.

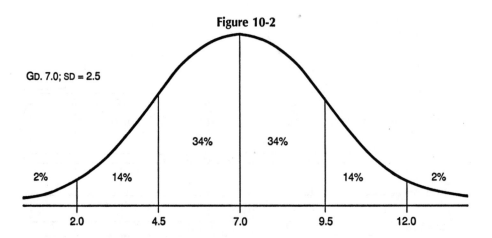

Figure 10-2

GD. 7.0; SD = 2.5

Notice in Figure 10-3, not only how the range increases but also how the slow learner falls further and further behind the average, while the faster learner moves further and further ahead. Hence, the higher the grade level, the greater the range. This increase in range can be clarified through the illustration in Figure 10-4, showing three children who have participated in one year of instruction in reading.

For the sake of the example, Figure 10-4 begins with the unreal assumption that all three children began first grade at exactly zero reading level, neither above nor below that zero point. Having had good average instruction for one year, Child A makes one year of progress in reading. Meanwhile, Child B, with the same good instruction plus extra help and working as hard as possible, gained half a year—and half a year was good progress for that child. Child C, with the same kind of instruction, but with a good background, interest, and aptitude, gained two years in the one year. At the end of the first year, the group has a range in reading levels of one and a half years. Extend this graph for a second year, and you will find a range of three years.

Figure 10-3

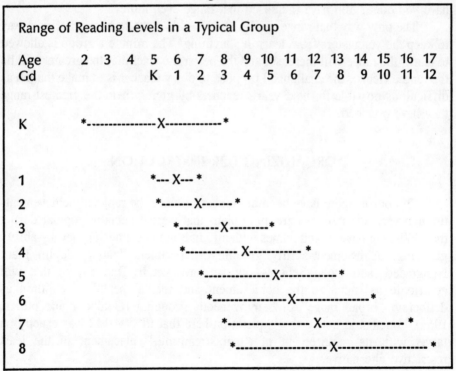

Range of Reading Levels in a Typical Group

Age	2	3	4	5	6	7	8	9	10	11	12	13	14	15	16	17
Gd				K	1	2	3	4	5	6	7	8	9	10	11	12

K   *---------------X-------------*

1   *--- X--- *

2   *-------- X------- *

3   *---------- X---------*

4   *------------ X------------ *

5   *--------------- X-------------- *

6   *----------------- X-----------------*

7   *------------------- X------------------- *

8   *---------------------- X--------------------- *

Figure 10-4

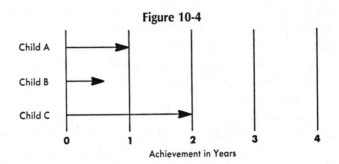

Child A

Child B

Child C

0   1   2   3   4

Achievement in Years

Figures 10-3 and 10-4 illustrate an often forgotten point: Not only do students differ in their placement at a given time, but they also differ in their *rate* of progress. One may gain two years per year while another gains half a year per year. Then why not, as critics have suggested, do a better job of teaching reading so that we won't have children below grade level? I'm certain we are all in favor of improving reading instruction, but that will not remove the differences. In fact, it will aggravate the problem. Suppose the teacher in Figure 10-4 did a superior job of teaching that year, so the children would learn at least 20 percent better. Add 20 percent to each child's achievement and what have you done? You have increased that range even more.

The only way that range can be contained is if the teacher can find a way to keep the youngsters from learning anything! The minute a group is allowed to learn, the range will increase, and the better the teaching, the greater will be the range. Hence, the challenge I propose to every teacher is to make the job as difficult as possible for next year's teachers by giving them the greatest range they have ever had.

ORGANIZING FOR INSTRUCTION

Of course, there have been attempts to reduce the range of achievements through various interclass grouping plans that were especially popular during the 1960s. We have played games with all kinds at the elementary level—ability grouping, achievement-ability grouping, departmentalization, Joplin Plan, Nongraded, and Open School—but we have yet to find a plan that will contribute as much to the achievement and mental health of children as deliberate "broad range" or heterogeneous grouping (Goldberg and others, 1966). You should notice the implication here that P.L. 94-142 was exactly on target with its requirement of "mainstreaming," placement in the least restrictive alternative.

Most efforts at special interclass grouping are not only a waste of time and energy, but they often hide differences that still remain by eliminating a few children who obviously deviate. We fool ourselves if we think we can "homogenize" children. We have known for decades that, even by grouping three classes "homogeneously" on the basis of their reading scores, we reduce the range only 5 to 10 percent (Wrightstone, 1957; Balow and Curtin, 1966; Clarke, 1958). Furthermore, some plans practically eliminate instructional time: Thurlow and others (1984) reported on 35 classes of second graders who had 120 minutes per day allocated for reading in a Joplin-type plan. The largest portion of their time was spent in transition, with the next largest on worksheets. In terms of behavior, of the 120 minutes, youngsters spent 8 minutes in silent reading, 2 in oral reading!

I still find no better statement on grouping than that made by Shane (1960): "An able teacher, given freedom to work creatively, is more important by far than any mechanical scheme, however ingenious."

Let's take a look at intraclass grouping—the grouping a teacher does with a collection of children within the classroom. Figure 10-5 shows a third grade class with its typical range in reading levels from first grade to beginning fifth grade. Also shown are the usual three reading groups—three only because most teachers know they can handle more than two groups, but four get unwieldy. Besides, the low group is not usually a group anyhow; it is a collection of four or five widely spread individuals.

Beginning teachers sometimes have a problem in management of their groups, usually because they seem to think that all pupils must "have reading" at the same time. Even though it is true that one group can be completing practice materials in reading and a second group reading silently while the teacher works with a third group, this is not necessary. It is here again that writing can play an important part as students who are not with the teacher work alone, in pairs, or in small groups on their written compositions. Independent groups may also be completing math practice materials, reading

Figure 10-5

Reading Level		Skill Needs
Low grade 5	⟶	
High grade 4	⟶	
Low grade 4	⟶	
High grade 3	⟶	
Low grade 3	⟶	
High grade 2	⟶	
Low grade 2	⟶	
High grade 1	⟶	

library books, writing, preparing to dramatize a play, or what have you, while a third group works with the teacher.

I see no problem with the "magic" three reading groups as a first step toward individualization under one *essential* condition: If all children in the group use the same book—and they usually do—that book must be no more difficult than the reading level of the poorest reader in the group. Any child can learn anything you want to teach from material that is easier than it needs to be; none can learn from material that they can't read!

Specifically, in terms of Figure 10-5, at the beginning of third grade, the two top groups can be using the regular third grade text; they are broken into separate groups only because of numbers. If the range in the lower group is too great, you might use different books with the "high grade 2" child and the "high grade 1" child.

Implied here also is the fact that—while the research itself is mixed—I see no point in accelerating children in a basal reading program since I see that basal as nothing more than a vehicle, for the convenience of teachers, to teach basic skills. The other *half* of the reading program—literally 50 percent—should be in the enjoyable application and practice of the skills in library books. And it is here that children can go off in all directions, with the third grader reading college texts in the unlikely event that he or she would enjoy them. Contrary to what some adults think, it is not true that "the harder the book, the more they learn"—too "hard" and they learn nothing but to dislike and to shun reading entirely.

Also shown in Figure 10-5 is the traditional assumption that children are grouped by reading level, and that at the given reading level they need the skills provided for in the teacher's guide at that level. We know this is not necessarily so. The child reading at third grade level may still need some of the skills at second grade and may even have mastered some of the "fourth grade" skills.

This further step toward improving the teaching of reading is to separate "reading level" from "reading skills" since there is no one-to-one relationship between the two. We must determine reading level in order to give children appropriate instructional material—material they can read. Then the job still remains to diagnose in terms of skills and to provide flexible grouping for the teaching of the skills needed by any collection of individuals.

It is in this change in grouping patterns from the nearly permanent grouping by reading level to the flexible, temporary grouping by skill needs that management systems serve a purpose. Management systems are available with basal reading programs, and some are available as separate components. They provide for pretesting of skills to determine need, direction to resources for teaching and practice, posttesting, and record keeping. Figure 10-6 is a schematic of a management system, showing the process, from teaching selection of an objective and pretest on appropriate skill through recording on

Figure 10-6

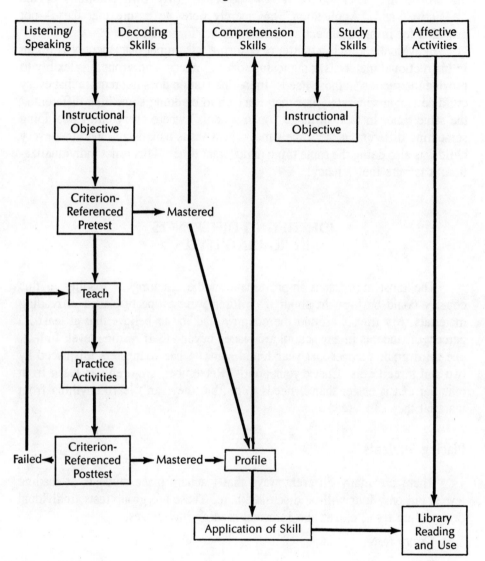

the profile and selection of a new objective. (My own additions of the "Affective" and "Application" are merely notes to assure that these—not provided for in management systems—are not forgotten.)

Individualization is a matter of ensuring this proper placement of children in instructional materials, diagnosing for skill needs, and grouping flexibly to provide instruction in those needs. Individualization does not require that every child be taught separately nor that every child be doing something different at the same time. In fact, in those "open schools" where every child was doing something different at the same time, repeat visits usually revealed that every child was also doing the same thing at different times. This is not individualization; it is pure inefficiency!

IDENTIFYING DIFFERENCES IN READING LEVELS

The most significant improvement in the teaching of reading in this country could be brought about if children were properly placed in reading materials. My travels around the country lead me to believe that at least 20 percent of students in any school are placed beyond their reading level. In fact, one third grade teacher last year found some of her youngsters misplaced by two and three levels. Check your pupils! Remember, children can learn from material that is easier than it needs to be, but they can't learn anything from material they can't read.

Placing Students

There are many different ways that teachers place students at reading levels, but only four will be discussed here. These are group tests, individual oral reading tests, cloze, and informal reading inventories.

Group Tests

The identification of an individual's reading level cannot be done with a group test. Most group tests tend to overestimate the instructional level of an individual, but there is no rule of thumb to suggest by how much. Furthermore, the standard error on the better group tests is usually about four months, which means that odds are only two out of three (67 percent) that the individual's true reading level is plus or minus four months of the earned grade equivalent. In other words, if a child scores a grade equivalent of 3.5 on a reading test, odds are two out of three that the true reading level is between 3.1 and 3.9. For more accuracy, double the standard error and odds are nine out of ten (still not the 95 percent minimum we want from research) that the individual's true level is between 2.7 and 4.3!

Grade equivalents are rather deceiving statistics anyhow, leading the International Reading Association to go on record as opposing their use. Too many people believe that a child who scores 3.5 on a reading test is reading like a typical third grader in midyear. Even ignoring the standard error for the time being, this interpretation comes close to being true only if the child is a third grader in midyear who earned that score on a test normed on third graders in midyear. For any other child, that score is merely a statistical extrapolation from averages of the norming sample, a statistical invention that relates to no real child. That score for a sixth grader merely means the child is not a good reader; for a first grader, the child is a superior reader—and certainly not that the first grader should be reading with third graders.

All this is not to suggest that we abandon group tests. Group tests provide important information about groups. They can serve as a dipstick to clarify how the school district, school, or grade level is doing this year as compared to previous years or to national norms. They can also be used to survey or screen large groups of children to make *tentative* identification of those who may need special help in reading. The point is, however, that they should not be used to determine the instructional level of individuals.

Individual Oral Reading Tests

Individual oral reading tests seem to be the best method for identifying instructional reading level. And this need not be so frightening or time-consuming as it might sound. There is seldom a reason for testing every child in a classroom to determine the reading level of each. Any teacher ought to have a pretty good idea of the top 40 to 50 percent of the children who are reading at grade level or above and who can read the grade level materials effectively. For such students, there is no reason they cannot continue in whatever grade level materials are being used for teaching reading. It is academic, in terms of instructional materials, *how much* above grade level they are reading. Hence, individual tests need be administered only to those about whom the teacher has a question—those who may not be able to read at grade level.

There are numerous individual reading tests available, from the many formalized "informal" reading inventories to the oral reading tests by Durrell, by Gilmore, and by Gray. Once more, however, I wouldn't use any of these. Each of these has its own error. Based on whatever grade equivalent is arrived at from the fallible test, a teacher must then find a book designated as that reading level—a designation based on a very fallible readability formula. This is about like measuring a door opening with one elastic rule and measuring the potential frame with another! The only way to be certain of a good fit is to measure the child with the material under consideration. Then, if the child can read it, the child can read it!

Cloze

To determine reading level with potential material, some have suggested gaining the advantage of group testing by making a cloze exercise from the material. This is a matter of taking a minimum of 250 words from the selection, replacing every fifth word with a blank, and keeping all blanks identical in length. Students are to fill in the blanks. Only exact replacements are considered correct; synonyms arc "errors," although misspellings are acceptable. The material is considered to be at instructional level if the student has between 45 and 55 percent correct exact replacements.

While this technique can be used in content areas as well as in any kind of reading material, I hesitate to use it to determine instructional level. For one thing, the level of accuracy varies with different research studies. Probably more important, cloze apparently does not measure comprehension beyond the sentence level: students who were given versions of a selection with the sentences scrambled did as well as those with unmutilated versions of the selection (Shanahan and others, 1982). Any examination of a cloze exercise will reveal that a large percentage of deleted words will be structure words that can be determined merely from knowledge of the structure of English sentences.

This is not to suggest that cloze is useless. It can be used for ranking materials, and it certainly is another good instructional technique for teaching use of context (Jongsma, 1980). However, for it to be effective, one must "teach" with it. Earlier investigations indicated that cloze was not an effective technique for increasing use of context, but those investigators merely gave practice by distributing exercises, having students complete them, and checking their accuracy—no instruction took place (Jongsma, 1971).

Informal Reading Inventories

I believe the best technique we have available for determining instructional reading level—and certainly not an infallible one—is that of using an Informal Reading Inventory (IRI) made from the material being considered for instruction. This is a technique that can also be used in the content areas with social studies, science, or any other reading material.

IRI Procedures

Most basal reading series have their own placement tests, which are usually equivalent to an IRI. If you have no tests available, you can still check on the appropriateness of a book by picking a section of one hundred words and asking the child, "Please read this to me. When you're finished, I'll ask you a few questions about it."

With your own copy of the selection, keep track of the errors— "miscues," if you prefer—that the youngster makes. Then ask four questions about that selection. These questions can be purely literal since you merely want to find out if the child understood what was read. Instructional level is that level at which the reader can read orally with 95 percent word accuracy and 75 percent comprehension (Betts, 1946). In other words, if the individual makes more than five errors in the oral reading of the hundred-word selection, or misses more than one of the four questions, that material is too difficult. Then you must get easier material and try it in the same manner.

It is usually a good idea to tape the testing, unless you are merely spot-checking. Then you can go back to double check the errors you recorded. The following suggestions for recording errors are based on a composite of the usual kinds of markings, so any reading teacher could pick up your test record and understand your scoring:

1. *Omission* of a word, phrase, punctuation—circle the omission.
2. *Hesitation* of two seconds or more—place a check mark above the word. (This is for information only; it is usually not counted as an error.)
3. *Refusal*—after five seconds, add a second check mark above the word and pronounce it.
4. *Insertion, reversal, substitution, mispronunciation* (saying anything that isn't there)—phonetically write in what was said.

In addition, *repetitions* can be marked by drawing a line over the entire portion repeated, but these are usually not counted as errors. Also, if a child makes an error, for example, a mispronunciation, and then self-corrects, you might put *SC* over the error. This is very positive behavior; however, it should still be counted as an error since it most likely would not have occurred had the material been easier.

If you are placing students in a basal reading series, you might want to make your own battery of IRI tests by picking representative hundred-word selections (fifty at preprimer and primer levels) from each level of the series. In testing, begin with a level that you are certain is easy for the student since there is nothing worse than beginning at frustration level, getting the youngster upset, and having to back down to lower levels. Also, despite the fact that most commercial IRI's begin with a "graded word list" to guide you to the appropriate starting paragraph for oral reading, such graded lists are not very accurate (McKenna, 1983), so you are probably better advised to merely plan on a minute or so extra and begin at what you know will be an easy level for the student being tested. Furthermore, in so doing, you are beginning with real reading instead of a word list.

If you plan to use a battery, whether a series of selections from subsequent levels of a basal or from a series of high-interest/low-vocabulary books, begin at a level you know is easy. After successful reading and answering of the four questions at that level, progress to the next level in the same manner. You will have the student continue to progressively higher levels until the level at which there are more than five word-accuracy errors or more than one comprehension error. Such is frustration, and the last previous successful level is instructional level.

In the scoring, be stringent. If you are "tough" in the scoring, you will be "easy" in the placement. In fact, perhaps the 95 percent criterion for word accuracy may result in placement that is too difficult (Forell, 1985; Hoffman and others, 1984). Common sense verifies the research once more. Consider the fact that the adult books you and I read have four hundred to five hundred words on a page. Even using the lower figure, a 5 percent word error would be twenty words on a page! How much reading would you do if twenty words on every page were completely foreign to you? And again, it is better to err by placing a child in a level easier than needed than to place that student in material at a frustration level.

Analysis of errors may yield some insights about the child's behavior in reading. For example, suppose the text sentence was "The girls ran down the street." If one child's errors consistently followed the pattern of calling *street* "string," or *girls* "grass," you would be identifying one who used phonics but paid little or no attention to context and did not read for meaning. Conversely, there are some who are such context guessers that *street,* for example, might be read as "alley."

Some students demonstrate a great number of hesitations, showing a lack of security, while others repeat a lot, often before a difficult word—as if they want to back up to get a running start. Further than that, the involved classification system of a *Reading Miscue Inventory* (Goodman and Burke, 1972) seems overly tedious for what it offers.

Pacing Students

Once youngsters have been placed properly in materials at their reading level for instructional purposes, theoretically (but unfortunately not realistically in most schools) there would never be a reason to retest for placement as long as children were paced at their own rate in the materials. Some learn skills faster than others, some are more interested, and some read more. Such individuals will move to higher levels at a regular pace. For those who don't move as quickly, it is still important that skill instruction and the enjoyable application and practice of those skills in library reading be part of their program, just as it is part of the program for better readers. In fact, use of library books and the many writing activities that can be related are excellent assurances that the basal will be properly paced.

Proper pacing will assure that children do not become misplaced in instructional materials once they have been properly placed through the use of an IRI. To move children too rapidly through instructional materials not only frustrates them, but it also "destroys" that material as a possible vehicle for instruction by next year's teacher who will have the children at a time when that material may be appropriate.

Naturally, the reverse is also possible: Children may be paced so slowly that they do not grow in reading skills as rapidly as they could and should. This situation, however, is less frustrating and, if library books are available, less likely to inhibit the reading development of the youngsters; they will continue to grow in spite of the snail's pace of the program.

DIAGNOSING SKILL NEEDS

As pointed out in the discussion of grouping patterns, children differ in their skill development just as they differ in reading levels. While teachers certainly should not get lost—or buried—in bookkeeping the hundreds of petty items that management systems sometimes list as "reading skills," they should be aware of each child's level of development in all the important skills and should be diagnosing specifically for those skills.

For example, Chapter 3 discussed means for diagnosing language skills and needs. When children actually get into reading itself, the first items usually taught are the use of context and consonant letter-sound associations. In listening to the oral reading of an IRI, the teacher should be able to determine if the youngster is or is not using context. Are the word errors the child makes meaningful errors (ones that make sense in the context), or do they more likely approximate the sounds of the letters in the word in print and completely ignore the context?

Diagnosing for Phonics

Many phonics tests are available commercially. However, these tests, if administered as directed, require encoding (spelling), not decoding (reading). Figure 10-7 is an example of the answer sheet of a phonics test for initial

Figure 10-7

Date _____				Name _____
A Initial Consonants				**Pronunciation Guide**
1	gam	fam	tam	nam	FAMily
2	rem	lem	sem	bem	REMedy
3	hol	sol	mol	col	COLumn
4	tig	kig	sig	hig	SIGnal
5	com	lom	rom	wom	LOMbard
6	biz	diz	miz	riz	BUsy
7	yaf	waf	taf	zaf	TAFfy
8	nug	gug	fug	kug	CUp
9	fep	bep	dep	tep	DEPth
10	yen	fen	jen	ken	YEN
11	rad	nad	gad	jad	JAm
12	nof	mof	tof	sof	NOt
13	dud	pud	fud	hud	PUDdle
14	vip	bip	gip	pip	GIll
15	lex	nex	bex	wex	WEt
16	bab	hab	lab	pab	HABit
17	vil	ril	nil	wil	VILlage
18	fot	yot	mot	bot	MOTley
19	nom	zom	dom	rom	ZOMbie
B Initial Consonant Digraphs				**Pronunciation Guide**
1	thap	knap	shap	whap	SHAck
2	drob	chob	clob	shob	CHOp
3	shek	drek	thek	knek	THEspian
4	drib	shib	knib	whib	WHIp
5	shas	thas	clas	chas	THAt
C Simple Vowels I				**Pronunciation Guide**
1	vop	vep	vap	vip	VAPid
2	fip	fup	fop	fep	rIP
3	lem	lim	lum	lom	LOMbard
4	dif	duf	daf	def	DUFfie
5	bom	bem	bim	bam	gEM
6	gef	gaf	gof	guf	GAFF
7	tiz	tuz	toz	tez	TIZzy
8	yit	yat	yut	yot	YUm
9	juck	jock	jeck	jick	JOCKey
10	paf	pif	pof	pef	PEt

Figure 10-7 (Continued)

D	Simple Vowels II				Pronunciation Guide
1	baipe	beip	beap	boap	pEP
2	zaid	zead	zawd	zaed	tAWDry
3	baup	boop	baip	bewp	pAUPer
4	jowk	jiek	jaik	jook	lOOK
5	sut	sewt	suet	seit	pUT

E	Complex Vowels				Pronunciation Guide
1	voy	vay	vuy	voay	hAY
2	koat	keut	koit	keat	mEAT
3	lai	lea	lau	lue	dUE
4	za	ze	zo	zu	ZEbra
5	vay	voy	vey	viy	VOYage
6	daf	dif	dafe	dufe	sAFE
7	saif	soaf	seef	sawf	bEEF
8	sije	soje	sij	suje	SIzE
9	luej	loaj	liej	laij	LAId
10	koog	keag	kaig	koig	COOl
11	bown	boan	bewn	beun	dOWN
12	soid	soud	sied	soed	lOUD
13	nove	neve	nov	nive	rOVE
14	fow	foi	fy	fui	deFY
15	teze	taze	tuz	tuaz	TOOth
16	leag	loug	laeg	loig	LOIn
17	vo	va	ve	vu	VOcal

F	Initial Consonant Clusters				Pronunciation Guide
1	bram	flam	blam	stam	BLAck
2	spem	glem	scem	grem	SPEck
3	crol	slol	prol	drol	DROp
4	clig	blig	plig	spig	PLInk
5	trom	brom	swom	drom	BROnze
6	scaz	spaz	claz	praz	SCAb
7	flaf	glaf	fraf	plaf	FRAn
8	scug	trug	crug	stug	STUb
9	frim	flim	plim	blim	FLIp
10	grep	brep	glep	frep	GLEn
11	swen	pren	slen	clen	SWEAt
12	crad	stad	swad	trad	TRAp
13	crof	grof	clof	stof	CROck
14	swud	slud	scud	brud	SLUg

Figure 10-7 (Continued)

F	Initial Consonant Clusters *(cont'd)*				Pronunciation Guide
15	plip	glip	prip	spip	PRIck
16	drex	crex	frex	clex	CLEm
17	drot	frot	grot	glot	GROTto
18	trun	smun	swun	grun	SMUg
19	snit	stit	smit	blit	SNIff

Copyright © 1972 by Robert L. Hillerich.

consonant sounds, digraphs, clusters, and vowels. These tests are spelling tests when administered as directed on a group basis. Typically, children are each given pupil answer sheets, as in Figure 10-7, but without the pronunciation guide or the answers circled. Then they are told, "Look at the first row. Draw a circle around the one that begins like *fish* and *fun.*"

Tested in this manner, youngsters are demonstrating spelling skill, not reading skill, since they hear the sound at the beginning of a word and then must find a word that begins with the letter most often representing that sound. Not only is this spelling, but it is also multiple-choice spelling, an even easier task. In decoding (reading), one operates in the reverse fashion: The reader sees a letter and—out of the whole world of sound—must decide what sound that letter represents. Poor readers at junior high demonstrated that this was about ten times more difficult than the multiple-choice spelling.

The test in Figure 10-7—or any commercial phonics test—can be converted to a reading test if administered individually: Sit down with the child to be tested, show the *answer* sheet, and tell the child, "I'm going to read all the words in each row except the one with the circle around it. Then you read that one."

You read "gam, tam, nam" and point to *fam.* If the student says "fam," obviously that youngster has established the sound association for the consonant *f.* Again, not every child should be tested; test only those about whom there is a question in terms of their consonant-sound associations.

Vowel understandings may also be diagnosed, not to determine what rules to teach, but to identify those children who can profit from more experience in exploring the possible representations of vowel sounds, as discussed in Chapter 5.

Application

Of course, all the diagnosing, teaching, and practice of phonics in the world is to no avail if students are not shown how to *apply* the skills, as discussed in connection with the word introduction technique in Chapter 5. In clinics and in classrooms, I have seen some poor students who knew more phonics than I would ever want to learn, but they still could not read. They didn't know what those skills, on which they and their teacher had worked so hard, had to do with reading the book in front of them.

While part of the application comes merely from understanding what reading is all about—from just enjoying good library reading—another part can come directly from instruction by the teacher. Students need a summarizing of "What do I do when I come to a word I don't know?" This can also be posted on a chart for all to see. In essence, the decoding strategy that should become automatic with them is:

1. Context
2. Phonics
3. Structural analysis
4. Dictionary

Put more clearly, students should know that the first step in approaching a word not immediately recognized is to use context in order to narrow the possibilities: "What word could I anticipate or expect this to be?" This requires use of both the semantic and syntactic context—meaning and part of speech.

Next, phonics will be used, where consonant generalizations are usually most helpful and adequate if the word is within the listening/speaking vocabulary. If more phonics help is needed, consideration of the possible representations of the vowels is possible.

In the case of words outside the listening/speaking vocabulary, structural analysis is sometimes helpful, most often in the case of recognizing two known words in a compound or in recognizing the meaning of an affix and base. Once in a while, chunking of syllables can assist in pronunciation of a word vaguely within the oral vocabulary, thereby leading to meaning.

In the event these techniques fail to yield the meaning of the word, the only viable alternative is reference, using a dictionary. Even here, use of context is a necessary adjunct skill.

Diagnosing for Higher Level Skills

Diagnosing for dictionary, comprehension, or study skills is best done by criterion-referenced testing, that is, by asking individuals to perform the intended task and observing whether they can or cannot do it. There is no group test that can provide a clear diagnostic picture of these skills, as noted in Farr's summary (1986).

Testing dictionary skills can be done, for example, in many different degrees, from asking a child to alphabetize a group of five or six words, to providing a strange word in context and asking for its meaning. In beginning at higher levels such as the latter, if an individual cannot perform as expected, it is necessary to move to progressively more basic levels until the handicapping deficit is discovered.

Similarly, if you want to know whether a child can identify the topic of a paragraph, the best way to find out is to provide a paragraph *at the appropriate reading level* and ask for the "topic," or what the paragraph is about if the term "topic" has not been taught. Example questions for identifying the comprehension skills were presented in Chapters 7 and 8. In fact, to review diagnosis of all the skills would, in effect, require a repetition of the contents of this book.

Care must be taken in diagnosing to sample a given skill several times with a child to be certain that the correct answer wasn't given by chance to a single sampling of that skill. This limited sampling of each skill is apparently one of the weaknesses of group tests.

A second major weakness of group tests that can be avoided on a personal basis has to do with follow-up. Care must be taken to question youngsters about *why* they answered as they did. For example, consider the process if you want to ask a child to draw a conclusion after reading the following selection:

> The boy ambled down the street. He gazed in one
> store window after another. Tarrying by store
> after store, he shuffled home.

As stated in Chapter 7, the obvious question might be, "Was the boy in a hurry?" If an individual responds as expected, with this and several other selections, that child apparently can draw conclusions at this reading level. However, if the youngster said the character was in a hurry, don't assume that the reader can't draw conclusions. The child may have associated *ambled* with *rambled, gazed* with *glanced, tarrying* with *hurrying,* and *shuffled* with another word having to do with hurrying. In other words, there are times when a basic skill can trip the youngster up and make that child appear lacking in some more sophisticated skill.

TEACHING CHILDREN FROM
DIFFERENT LANGUAGE BACKGROUNDS

As pointed out in Chapter 3 and verified in other research (Fillmore and Valadez, 1986), in order to learn to read a language, one must first speak and understand it. This point certainly applies as much or more to children with limited English proficiency (LEP) as it does to English speakers learning to read in their own language.

Fillmore and Valadez indicated that little research—and most of that in the 1970s—has been reported on this topic, possibly because of the political/ social overtones. The research that does exist indicates that the best way to start LEP students to read is to have them begin in their own language (L1) first. Modiano (1966) reported a study in Mexico, involving twenty-six schools, where half the classes were taught reading initially in L1 while the controls were taught in L2, which—in this case—was the national language. By the end of the second year in school, those who began reading instruction in L1 also read better in L2 than did youngsters who began in L2.

Hillerich (1972) reported a similar study, where Hispanic students were taught to read in Spanish first. They were taught to use the decoding strategy described in Chapter 4 that would then be used in reading in English, and they had a strong oral English program beginning in the summer before first grade. In comparison with a control group using the same instructional method but reading English from the beginning, children who began reading in Spanish were reading their native language as well as reading in English by the end of first grade. By the end of second grade, they were maintaining Spanish and were significantly higher in English reading comprehension than were their counterparts who began and read exclusively in English.

A second study, with tighter controls, indicated that the bilingual group made significantly greater gains by the end of first grade, and, by the end of second grade not only scored higher in reading achievement but were also higher on the SRA Achievement Test in English mechanics and English grammar as compared with children who began reading in English initially.

Such findings might seem contrary to evidence on the importance of time on task since children who begin reading in L2 certainly get more time on task on that language than do those beginning in L1 and then shifting to L2. However, research by Kolers (1968) partially explains this phenomenon: He found that with a bilingual person, two exposures to each of two words—one in L1 and one in L2—was as effective for remembering that word as were four exposures to the same word in either of the languages. For example, the Spanish–English-speaking bilingual, exposed to *fountain* twice and *fuente* twice, is as likely to remember either as he or she would be if exposed to *fountain* four times or to *fuente* four times. The reader appears to store meanings for words rather than the visual images of the words.

Other factors also seem important if this approach is to be successful. Not only does experience in one language carry over to the other, but learning to read in the native language seems to provide some understanding of what "reading" is. While a certain minimal competency is essential in L2 before learning to read that language, receptive competency is much more important and more highly related to success in reading than is expressive competence (Hillerich, 1984). Furthermore, the goal is not to exchange one language for another. It is to maintain the native language and culture while becoming proficient in a second language and contributing to a second culture.

The ESL methodology is clearly established. One learns a second language by behaving in it, not by being talked to about it and not by merely learning vocabulary labels. Furthermore, translation is not as effective as immersion in the language (Legarreta, 1979). Similarly, individuals should be spoken to normally, not louder, slower, or in broken rhythms. It is important to use the natural patterns of English sentences from the outset.

Some excellent guides for developing oral English are available from a number of publishers. Two good ones are:

Understanding English by Louise Lancaster. Houghton Mifflin.
I Like English, Book 1, by Gay and Sintetos. Scott Foresman.

In addition, young children can also benefit from *Ready Steps* and the *Peabody Language Development Kit,* as discussed in Chapter 3.

Students must get a great deal of experience in talking and listening in English. Since the classroom teacher with one or two LEP students doesn't have this kind of time, the program can still be conducted, with a minimum of instruction on the use of teacher's guides, by older students or parent volunteers.

Finally, any teacher working with children from other language backgrounds needs some understanding of the child's cultural heritage and must be aware of points of conflict in the child's native language and English. For example, English idioms are a problem, regardless of L1. There is no way to interpret an idiom, even if children understand the meaning of every word used unless they know that idiom: "He stuck his nose in someone else's business" or "Don't stick your neck out."

Children from a more inflected language, such as Spanish, will have difficulty with English word order as well: "Casa rosa" becomes "red house" in English. Furthermore, as teacher, you must decide on priorities—which is the prime instructional task, speech correction or reading instruction? The Hispanic, who did not have /sh/ in the native language, will tend to refer to *ship* as "chip." Eventually, as experience is gained in English, /sh/ and /ch/ will become confused and people will be said to sit on a "shair." Such pronunciations normally do not interfere with understanding and therefore should *not* be considered reading problems or even reading "errors." In fact, more will be said about this entire speech/language situation in the next section.

In their writing, LEP students should be treated just like any fledgling writers, having their attention focused on composing rather than on the surface problems with spelling and other mechanics. This composing effort will be supportive of learning in both reading and oral English as they attend to the task of communicating in the patterns and vocabulary of English. You should expect spelling initially to reflect the pronunciations of the oral L1. Correction of this phonetic spelling will not be achieved by merely attempting to substitute a new phonetic spelling. Assurance of correct spelling—a legitimate concern once competency in the vocabulary and syntax of English is achieved—comes only through memorization of the spellings of a basic core of English words and ability to use the dictionary for the remainder (Hillerich, 1985).

TEACHING CHILDREN FROM
BLACK DIALECT

The principles discussed in connection with children from different language backgrounds do not necessarily apply in the case of children who speak black dialect (BD). In fact, Rystrom (1970) demonstrated in a study of four first-grade classrooms that trying to teach English as a second language to children from BD did nothing but confuse them: It had a negative effect on their learning to read. The points of overlap in "standard" English (SE) and BD are prevalent since both are variations of the same language.

Any discussion of BD should begin with clarification of "standard" English and "dialect." "Standard" English we all know: It is that perfect English that you and I speak! A dialect is merely a regional, social, or cultural variation of a common language. Like it or not, we all speak a dialect, despite the negative connotation some have for the word. In fact, we all speak an idiolect—our own personal variation of that dialect. We are all linguistically different. This uniqueness of individual speech is even identifiable in the cooing of infants.

Part of the confusion about dialect undoubtedly relates to early efforts to explain BD in terms of its discrepancies from SE. It should be clear from the outset that BD is not an inferior or cheap imitation of SE. It apparently originated as a West African pidgin English, that is, as a *lingua franca* by means of which the adults from a variety of African tribes could communicate among themselves.

Like other pidgins, which are the languages of commerce, BD has its own rules and is not a distortion of another language. As with most pidgins, BD had a tendency to eliminate redundancy: Why use the *s* to mark a plural if it is already marked with another word, for example, *two,* in "two pencil"?

According to Dillard (1972), a clear history of the elements of BD was difficult to assemble because of the confusion of early sources. The slaves in this country also had different social levels: House servants and mechanics spoke one level of BD; field workers spoke plantation Creole; and the newly arrived, the West African pidgin English.

As stated in the previous section, any teacher who hopes to teach individuals from a different language—or, in this case, from a different dialect—must understand that language or dialect. Dialects may differ in terms of phonology (pronunciation), syntax (the rules for organizing words in sentences), and vocabulary. The latter is no more a concern than use of slang or jargon among different groups. However, lack of understanding of the differences in phonology or syntax can be a problem. Some of the major characteristics of BD phonology are presented in Figure 10-8.

Figure 10-9 lists some of the major syntactic differences between BD and SE. Two excellent sources for more information on the characteristics of BD are Dillard (1972) and Smitherman (1977). The latter also provides examples of BD along with clarification of the culture itself.

Again, remember priorities. The black child who does not pronounce the past marker in normal speech should not be considered as making an error if he or she does not pronounce it in reading. The question, as far as reading is concerned, is: Did the child notice the past marker, that is, comprehend its meaning? Besides, there are many instances in the normal speech of SE speakers where final consonants—not to mention *-ing*—are not enunciated: "past town" loses a /t/, "rowed down" loses a /d/, and so on.

There is no point, in a school setting, in attempting to "correct" the speech patterns of young children. To do so is to criticize them, their parents, and their heritage. It is also a good way to have them stop talking, when the important thing is to get them to use language—whatever the language or dialect they have to begin with. Whenever we react to *how* they speak instead of to *what* they are saying, we are not only discouraging further efforts, but we are also providing erroneous signals as to the purpose for language. Besides, all traditional efforts at "correcting" word usage have failed miserably: While the teacher presented two hundred practices with "I don't have a..." the child was going home and getting two hundred practices with "I ain't got no..." And isn't it good that we did fail? Imagine what would have happened to that inner-city youngster who walked out of school onto the street speaking as the teacher wanted him to speak!

All of the above is not to suggest that anything goes, that SE is not important, or that we want to keep some Americans "in their place." It is to suggest the fact that change will not take place until early adolescence or the teen years, when social pressures are such that the individual *wants* to participate with another linguistic group (Williams, 1970). This means that the educator's task is to keep youngsters talking so they can use and expand whatever language they have and to provide a model of SE. Middle grade

Figure 10-8

1. r-lessness (/r/ is dropped or replaced with /ə/)

Black Dialect	New England Dialect
(Drop /r/, except in initial position)	(Drop /r/ before consonant or in final position)
tore = toe	tore = toe
guard = god	guard = god
nor = gnaw	nor = gnaw
four times = foe time	four times = foe times
four o'clock = foe o'clock	four o'clock = four o'clock
Carol = Cal	

2. l-lessness (moved to a /w/ glide or disappears)

   toll = toe   help = hep
   tool = too   fault = fought
   all = awe   haul = haw

3. Reduction of clusters, especially after stressed vowels (*st, ft, nt, nd, ld, zd, md*)

   past/passed = pass
   rift = riff
   meant/mend = men
   wind = wine
   hold = hole

4. Weakening of final consonant (/t/ and /d/ mostly; sometimes /g/ and /k/) (note effect on pronunciation of past marker!)

   boot = boo
   past/passed = pass
   seed/seat = see
   road/rowed = row

5. Vowel shifts

/i/ = /e/ before nasals:	pin = pen; beer = bear
/e/ = /a/ before /l/:	peel = pail
/u/ = /o/ before /r/:	poor = poe
/oi/ = /o/:	oil = awe
/th/ = /f/:	Ruth = roof

teachers can begin to provide experience in translating up and down the linguistic ladder from formal to slang, helping youngsters realize that a given expression is not "right" or "wrong"; it is appropriate—socially acceptable— in a given situation or it is not. For example, just about any English speaker would consider it socially acceptable at a picnic for one to yell across the field,

Figure 10-9

Characteristic	Standard English	Black Dialect
Plural	fifty cents, three toys	fifty cent, three toy
Possessive	Tom's bike, his book	Tom bike, he book
Verb: Third person singular	He works here.	He work here.
Verb: agreement	She has a bicycle.	She have a bicycle.
Verb: 0 (zero) copula	He is working (now). He is working (every day).	He working (now). He be working (every day).
Verb: "is" as question marker	Are they sick? They are sick	Is they sick? They sick.
Verb: Past tense	Yesterday he worked.	Yesterday he work.
Future	I'll go home.	Ima go home.
Verb: Negative	She isn't going. She didn't go. I don't have any.	She don't go. She ain't go. I don't got none.
Preposition	He is over at the store. He works at Public Park.	He over to the store. He work Public Park.
Pronoun: Substitution	We have to go.	Us got to go.
Nongender 0 relative or substitution of *what*	That girl is tall. He has a friend who plays games.	That girl he tall. He have a friend play games. He have a friend what play games.
repeat subject "If" construction	John went to town. I asked if he did it.	John he go to town. I ask did he do it.
Deletion of unaccented	except, you're/we're	'cept, you/we
Substitution	Here are two birds.	Higo two bird.

"Hey, Joe, toss me the ball!" Yet I doubt that many would consider the identical pattern acceptable at the dinner table: "Hey, Joe, toss me the rolls!" Such experiences with language open the doors so that the individual can become bidialectical and can make judgments about the use of SE when it is desirable.

In teaching reading to children from BD, what kinds of materials and approaches should be used? Should those materials be written in BD spelling and syntax? Most educators are opposed to this position. Since BD has no written form, any more than a Boston or a Midwest dialect has its own spellings, standard spelling can just as well represent BD pronunciation as it does SE pronunciation. Besides, there is no one-to-one correspondence between sound and symbol in English spelling: *right* is no closer to SE /rīt/ than it is to BD /rat/.

Recognizing that we should use standard spelling, the question still remains, should children in the initial stages of reading learn from materials in BD syntax or in SE syntax? The overwhelming evidence is that BD speakers understand SE equally with BD (Simons and Johnson, 1974; Liu, 1975–76) regardless of their productive skill in the oral language, and it is the receptive ability that relates more closely to success in reading (Hillerich, 1984).

What then is the problem with BD? The basic problem has nothing to do with any handicapping effects inherent in BD; it has to do with school people's attitudes toward it. My own experience can be supported by a multitude of other reports: Teachers of BD speakers—certainly with all of the very best intentions—want them to "talk right." They know that "nonstandard" English is an economic handicap, but they seem to forget that inability to read is an even greater handicap. Let's care for first things first.

As a demonstration of the influence of attitude, several investigators, such as DeStefano (1973), have taught teachers BD and then had them interview youngsters to classify them as having or not having characteristics of BD. Consistently in such studies, a *few* characteristics of BD in the speech of a black youngster resulted in classification as a BD speaker, while essentially those same elements in the speech of a white did not!

It is now mainstream thinking among educators that the most important first step is to accept whatever dialect the young child brings to school (Alexander, 1980; Padak, 1981): Teachers should no more correct the BD speaker's rendition of *He parked the car* as "He park the car," than they would correct the Bostonian's rendition as "He paked the ca." It should go without saying that this acceptance of pronunciation applies equally to any other dialect considered less prestigious in another community.

Furthermore, if we truly believe that reading is a meaning-getting process, then we must also go the next step with beginning readers: We must accept not only their pronunciation, but we must also accept their syntax and see its use in reading as a higher level of comprehension (Zimet, 1978). For example, suppose the child is to read the sentence *She is working*. If the BD speaker reads, "She be working," I would compliment that youngster for excellent reading in that the child had comprehended and read the way he or she would talk. On the other hand, if surrounding context indicated that she just happened to be working that day and didn't normally work, I'd then probe and be concerned about an "error." Then the child should have read "She working," not "She be working." In other words, the child did not comprehend and therefore made a mistake as indicated by the dialect itself.

Of course, in order to work with children in this manner, the teacher must understand the dialect. But is it asking too much of us as teachers to understand the language of those with whom we work? And if we truly want children to read for meaning, we should be concerned that they internalize what they read and read it as they would say it, rather than be pleased with the word-for-word monotone renditions we too often hear in first grade classrooms.

The comments made about writing and spelling in connection with the discussion of other language backgrounds apply equally to BD speakers. Furthermore, manipulation of language in writing not only increases familiarity with the forms of the language, but it also offers the same advantage offered through its use in the content areas: It helps writers realize how much they know and don't know about that language.

This has been a book focusing on reading instruction within the language arts. Even more, it has been an attempt to discuss the development of reading/writing/speaking/listening as means of communication—enjoyable communication. Let's help our children to discover this!

References

Ackerman, Margaret. 1973. "Acquisition and Transfer Value of Initial Training with Multiple Grapheme-Phoneme Correspondences." *Journal of Educational Psychology* 64:28–34.

Alexander, Clara F. 1980. "Black English Dialect and the Classroom Teacher." *The Reading Teacher* 33 (February): 571–77.

Alvermann, Donna E.; Lynn C. Smith; and John E. Readence. 1985. "Prior Knowledge and the Comprehension of Compatible and Incompatible Text." *Reading Research Quarterly* 20 (Summer): 420–36.

Annis, Linda, and J. Kent Davis. 1975. "The Effect of Encoding and an External Memory Device on Note Taking." *Journal of Experimental Education* 44 (Winter): 44–46.

Applebee, A.N.; F. Lear; and A. Auten. 1981. "Learning to Write in the Secondary School: How and Where." *English Journal* 70 (September): 78–82.

Arbuthnot, May Hill. 1966. "Developing Life Values through Reading." *Elementary English* 43:10–16.

Aukerman, Robert C. 1984. *Approaches to Beginning Reading*. New York: Wiley.

Bailey, Mildred. 1967. "The Utility of Phonic Generalizations in Grades One through Six." *The Reading Teacher* 20: 413–18.

Balow, B., and J. Curtin. 1966. "Ability Grouping of Bright Pupils." *Elementary School Journal* 66 (March): 321–26.

Barbe, Walter B. 1961. *Educator's Guide to Personalized Reading Instruction*. Englewood Cliffs, NJ: Prentice-Hall.

Barnes, Buckley R., and Elmer V. Clawson. 1975. "Do Advance Organizers Facilitate Learning? Recommendations for Further Research Based on an Analysis of 32 Studies." *Review of Educational Research* 45 (Fall): 637–59.

Barrett, Thomas. 1968. "Taxonomy of Cognitive and Affective Dimensions of Reading Comprehension." In *Innovation and Change in Reading Instruction*, ed. Helen M. Robinson, 19–23. Chicago: National Society for the Study of Education.

Baumann, James F. ed. 1986. *Teaching Main Idea Comprehension*. Newark, NJ: International Reading Association.

Betts, Emmett. 1946. *Foundation of Reading Instruction*. New York: American Book.

Blazer, Bonita. 1984. *The Development of Writing in Kindergarten: Speaking and Writing Relationships*. Doctoral dissertation, University of Pennsylvania.

Bliesmer, Emory, and Betty Yarborough. 1965. "A Comparison of Ten Different Beginning Reading Programs in First Grade." *Phi Delta Kappan* 46: 500–503.

Bloom, Benjamin S., ed. 1956. *Taxonomy of Educational Objectives, Handbook I: Cognitive Domain*. New York: David McKay.

Bond, Guy, and Robert Dykstra. 1967. "The Cooperative Research Program in First-Grade Reading Instruction." *Reading Research Quarterly* 2: 5–142.

Boodt, Gloria M. 1984. "Critical Listeners Become Critical Readers in Remedial Reading Class." *The Reading Teacher* 37 (January): 390–94.

Braam, Leonard S., and Allen Berger. 1968. "Effectiveness of Four Methods of Increasing Rate, Comprehension, and Flexibility." *Journal of Reading* 2 (February): 346–52.

Brzeinski, Joseph E. 1964. "Beginning Reading in Denver." *The Reading Teacher* 18: 16–21.

Buchanan, Cynthia D., and M.W. Sullivan. 1963. *Programmed Reading*. New York: McGraw-Hill.

Canney, George, and Robert Schreiner. 1976–77. "A Study of the Effectiveness of Selected Syllabication Rules and Phonogram Patterns for Word Attack." *Reading Research Quarterly* 12: 102–24.

Carpenter, Ethelouise. 1961. "Readiness Is Being." *Childhood Education* 38: 114–16.

Carroll, John B.; Peter Davies; and Barry Richmond. 1971. *The American Heritage Word Frequency Book*. Boston: Houghton Mifflin.

Chaille, Christine; Donna Barnes; Thelma Bessel-Browne; and Karen Quigley, 1984. "Effects of Early Childhood Education Programs," *Research Roundup*. National Association of Elementary School Principals. 1 (November): 1–4.

Chall, Jeanne. 1967. *Learning to Read: The Great Debate*. New York: McGraw-Hill.

Chaney, Frances. 1979. "Materials Testing: Ready Steps." *Early Years* 9 (May): 56–57.

Christensen, Clifford, and Kalmer Stordahl. 1955. "The Effect of Organizational Aids on Comprehension and Retention." *Journal of Educational Psychology* 46: 65–74.

Clarke, S.C.T. 1959. "The Effect of Grouping on Variability in Achievement at Grade III Level." *Alberta Journal of Educational Research* (September): 162–71.

Cline, Ruth K.J., and George L. Kretke. 1980. "An Evaluation of Long-Term SSR in the Junior High School." *Journal of Reading* 23: 503–506.

Clymer, Theodore. 1963. "The Utility of Phonic Generalizations in Primary Grades." *The Reading Teacher* 16: 252–58.

Cohen, S. Alan. 1969. "Studies in Visual Perception and Reading in Disadvantaged Children." *Journal of Learning Disabilities* 2: 498–503.

Cohn, Marvin. 1974. "Letter Recognition Difficulties: Their Real Nature." Paper presented at International Reading Association Annual Convention, New Orleans, May, 1974.

Coleman, E.B. and G. Morris. 1978. "Generalization Tests: A Terminology that Focuses Attention on Fixed-Effect Restrictions." *Journal of Reading Behavior* 10: 377–92.

Cunningham, Patricia M.; Richard W. Cunningham; and Richard C. Rystrom. 1981. "A New Syllabication Strategy and Reading Achievement." *Reading World* 20: 208–14.

Dale, Edgar. 1965. "The Critical Reader." *The Newsletter* 30: 1.

Davey, Beth. 1983. "Think Aloud—Modeling the Cognitive Processes of Reading Comprehension." *Journal of Reading* 27 (October): 44–47.

de Hirsch, Katrina; Jeannette J. Jansky; and William S. Langford. 1966. *Predicting Reading Failure*. New York: Harper and Row.

Deighton, Lee C. 1959. *Vocabulary Development in the Classroom*. New York: Teachers College Press.

Denham, Carolyn, and Ann Lieberman, eds. 1980. *Time to Learn*. Washington, DC: National Institute of Education.

DeStefano, Johanna. 1973. *Language, Society, and Education: A Profile of Black English*. Worthington, OH: Charles A. Jones Publishing.

Dewey, Godfrey. 1970. *Relative Frequency of English Spellings*. New York: Teachers College Press.

Dillard, J.L. 1972. *Black English*. New York: Random House.

Dolch, Edward W. 1939. *A Manual for Remedial Reading*. Champaign, IL: Garrard Publishing.

Donaldson, Margaret. 1978. *Children's Minds*. New York: W.W. Norton.

Downing, John. 1964. *The Initial Teaching Alphabet*. New York: Macmillan.

Durkin, Dolores. 1978–79. "What Classroom Observations Reveal about Reading Comprehension Instruction." *Reading Research Quarterly* 14: 481–533.

————. 1974–75. "A Six-Year Study of Children Who Learned to Read in School at the Age of Four." *Reading Research Quarterly* 10: 9–61.

————. 1963. "Should the Very Young Be Taught to Read? They Should Have the Opportunity." *National Education Association Journal* 52: 20–24.

Durrell, Donald; Alice Nicholson; Arthur Olson; Sylvia Gavel; and Eleanor Linehan. 1958. "Success in First Grade Reading." *Journal of Education* 140.

Eames, Thomas. 1962. "Physical Factors in Reading." *The Reading Teacher* 15: 427–32.

Education Commission of the States. 1980–81. *NAEP Newsletter* 13 (Winter): 1–3.

Educational Testing Service. 1985. *The Reading Report Card*. Princeton, NJ: Educational Testing Service.

Eeds, Maryann, and Ward A. Cockrum. 1985. "Teaching Word Meanings by Expanding Schemata vs. Dictionary Work vs. Reading in Context." *Journal of Reading* 28 (March): 492–97.

Ehri, Linnea C.; Nancy D. Deffner; and Lee S. Wilce, (1984). *Journal of Educational Psychology* 76 (October): 880–93.

Elkind, David. 1986. "Formal Education and Early Childhood Education: An Essential Difference." *Phi Delta Kappan* 67 (May): 631–36.

————. 1981. *The Hurried Child*. Menlo Park, CA: Addison-Wesley.

Emans, Robert. 1967. "The Usefulness of Phonic Generalizations Above the Primary Grades." *The Reading Teacher* 20; 419–25.

Farr, Roger. 1986. *Reading: What Can Be Measured?* Newark, NJ: International Reading Association.

Farr, Roger; Leo Fay; and Harold Negley. 1978. *Then and Now: Reading Achievement in Indiana (1944–45 and 1976)*. Bloomington: Indiana University Press.

Feldman, Mary Jane. 1985. "Evaluating Pre-Primer Basal Readers Using Story Grammar." *American Educational Research Journal* 22 (Winter): 527–47.

Ferguson, Anne M., and Jo Fairburn. 1985. "Language Experience for Problem Solving in Mathematics." *The Reading Teacher* 38 (February): 504–507.

Fields, Marjorie V., and Deborah V. Hillstead. 1986. "Reading Begins with Scribbling." *Principal* 65 (May): 24–27.

Fillmore, Lily W., and Concepcion Valadez. 1986. "Teaching Bilingual Learners." In *Handbook of Research on Teaching* (3rd ed.), ed. Merlin C. Wittrock, pp. 648–85. New York: Macmillan.

Fleisher, Lisa S.; Joseph R. Jenkins; and Darlene Pany. 1979. "Effects on Poor Readers' Comprehension of Training in Rapid Decoding." *Reading Research Quarterly* 15: 30–47.

Follman, John, and A.J. Lowe. 1973. "Empirical Examination of Critical Reading and Critical Thinking—Overview." *Journal of Reading Behavior* 5 (Summer): 159–68.

Forell, Elizabeth R. 1985. "The Case for Conservative Reader Placement." *The Reading Teacher* 38 (May): 857–62.

Fowler, Gerald L. 1982. "Developing Comprehension Skills in Primary Students through the Use of Story Frames." *The Reading Teacher* 36 (November): 176–79.

Fry, Edward. 1965. "Are Reading Readiness Materials Necessary in the First Grade?"

Paper presented at American Educational Research Association annual meeting, (February).

Gall, Meredith. 1984. "Synthesis of Research on Teachers' Questioning." *Educational Leadership* 42 (November): 40–47.

Gambrell, Linda B. 1983. "The Occurrence of Think-Time during Reading Comprehension Instruction." *Journal of Educational Research* 77 (November/December): 77–80.

Gambrell, Linda B.; W.R. Pfeiffer; and R.M. Wilson. 1985. "The Effects of Retelling upon Reading Comprehension and Recall of Text Information." *Journal of Educational Research* 78: 216–20.

Garner, R., and C. Kraus. 1982. "Good and Poor Comprehender Differences in Knowing and Regulating Reading Behaviors." *Educational Research Quarterly* 6: 5–12.

Gates, Arthur T. 1926. "A Study of the Role of Visual Perception, Intelligence, and Certain Associative Processes in Reading and Spelling." *The Journal of Educational Psychology* 17 (Fall): 433–45.

Gates, Arthur. 1961. *Reading Attainment in Elementary Schools: 1957 and 1937*. New York: Teachers College Press.

Gattegno, Caleb. 1962. *Words in Color*. Chicago: Learning Materials.

Gaver, Mary. 1963. *Effectiveness of Centralized Library Service in Elementary Schools*. New Brunswick, NJ: Rutgers University Press.

Gettinger, Maribeth, and Mary Alice White. 1979. "Which Is the Stronger Correlate of School Learning? Time to Learn or Measured Intelligence?" *Journal of Educational Psychology* 71: 405–12.

Gibson, Carol. 1972. "Prefixes and Suffixes: An Analysis of the Applicability of Generalizations as Related to a Selected List of Over 2,000 Commonly Used Words." Master's Thesis, National College of Education.

Glazer, Joan I., and Gurney Williams III. 1979. *Introduction to Children's Literature*. New York: McGraw-Hill.

Goldberg, Miriam L.; Harry A. Passow; and Joseph Justman. 1966. *The Effects of Ability Grouping*. New York: Teachers College Press.

Good, Thomas L., and Jere E. Brophy. 1969. *Analyzing Classroom Interaction: A More Powerful Alternative*. Austin, TX: The Research and Development Center for Teacher Education, The University of Texas at Austin, September.

Goodman, Yetta M., and Carolyn L. Burke. 1972. *Reading Miscue Inventory*. New York: Macmillan Company.

Gorelick, Molly C. 1965. "The Effectiveness of Visual Form Training in a Prereading Program." *Journal of Educational Research* 58: 315–18.

Hahn, Amos L., and Ruth Garner. 1985. "Synthesis of Research on Students' Ability to Summarize Text." *Educational Leadership* 42 (February): 52–55.

Hammill, Donald D., and Gaye McNutt. 1981. *The Correlates of Reading*. Austin, TX: Pro-Ed.

Hanna, Paul R., and others. 1966. *Phoneme-Grapheme Correspondences as Cues to Spelling Improvement*. Washington, DC: U.S. Office of Health, Education, and Welfare.

Hardy, Madeline; P.C. Smythe; R.G. Stennett; 1972. "Developmental Patterns in Elemental Reading Skills: Phoneme-Grapheme and Grapheme-Phoneme Correspondences." *Journal of Educational Psychology* 63: 433-36.

Harris, Albert J., and Edward R. Sipay. 1985. *How to Increase Reading Ability.* New York: Longman.

Harris, Theodore L., and Richard E. Hodges. 1981. *A Dictionary of Reading and Related Terms.* Newark, NJ: International Reading Association.

Harste, Jerome C.; Virginia A. Woodward; and Carolyn L. Burke. 1984. *Language Stories and Literacy Lessons.* Portsmouth, NH: Heinemann Educational Books. 1979.

Hassler, Donni M. 1979. "A Successful Transplant of Wait-Time and Questioning Strategies in Children's Oral Language Behaviors." ERIC ED 205–951.

Hayakawa, S.I. 1949. *Language in Thought and Action.* New York: Harcourt, Brace and World.

Hazard, Paul. 1947. *Books, Children and Men.* Boston: Horn Book.

Henderson, H.K. 1981. "A Comparison of the Effects of Practice with Signaled or Open Sentence Combining Exercises within Varying Instructional Time Frames." Doctoral dissertation, University of Houston. Dissertation Abstracts International 41, 55009A.

Hillerich, Robert L. 1987. "Reading Central: Selecting and Using Picture Dictionaries." *Teaching K–8* 17 (April): 24–26.

———. 1986. "Reading Central: World Introduction." *Early Years* 16 (February): 13–14.

———. 1985. *Teaching Children to Write, K–8: A Complete Guide to Developing Writing Skills.* Englewood Cliffs, NJ: Prentice-Hall.

———. 1984. "The Language Arts Connection: Communication." Paper presented at the Tenth Annual National Educators Conference. South Bend, IN: University of Notre Dame.

———. 1983a. *The Principal's Guide to Improving Reading Instruction.* Newton, MA: Allyn and Bacon.

———. 1983b. "Critical Reading: Beyond the Questions." Presentation at the Fifth Great Lakes Regional Conference of International Reading Association, Springfield, IL, October 6, 1983.

———. 1982. *Spelling: An Element in Written Expression.* Columbus, OH: Charles E. Merrill.

———. 1981. "Recognition Vocabularies: A Research-Based Caution." *Elementary School Journal* 81: 313–17.

———. 1980a. "Pacemaker Core Vocabulary 1—The First Readability Study." In *Pacemaker Core Vocabularies.* Belmont, CA: Fearon Pitman, 63–67.

———. 1980b. "Sight/Recognition Vocabularies: What's the Word?" Bowling Green, OH: Bowling Green State University.

———. 1978a. *A Writing Vocabulary of Elementary Children.* Springfield, IL: Charles C. Thomas.

———. 1978b. "A Diagnostic Approach to Early Identification of Language Skills." *The Reading Teacher* 31 (January) 357–64.

———. 1974a. *PDQ: A Diagnostic Approach to Early Identification of the Pre-Reading Language Needs for Four- and Five-Year-Olds.* Wilmette, IL: Eduscope. (Now published as *Ready Steps Language Survey,* Houghton Mifflin, 1986).

———. 1974b. "Word Lists—Getting It All Together." *The Reading Teacher* 27: 353–60.

———. 1973. "Use of the Computer for Instructional Purposes: Review and

Recommendations." National College of Education.

————. 1973. "Starter Words: A More Efficient Beginning Vocabulary." *Illinois Reading Council Journal* 2: 3–5.

————. 1972. "Beginning Reading for Spanish-Speaking Children." *The Instructor* 81: 19–22.

————. 1970. "Teaching about Vowels in Second Grade." *Illinois School Research* 7: 35–38.

————. 1967. "Vowel Generalizations and First Grade Reading Achievement." *Elementary School Journal* 67: 246–50.

————. 1966. "Bringing Together Children and Books: A Decentralized School Library." *National Elementary Principal* 46: 32–35.

————. 1966a. "An Interpretation of Research in Reading Readiness." *Elementary English* 43: 359–64, 372.

————. 1966b. "Predictive Value of Letter Name Test, Preliminary Study." Glenview, IL: Public Schools Bulletin.

————. 1965. "Pre-Reading Skills in Kindergarten: A Second Report." *Elementary School Journal* 65: 312–17.

————. 1963. "Dare We Evaluate Paradise?" In *New Directions in Kindergarten Programs.* Cambridge, MA: Lesley College.

Hillerich, Robert L. and Timothy G. Johnson. 1978, 1986. *Ready Steps.* Boston: Houghton Mifflin.

Hillocks, George, Jr., and Larry H. Ludlow. 1984. "A Taxonomy of Skills in Reading and Interpreting Fiction." *American Educational Research Journal* 21 (Spring): 7–24.

Hoffman, James V., and others, 1984. "Guided Oral Reading and Miscue Focused Verbal Feedback in Second-Grade Classrooms." *Reading Research Quarterly* 19 (Spring): 367–84.

House, Ralph W. 1944. "Do Pupils Learn to Use Diacritical Marks?" *Journal of Educational Research* 37: 352–55.

Huck, Charlotte S. 1986. *Children's Literature in the Elementary School.* New York: Holt, Rinehart and Winston.

Huff, Darrell. 1954. *How to Lie with Statistics.* New York: W.W. Norton.

Humphrey, Jack W. 1986. "Full-Day Kindergarten Survey." Evansville, IN, 1 page. August 1, 1986.

————. 1983. *A Longitudinal Study of the Effectiveness of Full-Day Kindergarten.* Evansville, IN: Evansville-Vanderburgh School Corporation.

Hunt, Kellogg W. 1965. *Grammatical Structures Written at Three Grade Levels.* Champaign: National Council of Teachers of English.

Ibeling, Fred. 1961. "Supplementary Phonics Instruction and Reading and Spelling Ability." *Elementary School Journal* 62: 152–60.

Ilg, Frances L., and others. 1978. *School Readiness.* New York: Harper and Row.

Irwin, Judith W., ed. 1986. *Understanding and Teaching Cohesion Comprehension.* Newark, NJ: International Reading Association.

Jansky, Jeannette, and Katrina de Hirsch. 1972. *Preventing Reading Failure.* New York: Harper and Row.

Jenkins, Joseph R.; R.B. Bausell; and Linda M. Jenkins. 1972. "Comparisons of Letter Name and Letter Sound Training as Transfer Variables." *American Educational Research Journal* 9 (Spring): 75–86.

Jensen, Norma, and Ethel King. 1970. "Effects of Different Kinds of Visual Motor Discrimination Training on Learning to Read Words." *Journal of Educational Psychology* 61: 90–96.

Johnson, Nancy S., and Jean M. Mandler. 1980. "A Tale of Two Structures: Underlying and Surface Forms in Stories." *Poetics* 9: 51–86.

Jongsma, Eugene A. 1980. *Cloze Instruction Research: A Second Look*. Newark, NJ: International Reading Association.

————. 1971. *The Cloze Procedure as a Teaching Device*. Newark, NJ: International Reading Association.

Kelley, Kathleen R. 1984. *The Effect of Writing Instruction on Reading Comprehension and Story Writing Ability*. Doctoral dissertation, University of Pittsburgh. DA8421346.

Kiewra, Kenneth A. 1984. "Acquiring Effective Notetaking Skills: An Alternative to Professional Notetaking." *Journal of Reading* 27 (January): 299–302.

Kimmel, Thomas. 1973. *What Critical Reading Skills Are Important in Evaluating Informative and Persuasive Writing as Represented by News, Opinion, and Advertisements in Print?* Master's thesis, National College of Education.

Kneedler, Peter. 1985. "California Assesses Critical Thinking." In *Developing Minds*, ed. Arthur L. Costa, pp. 276–80. Alexandria, VA: Association for Supervision and Curriculum Development.

Kolers, Paul A. 1968. "Bilingualism and Information Processing." *Scientific American* 21: 78–85.

Kucera, Henry, and W. Nelson Francis. 1967. *Computational Analysis of Present-Day American English*. Providence, RI: Brown University Press.

LaFontaine, Denise. 1984. *Do Metacognitive Differences Exist Between Fifth Grade Good and Poor Comprehenders?* Master's thesis, Bowling Green State University.

Langer, Judith A. 1984. "Examining Background Knowledge and Text Comprehension." *Reading Research Quarterly* 19 (Summer): 468–81.

Laubach, Frank, (1947). *Teaching the World to Read*. New York: Friendship Press.

Lazar, May. 1957. "Individualized Reading: A Dynamic Approach." *The Reading Teacher* 11: 75–83.

Legarreta, D. 1979. "The Effects of Program Models on Language Acquisition by Spanish Speaking Children." *TESOL Quarterly* 13: 521–34.

Levin, Harry, and J.A. Watson. 1963. *A Basic Research Program on Reading*. Ithaca, NY: Cornell University Cooperative Research Grant No. 639.

Liu, Stella. 1975–76. "An Investigation of Oral Reading Miscues Made by Nonstandard Dialect Speaking Black Children." *Reading Research Quarterly* 11: 193–97.

Loban, Walter D. 1976. *Language Development: Kindergarten Through Grade Twelve*. Urbana, IL: National Council of Teachers of English.

————. 1963. *The Language of Elementary School Children*. Champaign, IL: National Council of Teachers of English.

Lucking, Robert A. 1975. "Comprehension and a Model for Questioning." April. ERIC ED 110–988.

Lyttek, Elaine. 1974. "A Comparative Study of Second Graders Taught by a Linguistic and Basal Reading Approach and Their Ability to Use Phonograms as Cues to Unlocking New Words." Master's thesis, National College of Education.

McConkie, George W.; Keith Rayner; and Steven J. Wilson. 1973. "Experimental Manipulation of Reading Strategies." *Journal of Educational Psychology* 65: 1–8.

McDaniel, Mark A., and Michael Pressley. 1984. "Putting the Keyword Method in Context." *Journal of Educational Psychology* 76 (August): 598–609.

McHugh, Walter J. 1962. "Indices of Success in First Grade Reading." Paper presented at American Educational Research Association annual meeting, February.

McKenna, Michael C. 1983. "Informal Reading Inventories: A Review of the Issues."

The Reading Teacher 36 (March): 670–79.

McNeil, David. 1970. *The Acquisition of Language.* New York: Harper and Row.

Mandler, G. 1967. "Organization and Memory." In *The Psychology of Learning and Motivation*, K.W. Spence, and J.T. Spence, eds. New York: Academic Press.

Manning, Gay, and Maryann Manning. 1984. "What Models of Recreational Reading Make a Difference?" *Reading World* 23 (May): 375–80.

Marchbanks, Gabrielle, and Harry Levin. 1965. "Cues by Which Children Recognize Words." *Journal of Educational Psychology* 56: 57–61.

Marsh, G., and P. Desberg. 1978. "Mnemonics for Phonics." *Contemporary Educational Psychology* 3: 57–61.

Marzano, Robert J., and others. 1976. "Are Syllabication and Reading Related?" *Journal of Reading* 19: 545–47.

Meisels, Samuel J. 1987. "Uses and Abuses of Developmental Screening and School Readiness Testing." *Young Children* 42 (January): 4–6, 68–73.

Menyuk, Paula. 1971. *The Acquisition and Development of Language.* New York: Prentice-Hall.

Miller, John W.; Michael C. McKenna; and Dennis J. Kear. 1982. "An Examination of the Efficiency of Four Reading/Study Techniques." *Journal of Reading* 26 (December): 239–42.

Minnesota Department of Education. "Full-Day Alternate-Day Kindergarten: A Report on Research." St. Paul: Minnesota Department of Education, October.

Modiano, Nancy. 1966. *A Comparative Study of Two Approaches to the Teaching of Reading in the National Language.* Cooperative Research Project No. S-237, U.S. Department of Health, Education and Welfare. New York: New York University.

Moffett, James, and Betty Jane Wagner. 1983. *Student-Centered Language Arts and Reading, K–13.* Boston: Houghton Mifflin.

Morgan, Elmer F., and Morton Lightfoot. 1963. "A Statistical Evaluation of Two Programs of Reading Instruction." *Journal of Educational Research* 56: 99–101.

Morphett, Mabel V., and Carleton Washburne. 1931. "When Should Children Begin to Read?" *Elementary School Journal* 31: 496–503.

Morrison, Coleman. 1964. "A Comparison Between Reported and Recommended Practices Related to Selected Aspects of Kindergarten and Beginning Reading Programs." Paper presented at American Educational Research Association annual meeting.

Morrow, Lesley M. 1985. "Reading and Retelling Stories: Strategies for Emergent Readers." *The Reading Teacher* 38 (May): 870–75.

Moskowitz, Breyne A. 1978. "The Acquisition of Language." *Scientific American* (November): 92–108.

Mower, Morris L., and LeRoy Barney, 1968. "Which Are the Most Important Dictionary Skills?" *Elementary English* 45: 468–70.

Muehl, Siegmar. 1962. "The Effects of Letter-Name Knowledge on Learning to Read a Word List in Kindergarten Children." *Journal of Educational Psychology* 53 (May): 181–86.

Munday, Leo A. 1979. "Changing Test Scores, Especially since 1970." *Phi Delta Kappan* 60 (March): 496–99.

———. 1979a. "Changing Test Scores: Basic Skills Development in 1977 Compared with 1970." *Phi Delta Kappan* 60 (May): 670–71.

Murphy, Richard T., and Lola R. Appel. 1984. *Evaluation of the Writing to Read Instructional System 1982–1984*. Princeton, NJ: Educational Testing Service, November.

Murray, Corallie. 1974. "An Inquiry into the Use of Phonograms in Decoding by First and Second Grade Children." Master's thesis, National College of Education.

Nagy, William E., and Richard C. Anderson. 1982. "How Many Words Are There in Printed School English?" Technical Report No. 253. Urbana: Center for the Study of Reading. ED 218–596.

Nagy, William E.; Patricia A. Herman; and Richard C. Anderson. 1985. "Learning Words from Context." *Reading Research Quarterly* 20 (Winter): 233–53.

National Assessment of Educational Progress. 1985 (undated). *The Reading Report Card*. Princeton, NJ: Educational Testing Service.

———. 1981. *Reading, Thinking and Writing*. Denver, CO: Educational Commission of the States, October.

National Commission on Excellence in Education. 1983. *A Nation at Risk*. Washington, DC: U.S. Department of Education, April.

National Council of Teachers of English. 1978. "Censorship: Don't Let It Become an Issue in Your Schools." *Language Arts* 55: 230–42.

Nebraska State Board of Education. 1984. "Position Statement on Kindergarten." Omaha: Nebraska State Board of Education, November.

Nicholson, Alice. 1957. "Background Abilities Related to Reading Success in First Grade." Ph.D. Dissertation, Boston University, 1957.

Norton, Donna E. 1983. *Through the Eyes of a Child*. Columbus, OH: Charles E. Merrill.

Olson, Arthur V., Jr. 1957. "Growth in Word Perception as it Relates to Success in Beginning Reading." Ed.D. dissertation, Boston University.

Ortony, A.; T.J. Turner; and N. Larson-Shapiro. 1985. "Cultural and Instructional Influences on Figurative Language Comprehension by Inner-City Children." *Research in the Teaching of English*, 19: 25–36.

Padak, N.D. 1981. "The Language and Educational Needs of Children Who Speak Black English." *The Reading Teacher* 35: 144–51.

Pallman, M. 1983. "Verbal Language Processes in Support of Learning Mathematics." *Mathematics in College*, (Winter): 49–55.

Pearson, P. David. 1985. "The Comprehension Revolution: A Twenty-Year History of Process and Practice Related to Reading Comprehension." Reading Education Report No. 57, Center for the Study of Reading. Champaign: University of Illinois.

Pearson, P. David, and Dale D. Johnson. 1978. *Teaching Reading Comprehension*. New York: Holt, Rinehart and Winston.

Pellegrini, A.D., and Lee Galda. 1982. "The Effects of Thematic-Fantasy Play Training on the Development of Children's Story Comprehension." *American Educational Research Journal* 19 (Fall): 443–52.

Peters, Charles W. 1975–76. "The Effect of Systematic Restructuring of Material upon the Comprehension Process." *Reading Research Quarterly* 11: 87–111.

Powell, William R. 1966. "Classroom Libraries: Their Frequency of Use." *Elementary English* 43: 395–97.

Pressley, Michael; Joel R. Levin; and Harold D. Delaney. 1982. "The Mnemonic Keyword Method." *Review of Educational Research* 52 (Spring): 61–91.

Rand, Muriel K. 1984. "Story Schema: Theory, Research and Practice." *The Reading Teacher* 37 (January): 377–82.

Rinsland, Henry. 1945. *A Basic Vocabulary of Elementary School Children.* New York: Macmillan.

Robinson, Francis P. 1961. *Effective Study.* New York: Harper and Brothers.

Robinson, H. Allan. 1978. *Teaching Reading and Study Strategies.* Boston: Allyn and Bacon.

Rosenshine, Barak V. 1980. "Skill Hierarchies in Reading Comprehension." In *Theoretical Issues in Reading Comprehension.* Rand J. Spire, Bertram C. Bruce, and William F. Brewer, eds. Hillsdale, NJ: Lawrence Erlbaum Associates.

Rowe, Mary Budd. 1969. "Science, Silence and Sanctions." *Science and Children* 6: 11–13.

Rumelhart, David E. 1980. "Schemata: The Building Blocks of Cognition." In *Theoretical Issues in Reading Comprehension,* Rand J. Spiro, Bertram C. Bruce, and William F. Brewer, eds. Hillsdale, NJ: Lawrence Erlbaum Associates.

Russell, David. 1956. *Children's Thinking.* Boston: Ginn.

Rystrom, Richard. 1970. "Dialect Training and Reading: A Further Look." *Reading Research Quarterly* 5: 581–99.

Samuels, S.J. 1972. "The Effect of Letter-Name Knowledge on Learning to Read." *American Educational Research* Journal 9 (Spring): 65–74.

Sartain, Harry W. 1960. "A Bibliography on Individualized Reading." *The Reading Teacher* 13: 262–65, 270.

_____. 1960a. "The Roseville Experiment with Individualized Reading." *The Reading Teacher* 13: 277–81.

Schoephoerster, Hugh; Richard Barnhart; and Walter M. Loomer. 1966. "The Teaching of Prereading Skills in Kindergarten." *The Reading Teacher* 19: 352–57.

Shake, Mary C. and Richard L. Allington. 1985. "Where Do Teachers' Questions Come From?" *The Reading Teacher* 38 (January) 432–38.

Shanahan, Timothy. 1984. "Nature of the Reading-Writing Relation: An Exploratory Multivariate Analysis." *Journal of Educational Psychology* 76 (June): 466–77.

Shanahan, Timothy; Michael L. Kamil; and Aileen W. Tobin. 1982. "Cloze as a Measure of Intersentential Comprehension." *Reading Research Quarterly* 17: 229–55.

Shane, Harold. 1960. "Elementary Education—Organization and Administration." In *Encyclopedia of Educational Research,* ed. Chester W. Harris. New York: Macmillan, pp. 421–30.

Shaw, Jules H. 1964. "Vision and Seeing Skills of Preschool Children." *The Reading Teacher* 18: 33–36.

Sheldon, William. 1963. "Should the Very Young Be Taught to Read? Harm Might Result." *National Education Association Journal,* 52: 20–22.

Silberberg, Norman; Iver Iversen; and Margaret Silberberg. 1968. "The Predictive Efficiency of the Gates Reading Readiness Tests." *Elementary School Journal* 68: 213–18.

Silberberg, Norman E., and Margaret C. Silberberg. 1977. "The Great Reading Score Deception." *Principal* 57 (October): 70–71.

Silberberg, Norman E.; M. Silberberg; and I. Iversen, (1972). "The Effects of Kindergarten Instruction in Alphabet and Numbers on First Grade Reading," *Journal of Learning Disabilities* 5 (Fall): 254–61.

Simons, Herbert D., and Kenneth R. Johnson. 1974. "Black English Syntax and

Reading Interference." *Research in the Teaching of English* 8 (Winter): 339–58.

Sloane, William. 1955. *Children's Books in England and America in the Seventeenth Century.* New York: King's Crown Press, Columbia University.

Smith, Charlotte T. 1978. "Evaluating Answers to Comprehension Questions." *The Reading Teacher* 31 (May): 896–900.

Smith, Nila B., and Ruth Strickland. 1969. *Some Approaches to Reading.* Washington, DC: Association for Childhood Education International.

Smitherman, Geneva. 1977. *Talkin and Testifyin.* Boston: Houghton Mifflin.

Spache, George D. 1965. "Innovations in Reading Instruction." In *Recent Developments in Reading,* ed. H. Alan Robinson. Chicago: University of Chicago Press.

Sparks, Paul, and Leo Fay. 1957. "An Evaluation of Two Methods of Teaching Reading." *Elementary School Journal* 57: 386–90.

Stein, Althea H. 1972. "Mass Media and Young Children's Development." In *Early Childhood Education,* ed. Ira J. Gordon. Chicago: National Society for the Study of Education.

Stotsky, Sandra. 1983. "Research on Reading/Writing Relationships: A Synthesis and Suggested Directions." *Language Arts* 60 (May): 627–42.

Styer, Sandra. 1972. "The Comparative Effectiveness of Two Methods of Teaching the Principle of Alphabetizing." *Elementary English* 49: 77–82.

Taylor, Barbara M. 1982. "Text Structure and Children's Comprehension and Memory for Expository Material." *Journal of Educational Psychology* 74 (June): 323–40.

Templin, Mildred. 1957. *Certain Language Skills in Children: Their Development and Interrelationships.* Minneapolis, MN: University of Minnesota Press.

Thorndyke, Perry W. 1977. "Cognitive Structures in Comprehension and Memory of Narrative Discourse." *Cognitive Psychology* 9 (January): 77–110.

Thurlow, Martha; Janet Graden; James E. Ysseldyke; and Robert Algozzine, 1984. "Student Reading During Reading Class: The Lost Activity in Reading Instruction," *Journal of Educational Research* 77 (May/June): 267–72.

Tierney, Robert J., and James W. Cunningham. 1984. "Research on Teaching Reading Comprehension." In *Handbook of Reading Research,* ed. P. David Pearson. New York: Longman.

Tuinman, Jaap; Michael Rowls; and Roger Farr. 1976. "Reading Achievement in the United States: Then and Now." *Journal of Reading* 19 (March): 455–63.

Van Allen, Roach. 1968. "How a Language Experience Program Works." In *A Decade of Innovations,* ed. Elaine C. Vilscek. Newark, NJ: International Reading Association.

Veatch, Jeanette. 1959. *Individualizing Your Reading Program.* New York: G.P. Putnam's Sons.

Wardhaugh, Ronald. 1969. *Reading: A Linguistic Perspective.* New York: Harcourt Brace Jovanovich.

———. 1966. "Syl-lab-i-ca-tion." *Elementary English* 43: 785–88.

White, Regine S., and Herb Karl. 1980. "Reading, Writing and Sentence Combining: The Track Record." *Reading Improvement* 17 (Fall): 226–32.

Whitehead, Robert J. (1984) *A Guide to Selecting Books for Children.* Metuchen, NJ: The Scarecrow Press, Inc.

Wiley, David, and Annegret Harnischfeger. 1974. "Explosion of a Myth: Quantity of Schooling and Exposure to Instruction, Major Educational Vehicles." *Educational Researcher* 3: 7–12.

Williams, Frederick. 1970. *Language and Poverty.* Chicago: Markham.

Williams, Joanna. 1968. "Successive versus Concurrent Presentation of Multiple Grapheme-Phoneme Correspondences." *Journal of Educational Psychology* 59: 309–14.

Williams, Joanna P.; Ellen L. Blumberg; and David V. Williams. 1970. "Cues Used in Visual Word Recognition." *Journal of Educational Psychology* 61: 310–15.

Wise, James. 1965. "The Effects of Two Kindergarten Programs upon Reading Achievement in Grade One." Ed.D. dissertation, University of Nebraska.

Wittrock, M.C. 1983. "Writing and the Teaching of Reading." *Language Arts* 60: 600–606.

Wolf, Lois. 1972. "Reading Readiness: An Experimental Study of the Effects of Specific Reading Skills Instruction on Sixty-Three Four-Year-Olds in Winnetka, Illinois." Master's thesis, National College of Education.

Wolf, Willavene; Charlotte S. Huck; and Martha L. King. 1967. *Critical Reading Ability of Elementary School Children.* Columbus: The Ohio State University Research Foundation.

Wrightstone, J. Wayne. 1957. *What Research Says to the Teacher: Class Orgaization for Instruction.* Washington, DC: National Education Association.

Yaden, David B., Jr., and Shane Templeton, eds. 1986. *Metalinguistic Awareness and Beginning Literacy.* Portsmouth, NH: Heinemann Educational Books.

Yap, Kim O. 1977. "Relationships between Amount of Reading Activity and Reading Achievement." *Reading World* 17 (October): 23–29.

Zimet, Sara G. 1978. "Dispelling Myths and Examining Strategies in Teaching Non-Standard Dialect Speakers to Read." ERIC ED 178–859. July.

Subject Index

Index of Names